Top Federal Tax Issues
FOR 2015 | CPE COURSE

CCH Editorial Staff Publication

Portland Community College

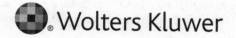

Wolters Kluwer

Contributors

Contributing Editors . . . . Glenn L. Borst, J.D., LL.M.;

James A. Chapman, J.D., LL.M.;

Jennifer R. Cordaro, J.D.;

Elena Eyber, J.D.;

Joy A. Hail, J.D.;

Kieran Murray, J.D., LL.M.;

Lawrence A. Perlman, CPA, J.D., LL.M.;

Deborah M. Petro, J.D., LL.M.;

Michael G. Sem, J.D.;

James Solheim, J.D., LL.M.;

Raymond G. Suelzer Jr., J.D., LL.M.;

George L. Yaksick, Jr., J.D.

Technical Review . . . . George G. Jones, J.D., LL.M.

Production Coordinator . . . . Gabriel E. Santana;

Jennifer Schencker

Production . . . . Lynn J. Brown

This publication is designed to provide accurate and authoritative information in regard to the subject matter covered. It is sold with the understanding that the publisher is not engaged in rendering legal, accounting, or other professional service. If legal advice or other expert assistance is required, the services of a competent professional person should be sought.

ISBN: 978-0-8080-3819-1

Printed in the United States of America

MIX
From responsible sources
FSC
www.fsc.org   FSC® C099992

Introduction

Each year, a handful of tax issues typically require special attention by tax practitioners. The reasons vary, from a particularly complicated new provision in the Internal Revenue Code, to a planning technique opened up by a new regulation or ruling, or the availability of a significant tax benefit with a short window of opportunity. Sometimes a developing business need creates a new set of tax problems, or pressure exerted by Congress or the Administration puts more heat on some taxpayers while giving others more slack. All these share in creating a unique mix that in turn creates special opportunities and pitfalls in the coming year and beyond. The past year has seen more than its share of these developing issues.

CCH's *Top Federal Tax Issues for 2015 CPE Course* identifies those recent events that have developed into the current "hot" issues of the day. These tax issues have been selected as particularly relevant to tax practice in 2015. They have been selected not only because of their impact on return preparation during the 2015 tax season but also because of the important role they play in developing effective tax strategies for 2015 and beyond. Some issues are outgrowths of several years of developments; others have burst onto the tax scene unexpectedly. Among the latter are issues directly related to the recent economic downturn and tax legislation designed to assist in a recovery. Some have been emphasized in IRS publications and notices; others are just being noticed by the IRS.

This course is designed to help reassure the tax practitioner that he or she is not missing out on advising clients about a hot, new tax opportunity; or that a brewing controversy does not blindside their practice. In addition to issue identification, this course provides the basic information needed for the tax practitioner to implement a plan that addresses the particular opportunities and pitfalls presented by any one of those issues. Among the topics examined in the *Top Federal Tax Issues for 2015 CPE Course* are:

- Employer Mandate of the Affordable Care Act
- Capitalization and Repairs—Compliance Rules
- Passive Activity Rules for Passthrough Entities and Owners
- Virtual Currency
- International Tax Reporting
- Retirement Plan Rollovers, Conversions, and Distributions
- Telecommuting and Traveling for Work
- Trusts: Income Tax Strategies
- Conservation Easements
- Tax Reform: Policy and Proposals

Study Questions. Throughout the course you will find Study Questions to help you test your knowledge, and comments that are vital to understanding a particular strategy or idea. Answers to the Study Questions with feedback on both correct and incorrect responses are provided in a special section beginning at ¶ 10,100.

Index. To assist you in your later reference and research, a detailed topical index has been included for this course.

Quizzer. This course is divided into four Modules. Take your time and review all course Modules. When you feel confident that you thoroughly understand the material, turn to the CPE Quizzer. Complete one, or all, Module Quizzers for continuing professional education credit.

Go to **CCHGroup.com/PrintCPE** to complete your Quizzer online. The CCH Testing Center website lets you complete your CPE Quizzers online for immediate results and no Express Grading Fee. Your Training History provides convenient storage for your CPE course Certificates. Further information is provided in the CPE Quizzer instructions at ¶ 10,200.

October 2014

CCH'S PLEDGE TO QUALITY

Thank you for choosing this CCH Continuing Education product. We will continue to produce high quality products that challenge your intellect and give you the best option for your Continuing Education requirements. Should you have a concern about this or any other CCH CPE product, please call our Customer Service Department at 1-800-248-3248.

COURSE OBJECTIVES

This course was prepared to provide the participant with an overview of specific tax issues that impact 2014 tax return preparation and tax planning in 2015. These are the issues that "everyone is talking about;" each impacts a significant number of taxpayers in significant ways.

Upon course completion, you will be able to:

- Identify entities that are applicable small, midsize, and large employers for purposes of the employer mandate;
- Recognize three safe harbors for affordability of coverage;
- Identify when to deduct materials and supplies;
- Recognize the significance of the de minimis safe harbor election, the small building-small taxpayer election, and book-capitalization election;
- Recognize the passive activity rules as they apply to rental activities conducted through passthrough entities;
- Identify the tests for material participation to partners and S corporation shareholders;
- Recognize the role of virtual currency;
- Identify the benefits and risks of using Bitcoins;
- Recognize the differences between the FBAR and FATCA reporting requirements;
- Recognize the civil and criminal penalties associated with noncompliance with the FATCA and FBAR requirements;
- Identify key features of today's retirement plan accounts and roads to building retirement assets;
- Identify plan assets that may use rollovers and the plans eligible to receive them;
- Recognize when a worker may deduct the cost of commuting;
- Identify the eligibility requirements for the home office deduction;
- Identify the rules used to make allocations of receipts and disbursements between principal and income;
- Recognize the mechanism by which trust distributions are taxed to the beneficiaries;
- Identify the requirements for a qualified conservation easement;
- Recognize the elements of a qualified appraisal;

- Identify many possible reforms for corporate, small business, and individual taxation; and

- Recognize the obstacles and concerns facing policymakers and lawmakers in addressing tax reform.

One **complimentary copy** of this course is provided with certain copies of CCH publications. Additional copies of this course may be downloaded from **CCHGroup.com/ PrintCPE** or ordered by calling 1-800-248-3248 (ask for product 10024491-0002).

Contents

MODULE 1: EMPLOYER/BUSINESS ISSUES—Chapter 1: Employer Mandate of the Affordable Care Act

¶ 101 WELCOME

This chapter explores the employer shared responsibility requirements (the "employer mandate.") The *Patient Protection and Affordable Care Act* (Affordable Care Act) created the employer mandate in 2010 and, in subsequent years, the IRS has provided guidance. Generally, the employer mandate will be fully phased in starting after 2016. Under transition relief, qualifying employers with at least 50 but fewer than 100 full-time employees, including full-time equivalent employees, are excused from share responsibility payments for 2015. Employers with fewer than 50 full-time employees are generally excused from any employer mandate responsibility irrespective of the year, although how full-time employees are counted may be at issue.

¶ 102 LEARNING OBJECTIVES

Upon completion of this chapter, you will be able to:

- Identify entities that are applicable small, midsize, and large employers for purposes of the employer mandate;
- Recognize three safe harbors for affordability of coverage;
- Identify terms of the employer mandate transition relief for 2015; and
- Identify the requirements for Code Sec. 6056 reporting by applicable large employers.

¶ 103 INTRODUCTION

The Affordable Care Act, signed into law by President Obama in 2010, continues to transform the delivery of health care and how Americans obtain health care insurance coverage. Individuals must carry minimum essential health care coverage (unless exempt) or make an individual shared responsibility payment (the "individual mandate.") The Affordable Care Act also requires certain employers to make a shared responsibility payment if they do not provide minimum essential coverage, among other criteria (the "employer mandate"). Like the individual mandate, the employer mandate includes many exemptions, most notably an exclusion for qualified small employers. Since enactment of the Affordable Care Act, the IRS, the U.S. Departments of Health and Human Services (HHS) and Labor (DOL) have issued proposed regulations, final regulations, and transition relief. The Obama Administration has also delayed the effective date of the employer mandate. All of these developments will be explored in this chapter.

> **COMMENT:** Closely related to the employer mandate are several other provisions in the Affordable Care Act, including employer/insurer reporting of health insurance coverage, reporting of the cost of health care coverage on employees' Forms W-2, *Wage Statement,* the Code Sec. 36B premium assistance tax credit, and the individual mandate. These related provisions are also highlighted in this chapter.

COMMENT: At the time this course was prepared, the Obama Administration had delayed the effective date of the employer mandate until 2015. However, midsize employers have been given additional time until 2016 under transition relief. Small employers—ones with fewer than 50 full-time employees or a combination of full-time and part-time employees that is equivalent to fewer than 50 full-time employees—are permanently exempted by the Affordable Care Act from the employer mandate.

COMMENT: The IRS has provided final regulations on the employer mandate for employers with workers who are members of a collective bargaining unit, individuals who are employed by temporary staffing firms, controlled groups, and employers with employees engaged in work both within and without the U.S. These rules are beyond the scope of this course.

¶ 104 ROLE OF THE EMPLOYER MANDATE IN THE AFFORDABLE CARE ACT

The starting point for understanding the employer mandate is the Affordable Care Act, which created Code Sec. 4980H. This provision provides for what is known as Code Sec. 4980H(a) liability and Code Sec. 4980H(b) liability.

Under Code Sec. 4980H, an applicable large employer must make a shared responsibility payment if either:

- The employer *does not offer*—or offers coverage to less than 95 percent (70 percent in 2015) of its full-time employees (or a combination of full-time and part-time employees that is equivalent to 95 percent of full-time employees) and their dependents—the opportunity to enroll in minimum essential coverage and one or more full-time employee is certified to the employer as having received a Code Sec. 36B premium assistance tax credit or cost-sharing reduction ("Section 4980H(a) liability"); or

- The employer *offers*—to all or at least 95 percent of its full-time employees (or a combination of full-time and part-time employees that is equivalent to 95 percent of full-time employees) and their dependents—the opportunity to enroll in minimum essential coverage under an eligible employer-sponsored plan and one or more full-time employees is certified to the employer as having received a Code Sec. 36B premium assistance tax credit or cost-sharing reduction ("Section 4980H(b) liability").

Section 4980H(a) and Section 4980H(b) carry similar elements. However, the provisions have important differences. For Section 4980H(a) liability to arise, the applicable large employer must generally fail to offer qualified employees (and dependents) the opportunity to enroll in minimum essential coverage under an eligible employer-sponsored plan. Section 4980H(b) contemplates that the employer does provide the opportunity to qualified employees (and dependents) the opportunity to enroll in minimum essential coverage but that at least one employee is deemed unable to afford the premiums without Code Sec. 36B assistance.

COMMENT: A cost-sharing reduction is advance payment of the Code Sec. 36B premium assistance tax credit.

EXAMPLE: Megacorp is an applicable large employer that offers health insurance coverage to its 350 full-time employees that is affordable and provides minimum value (discussed below). Jeremiah Yost is a full-time employee of Megacorp and elects not to enroll in its coverage, instead obtaining coverage through the marketplace. Jeremiah is the only employee of Megacorp to obtain coverage through the marketplace. Jeremiah is ineligible for the Code Sec. 36B premium assistance tax credit. Megacorp is not liable for the employer mandate because it offers coverage that is affordable and meets minimum value, and there is no employee who receives the Code Sec. 36B premium assistance tax credit to offset the cost of coverage through the marketplace. If no full-time employee receives a Code Sec. 36 premium assistance tax credit, Megacorp as an applicable large employer is not subject to the employer mandate.

EXAMPLE: Juarez Co. is an applicable large employer that offers health insurance coverage to its 210 employees that is affordable and provides minimum value. Olivia Hernandez is a full-time employee of Juarez and elects not to enroll in the employer's coverage for herself and her 13-year old daughter. Instead, Olivia obtains coverage for her daughter through the marketplace. Oscar Mendez is the only employee of Juarez to obtain marketplace coverage for a dependent. Oscar is ineligible for the Code Sec. 36B premium assistance tax credit. Juarez is not liable for the employer mandate because Oscar does not receive the Code Sec. 36B premium assistance tax credit. An applicable large employer is not liable for the employer mandate unless one or more full-time employees receive a Code Sec. 36 premium assistance tax credit.

COMMENT: After passage of the Affordable Care Act, some employers asked the IRS what the consequences, if any, would be to employers if they elected not to provide health insurance but reimbursed employees for premiums paid for health insurance through the marketplace. In early 2014, the IRS reminded employers that this type of arrangement would fail to satisfy insurance market reforms under the ACA. Therefore, employers would be subject to a $100 per day excise tax (or $36,500 per year).

Small Employers

Small employers—ones with fewer than 50 full-time employees (including full-time equivalent employees)—are always exempt from the Code Sec. 4980H employer shared responsibility requirements. There are no exceptions to this rule. A small employer may choose whether to offer health coverage. No liability under Code Sec. 4980H attaches in any event or if an employee (or employees) of the small employer obtains coverage through the marketplace.

EXAMPLE: Alliance Transportation Co. employs 36 employees. All employees work 40 hours each week. Alliance offers its full-time employees health care coverage. Thirteen full-time employees choose to obtain health insurance through the marketplace and five receive the Code Sec. 36B premium assistance tax credit. The remaining employees have other insurance arrangements. Alliance is not liable for an assessable payment under Code Sec. 4980H(a) or Code Sec. 4980H(b) because the company has fewer than 50 full-time employees.

Figure 1. Code Sec. 45R Small Employer Health Insurance Credit

Very small employers may be eligible for the Code Sec. 45R small employer health insurance tax credit. Generally, a qualified employer must:

Have no more than 25 full-time equivalent employees (25 full-time employees or a combination of full-time and part-time employees that equals 25) for the tax year;

Pay average annual wages of no more than $50,000 per qualified employee (indexed for inflation after 2013); and

Maintain a qualifying health care insurance arrangement. In tax years that begin after 2013, an employer must obtain coverage through the Small Business Health Options Program (SHOP) marketplace or be eligible for an exception. The employer must cover at least 50 percent of the cost of employee-only (not family or dependent) health care coverage for each of its employees.

Phaseout. The Code Sec. 45R is subject to phaseout if the number of qualified employees exceeds 10 or if the average annual wages for FTEs exceed $25,000 (as adjusted for inflation for tax years beginning after 2013; $25,400 for 2014). For an employer with both more than 10 qualified employees and average annual wages exceeding $25,000, the credit is reduced based on the sum of the two reductions.

Employees. The following types of employees are expressly excluded from being treated as employees for the Code Sec. 45R credit:

- Owners of the small business, such as sole proprietors, partners, shareholders owning more than 2 percent of an S corporation or more than 5 percent of a C corporation; spouses of these owners;

- Family members of these owners, including a children, grandchildren, siblings or step-siblings, parents or ancestors of a parent, step-parents, nieces or nephews, aunts, uncles, sons-in-law, daughters-in-law, fathers-in-law, mothers-in-law, brothers-in-law, or sister-in-laws. A spouse of any of these family members is also not be counted as an employee; and

- Seasonal workers.

Variable amount. For tax years 2010 through 2013, the maximum credit is 35 percent of health insurance premiums paid by qualified employers (25 percent for small tax-exempt employers). The credit is 50 percent for qualified employers (35 percent for small tax-exempt employers) after 2013 (but is scheduled to terminate after 2015). Starting in 2014, an employer may claim the credit for two consecutive taxable years, beginning with the first tax year in or after 2014 in which the employer attaches a Form 8941, *Credit for Small Employer Health Insurance Premiums,* to its income tax return, or in the case of a tax-exempt employer, attaches Form 8941 to Form 990-T, *Exempt Organization Business Income Tax Return.*

> **COMMENT:** The *Budget Control Act of 2011* requires a 7.2 percent reduction in refunds to tax-exempt employers claiming the refundable portion of the credit. The sequestration reduction rate is applied to refunds processed between October 1, 2013, and September 30, 2014.

STUDY QUESTION

1. A major difference between Code Sec. 4980H(a) and 4980H(b) liabilities for 2015 is:
    - **a.** Whether at least one employee receives the Code Sec. 36B premium assistance credit
    - **b.** The percentage of employees offered minimum essential coverage
    - **c.** The average salary of employees not offered minimum essential coverage
    - **d.** The size of the employer

¶ 105 APPLICABLE LARGE EMPLOYERS

The employer mandate applies to "applicable large employers." An *applicable large employer* with respect to a calendar year is an employer that employed an average of at least 50 full-time employees (or combination of full-time and part-time employees that equals at least 50) on business days during the preceding year. For purposes of determining whether an employer is an applicable large employer, full-time employees and full-time equivalent employees are taken into account. An employee is a *full-time employee* if he or she works on average at least 30 hours a week. The hours of service of part-time employees are taken into account by aggregating the number of hours of service of all part-time employees for each month and dividing by 120, the result of which is the number of full-time equivalent employees for the month.

COMMENT: A *part-time employee* for purposes of Code Sec. 4980H is an employee whom the employer reasonably expects to be employed on average less than 30 hours of service per week.

EXAMPLE: During each calendar month of 2015, Brashton Co. has 20 full-time employees, each of whom averages 35 hours of service per week, 40 employees, each of whom averages 90 hours of service per calendar month, and no seasonal workers. Each of the 20 employees who averages 35 hours of service per week counts as one full-time employee for each calendar month. To determine the number of Brashton's full-time employees (including full-time equivalent employees) for each calendar month, the total hours of service of the employees who are not full-time employees (but not more than 120 hours of service per employee) are aggregated and divided by 120. The result is that Brashton has 30 FTEs for each calendar month (40 × 90 = 3,600, and 3,600 ÷ 120 = 30). Because Brashton has 50 full-time employees (the sum of 20 full-time employees and 30 FTEs) during each calendar month in 2015, and because the seasonal worker exception is not applicable, Brashton is an applicable large employer for 2016.

COMMENT: After the IRS issued proposed regulations on the employer mandate, many stakeholders asked the agency to increase the threshold for triggering the employer mandate from 50 qualified employees to a higher number, such as 100. The IRS explained in the final regulations issued in 2014 that it could not increase the threshold because it is set by the Affordable Care Act.

Full-Time Employees/Full-Time Equivalent Employees

Measurement methods. As described earlier, the Affordable Care Act sets a 30-hour per week threshold for determining whether a worker is a full-time employee for purposes of the employer mandate. Under Code Sec. 4980H, an employee respect to any month, an employee who is employed on average at least 30 hours of service per week is a full-time employee. In the final regulations issued in 2014, the IRS provided two methods for determining whether a worker is a full-time employee:

- The monthly measurement method; and
- The lookback measurement method.

The monthly measurement method allows an employer to determine each employee's status by counting the employee's hours of service for each month. The lookback measurement method allows employers to determine the status of an employee as a full-time employee during a future period, based upon the hours of service of the employee in a prior period. Both the monthly measurement method and the lookback method use 130 hours of service in a calendar month as the monthly equivalent of at least 30 hours of service per week. Both of these methods set forth minimum standards for an employer to determine full-time employee status.

COMMENT: The IRS has placed some restrictions on use of the lookback measurement method. For example, an employer may not use it for seasonal employees while using the monthly measurement method for other employees.

COMMENT: Several bills have been introduced in Congress to increase the threshold for full-time status from 30 hours to 40 hours of service per week.

Those not considered employees under Code Sec. 4980H. The following are not included in measuring employees under Code Sec. 4980H:

- Leased employees;
- Sole proprietors;
- Partners in a partnerships;
- 2 percent S corporation shareholders;
- Direct sellers; and
- Real estate agents (Code Sec. 3508).

Seasonal Employees

Since enactment of the Affordable Care Act, questions arose about how to treat the services of seasonal employees. An employer, especially in the construction and retail trades, may employ a significantly larger number of employees at certain times of the year. The proposed reliance regulations (REG-113792-13) initially addressed the treatment of seasonal workers and the final regulations (TD 9672) further refine that treatment.

An employer is not an applicable large employer if the seasonal worker exception applies. This exception applies if:

- The employer's workforce exceeds 50 full-time employees (including full-time equivalent employees) for 120 or fewer days during the calendar year; and
- Its employees in excess of 50 employed during the 120-day period are seasonal workers.

Four calendar months counts as 120 days. Months or days for the 120-day rule do not have to be consecutive. Under the Affordable Care Act, the definition of *seasonal emplo* yee is made by reference to DOL regulations. Labor is performed on a seasonal basis when, ordinarily, the employment pertains to or is of the kind exclusively performed at certain seasons or periods of the year and that, from its nature, may not be continuous or carried on throughout the year. A worker who moves from one seasonal activity to another while employed in agriculture or performing agricultural labor is employed on a seasonal basis even though he or she may continue to be employed during a major portion of the year.

Variable-Hour Employees

Workers in the hospitality and retail trades often work variable hours. In the final regulations, the IRS explained that a worker is a variable-hour employee if, based on the facts and circumstances at the employee's start date, the employer cannot determine whether the employee is reasonably expected to be employed on average at least 30 hours of service per week during the initial measurement period because the employee's hours of service are variable or otherwise uncertain. The IRS described various factors, including:

- The extent to which the hours of service of employees in the same or comparable positions have actually varied above and below an average of 30 hours of service per week during recent measurement periods; and
- Whether the job was documented as requiring hours of service that would average at least 30 hours of service per week, fewer than 30 hours of service per week, or varying above and below an average of 30 hours of service per week.

EXAMPLE: Jacob Ruiz is hired on an hourly basis by NANO Co. to fill in for employees who are absent and to provide additional staffing at peak times. The employer expects that Jacob will average 30 hours of service per week or more for his first few months of employment while assigned to a specific project, but also reasonably expects that the assignments will be of unpredictable duration, that there will be periods of unpredictable duration between assignments, that the hours per week required by subsequent assignments will vary, and that Jacob will not necessarily be available for all assignments. NANO cannot determine whether Jacob is reasonably expected to average at least 30 hours of service per week for the initial measurement period. Accordingly, NANO may treat Jacob as a variable-hour employee.

COMMENT: All employers generally may determine when an employee has separated from service by considering all the facts and circumstances and by using a reasonable method consistent with the employer's general practices, such as *Consolidated Omnibus Budget Reconciliation Act* (COBRA) coverage, benefit plan rules, and state laws.

Volunteer Employees

In some positions, volunteers may receive compensation for their labor, such as a stipend or reimbursement of expenses. Under the final regulations, hours of service do not include hours worked as a "bona fide volunteer." A *bona fide volunteer* is any individual who performs his or her services for a governmental entity exempt from taxation and whose only compensation is reimbursement for reasonable expenses or reasonable benefits, such as length of service awards.

COMMENT: The most common group of bona fide volunteers envisioned by the final regulations is volunteer emergency responders.

EXAMPLE: Aidan Harrison is a certified emergency medical technician and volunteers at the Volunteer Fire and Rescue Squad, located in the town of Springfield, which officially sponsors the squad. Aiden volunteers for a total of 24 hours every month. He receives no monetary compensation for his services and pays for his own uniform and supplies. The town has traditionally presented volunteers with a small monetary award at the end of every five years of service. Aiden has completed five years of service as of July 31, 2014. His award is the type contemplated under the final regulations as being outside of the type of compensation that would bring Aiden within the scope of being an "employee" for purposes of the employer mandate.

Student Employees

Since enactment of the Affordable Care Act, educational organizations have requested special rules for determining the hours of service of employees who are also students of a school, college, or other educational institution. The final regulations provide that hours of service for Code Sec. 4980H purposes do not include hours performed by students in federal or other governmental work-study programs. Services by an unpaid intern would not count as hours of service for Code Sec. 4980H purposes under the general definition of hours of service to the extent that the student does not receive, and is not entitled to, payment.

EXAMPLE: Marcia Abernathy is a second-year student at the Nevada College of Veterinary Medicine. Marcia applied for and was accepted into a six-week internship at a local veterinary hospital. Marcia began interning on October 20, 2014, and performs various duties at the veterinary hospital two days each week, eight hours per day. Marcia will receive academic credit for the internship from Nevada College but no monetary compensation from the veterinary hospital. Marcia is an intern and not an "employee" for purposes of the employer mandate.

COMMENT: Educational organizations expressed concerns that schools would be reluctant to employ students in work-study programs and also discourage outside employers from offering internships to student if work-study students and unpaid interns were deemed to be under the umbrella of Code Sec. 4980H.

Members of Religious Orders

The Affordable Care Act did not address whether members of religious orders are employees. The final regulations provide a special rule: A religious order may exclude from its calculation of a worker's hours of service any work performed by an individual who is subject to a vow of poverty as a member of that order.

Adjunct Faculty

The final regulations provide a special rule for institutions of higher learning employing adjunct faculty members. These employers must use a reasonable method for crediting hours of service that is consistent with the overall purpose of the employer mandate.

One method, the IRS explained, would be to credit an adjunct faculty member of an institution of higher education with both:

- $2\frac{1}{4}$ hours of service (representing a combination of teaching or classroom time and time performing related tasks such as class preparation and grading of examinations or papers) per week for each hour of teaching or classroom time (in other words, in addition to crediting an hour of service for each hour teaching in the classroom, this method would credit an additional $1\frac{1}{4}$ hours for activities such as class preparation and grading); and, separately,
- An hour of service per week for each additional hour outside of the classroom the faculty member spends performing duties he or she is required to perform (such as required office hours or required attendance at faculty meetings).

COMMENT: The IRS explained that this is one but not the only method of treating adjunct faculty members. However, the IRS did not provide any other methods in the final regulations. Moreover, the IRS added that employers may rely on this method at least through the end of 2015.

Airline Employees

The IRS also provided a method for calculating hours spent on layovers by airline employees. Generally, employers must use a reasonable method for crediting hours of service that is consistent with the overall purpose of the employer mandate. The IRS explained that it is not reasonable for an employer to not credit a layover hour as an hour of service if the employee receives compensation for the layover hour beyond any compensation that the employee would have received without regard to the layover hour or if the employer counts the layover hour toward the required hours of service for the employee to earn his or her regular compensation.

On-Call Employees

Employees may be required to be "on-call" (available to come to work) in the course of their employment. As of the time this course was prepared, the IRS was continuing to study the treatment of on-call hours. In the interim, the IRS provided guidance in the final regulations. Employers must use a reasonable method to credit hours of service that is consistent with the employer mandate. The IRS explained that it is not reasonable for an employer to fail to credit an employee with an hour of service for any on-call hour for which payment is made or due, for which the employee is required to remain on-call on the employer's premises, or for which the employee's activities while remaining on-call are subject to substantial restrictions that prevent the employee from using the time effectively for the employee's own purposes.

Short-Term Employees/High-Turnover Positions

Neither the Affordable Care Act nor the IRS final regulations provide an exception for short-term employees or ones in high-turnover jobs. The IRS reported a concern about potential for abuse by employers using initial training period positions or other methods to artificially divide the tenure of an employee into one or more short-term employment positions to avoid application of Code Sec. 4980H. Similarly, the IRS declined to provide any special rules for employees in high-turnover positions. Any special treatment for employees hired into a high-turnover position could be an incentive for employers to terminate employees to ensure that the position remains a high-turnover position and thereby to avoid Code Sec. 4980H, the IRS cautioned.

STUDY QUESTION

---

2. The Code Sec. 4980H rules for measuring the number of full-time employees apply to:

    a. Part-time employees

    b. Bona fide volunteers

    c. Leased employees

    d. Students holding work-study positions

¶ 106 MINIMUM ESSENTIAL COVERAGE

Minimum essential coverage under the Affordable Care Act and IRS regulations includes the following:

- Employer-sponsored coverage (including COBRA coverage and retiree coverage);
- A grandfathered plan, which, generally, is a group health plan or health insurance coverage in effect on March 23, 2010;
- Coverage purchased in the individual market, including a qualified health plan offered by the Health Insurance Marketplace;
- Medicare Part A coverage and Medicare Advantage (MA) plans;
- Most Medicaid coverage;
- Children's Health Insurance Program (CHIP) coverage;
- Certain types of veterans health coverage administered by the Veterans Administration;
- TRICARE;
- Coverage provided to Peace Corps volunteers;
- Coverage under the Nonappropriated Fund Health Benefit Program;
- Refugee Medical Assistance supported by the Administration for Children and Families;
- Self-funded health coverage offered to students by universities for plan or policy years that begin on or before December 31, 2014 (for later plan or policy years, sponsors of these programs may apply to HHS to be recognized as minimum essential coverage); and
- State high-risk pools for plan or policy years that begin on or before December 31, 2014 (for later plan or policy years, sponsors of these programs may apply to HHS to be recognized as offering minimum essential coverage).

Employer Coverage

Employer-provided coverage (generally by any size employer) for purposes of the Affordable Care Act is generally treated as minimum essential coverage. There are two important criteria in determining when coverage is not minimum essential coverage. The coverage may be unaffordable or fail to meet minimum value standards. Additionally, some coverage is expressly treated as not providing minimum essential coverage, including coverage only for accident or disability income insurance, or any combination thereof; workers' compensation or similar insurance; and coverage for on-site medical clinics.

Minimum value. If employer-provided coverage fails to offer minimum value, an employee may be eligible to obtain coverage through the marketplace and, further, may be eligible for the Code Sec. 36B premium assistance tax credit. An employer plan is treated as failing to provide minimum value if the plan's share of the total allowed costs of benefits provided under the plan is less than 60 percent of those costs.

> **COMMENT:** The percentage of total allowed costs of benefits is determined by reference to regulations issued by HHS. Employers may use an online calculator developed by HHS or may determine minimum value using a safe harbor. These actuarial analyses are beyond the scope of this chapter.

Affordability. An employer plan may be treated as providing minimum essential coverage but is deemed unaffordable to the employee. An employer plan is treated as providing affordable coverage if the employee's required contribution for self-only coverage does not exceed 9.5 percent of the taxpayer's household income for the tax year (9.56 percent for tax years beginning in 2015 as adjusted by the IRS to reflect the excess of premium growth over income growth). Employers need to determine whether the coverage offered—if they offer coverage—is affordable. The Code Sec. 36B premium assistance tax credit links affordability to an employee's household income. Because an employer generally will not know an employee's household income, the IRS has created three optional safe harbors:

- Form W-2 wages safe harbor—using this method, employers may calculate the affordability of the coverage based solely on the wages paid to the employee as reported on the employee's Form W-2.

> **EXAMPLE:** Adam Green is employed by Seagreen Company consistently from January 1, 2015, through December 31, 2015. Seagreen offers Adam and his dependents minimum essential coverage during that period that provides minimum value. The employee contribution for self-only coverage is $100 per calendar month, or $1,200 for the calendar year. For 2015, Adam's Form W-2 wages with respect to employment with Seagreen are $24,000. Because the employee contribution for 2015 is less than 9.56 percent of Adam's Form W-2 wages for 2015, the coverage offered is treated as affordable with respect to Adam for 2015 ($1,200 = 5 percent of $24,000).

- Rate of pay safe harbor—an employer's offer of coverage would be treated as affordable for the calendar month if the employee's required contribution for the calendar month for the lowest-cost self-only coverage that provides minimum value does not exceed:

—9.5 percent (9.56 for 2015) of an amount equal to 130 hours multiplied by the lower of the employee's hourly rate of pay as of the first day of the coverage period (generally the first day of the plan year) or

—The employee's lowest hourly rate of pay during the calendar month.

> **EXAMPLE:** Transair Corp. offers its full-time employees and their dependents minimum essential coverage that provides minimum value. For 2015, Tran-

sair uses the rate of pay safe harbor to establish premium contribution amounts for full-time employees paid at a rate of $7.25 per hour for each calendar month of the entire 2015 calendar year. Transair can apply the rate of pay safe harbor by using an assumed monthly income amount that is based on an assumed 130 hours of service multiplied by $7.25 per hour ($942.50 per calendar month). To satisfy the safe harbor, Transair would set the employee monthly contribution amount at a rate that does not exceed 9.56 percent of the assumed monthly income of $942.50. Transair sets the employee contribution for self-only coverage at $85 per calendar month for 2015. Because $85 is less than 9.56 percent of the employees' assumed monthly income at a $7.25 rate of pay, the coverage offered is treated as affordable under the rate of pay safe harbor for each calendar month of 2016 ($85 = 9.02 percent of $942.50).

- Federal poverty line safe harbor—an employer's offer of coverage would be treated as affordable if the employee's required contribution for the calendar month for the lowest-cost self-only coverage that provides minimum value does not exceed 9.5 percent (9.56 percent for 2015) of the monthly amount determined as the federal poverty line for a single individual for the calendar year, divided by 12.

EXAMPLE: Amber Williams is employed by Belmont Co. from January 1, 2015, through December 31, 2015. Amber is a full-time employee working more than 35 hours each week. Belmont offers Amber minimum essential coverage during that period that provides minimum value. Assuming that the federal poverty line for 2015 for an individual is $11,670, Belmont sets the monthly employee contribution for employee single-only coverage for each calendar month of 2015 at $70. The coverage under the plan is treated as affordable with respect to Amber, because the employee contribution does not exceed 9.56 percent of the federal poverty line.

COMMENT: If an employer offers multiple healthcare coverage options, the affordability test applies to the lowest-cost self-only option available to the employee that also meets the minimum value requirement.

COMMENT: An employee's election of coverage is treated as continuing into future years unless the employee affirmatively opts out of coverage.

COMMENT: Affordability of employer-provided coverage also is part of the calculation for the Affordable Care Act's individual shared responsibility payment under Code Sec. 5000A. Generally, an individual is exempt from the individual shared responsibility requirement for any month for which the individual does not have access to affordable minimum essential coverage. If the individual's required contribution for coverage for the month exceeds 8 percent of household income for the tax year, the coverage is deemed unaffordable. For plan years beginning in 2015, the percentage increases to 8.05 percent.

STUDY QUESTION

---

3. Why did the IRS develop the three safe harbors for employer plans?
   - **a.** Employers may not know their employees' household income
   - **b.** To apply different safe harbors for self-only coverage versus coverage for spouses or dependents
   - **c.** To exempt small employers from the employer mandate
   - **d.** To delay the effective date for applicable large employers to 2016

¶ 107 HOURS OF SERVICE

Employers must calculate each of their employees' hours of service. The calculations differ for employees who are paid an hourly wage and employees who are salaried. Hours of service also encompass time for which an employee is entitled to payment, including holidays, paid sick days, and military leave.

Hourly Basis

The employees of an applicable large employer may be paid on an hourly basis. For hourly employees, an employer is required to calculate actual hours of service from records of hours worked and hours for which payment is made or due.

Salaried Basis

For salaried employees, an employer may calculate the actual hours of service using the same method as for hourly employees. Alternatively, employers may use a days-worked equivalency, crediting the employee with eight hours of service for each day for which the employee would be required to be credited with at least one hour of service, or a weeks-worked equivalency, crediting an employee with 40 hours of service for each week for which the employee would be required to be credited with at least one hour of service.

In the final regulations, the IRS provided employers with some flexibility concerning salaried employees. An employer may change its method of calculating the hours of service of salaried employees for each calendar year. Additionally, an employer may use different equivalencies for different groups of salaried employees.

> **COMMENT:** Employers cannot manipulate the equivalencies so that the result is to treat a full-time employee as a part-time employee. Proposed regulations included an antiabuse rule that barred the use of equivalencies when the result would be a substantial understatement of an employee's hours of service, causing him or her not to be treated as a full-time employee. The final regulations expanded the antiabuse rule to also prohibit the use of an equivalency method if the result is to understate hours of service for a substantial number of employees, even if no given employee's hours of service are understated substantially and even if the understatement would not cause the employee to not be treated as a full-time employee.

Employers may, for example, use different measurement periods for employees who are members of a collective bargaining unit and employees who are not members of that unit. An employer also may use different measurement periods for employees in different collective bargaining units.

> **EXAMPLE:** Hydra Co. operates a power plant facility in which 326 full-time employees are part of a collective bargaining union represented by steamfitters' union. Another 115 employees are members of a collective bargaining unit represented by the iron workers' union. Finally, 33 employees are members of a collective bargaining unit represented by the office and professional employees union. Hydra may use different measurement periods for the various collective bargaining units.

¶ 108 NEW EMPLOYERS

Under the final regulations issued in 2014, the calculation of whether a new employer is an applicable large employer during its first calendar year is based on the reasonable expectations of the employer at the time that employer comes into existence.

EXAMPLE: On January 31, 2016, Grisson Co. is organized as a corporation with 3 employees. Prior to its incorporation, the owners purchased a factory that is expected to open within two calendar months of incorporation and to employ approximately 100 full-time employees. By March 15, 2016, Grisson has more than 75 full-time employees. Because Grisson can reasonably be expected to employ on average at least 50 full-time employees on business days during 2016, and actually employs an average of at least 50 full-time employees on business days during 2016, Grisson is an applicable large employer for calendar year 2016.

STUDY QUESTION

4. All of the following are methods employers may use to calculate salaried employees' annual hours of service *except:*

   a. Months-worked equivalency

   b. Actual hours of service

   c. Weeks-worked equivalency

   d. Days-worked equivalency

¶ 109 ASSESSABLE PAYMENTS

Applicable large employers responsible for either Section 4980H(a) or Section 4980H(b) liability will make a shared responsibility payment. This payment is known under the Affordable Care Act as an "assessable payment." Full-time equivalent employees are not included in the calculation of any assessable payment, either under Code Sec. 4980H(a) or Code Sec. 4980H(b), but are counted in determining whether the employer is an applicable large employer.

Section 4980H(a) Assessable Payment

The monthly assessable payment for the Section 4980H(a) liability is equal to 1/12 of $2,000 (inflation-adjusted starting in 2015) multiplied by the number of the employer's full-time employees (not counting full-time equivalent employees) minus 30 for any month in which any full-time employee have marketplace coverage and receive the Code Sec. 36B credit.

EXAMPLE: Belltown Co. employs 300 full-time employees in 2014. The company does not offer health coverage to employees. Twenty employees obtain coverage through the marketplace and all 20 individuals receive the Code Sec. 36B premium assistance tax credit. The monthly assessable payment for Belltown's Section 4980H(a) liability for 2015 is equal to 1/12 of $2,000 (inflation-adjusted) multiplied by the number of the Belltown's full-time employees minus 30 (or 270 employees in this case) for any month in which any full-time employees have marketplace coverage and receive the Code Sec. 36B credit.

Section 4980H(b) Assessable Payment

The monthly assessable payment for Section 4980H(b) liability is 1/12 of $3,000 (inflation-adjusted starting in 2015) for each month a full-time employee (not counting full-time equivalent employees) obtains coverage through the marketplace and receives the Code Sec. 36B premium assistance tax credit. The maximum amount of the Code Sec. 4980H(b) assessable payment is capped at the amount of the assessable payment that would have been assessed for a failure to provide coverage.

> **EXAMPLE:** Thruput Co. offers health coverage to all of its 200 full-time employees in 2014; 10 full-time employees obtain coverage through the marketplace and 7 of these individuals receive the Code Sec. 36B premium assistance tax credit. The assessable payment for Section 4980H(b) liability is 1/12 of $3,000 × 7 for each month the 7 employees obtain coverage through the marketplace and receive the Code Sec. 36B premium assistance tax credit. The maximum amount of the Code Sec. 4980H(b) assessable payment for Thruput would be capped at the amount of the assessable payment that would have been assessed for a failure to provide coverage.

> **COMMENT:** The Affordable Care Act provides an inflation adjustment for the assessable payment under Code Sec. 4980H(a) and 4980H(b) after 2014.

The IRS will advise employers if one or more of its employees have received a Code Sec. 36B premium assistance tax credit or cost-sharing reduction. At the time this course was prepared, the IRS had not yet provided details about how it will contact employers. The IRS has, however, indicated that it will likely not contact employers until after individual income tax returns are due (April 15, 2015). Individuals must report claims for the Code Sec. 36B premium assistance tax credit on their 2014 federal income tax returns. A Medicaid-eligible individual can always choose to leave the employer's coverage and enroll in Medicaid, and an employer will not be subject to an assessable payment for any employees enrolled in Medicaid.

> **COMMENT:** An employer may not deduct an assessable payment under Code Sec. 4980H(a) or Code Sec. 4980H(b).

¶ 110 DEPENDENTS

Many employer-sponsored health plans cover qualified dependents of the employee. Other plans do not. For 2014 and 2015, special transition relief is available.

Who Is a Dependent?

A dependent for purposes of Code Sec. 4980H is a child (a son or daughter of an employee who has not attained age 26). An employee's spouse is not a dependent. In the final regulations, the IRS reiterated that a grandchild is not a dependent for purposes of Code Sec. 4980H. A foster child or a stepchild is also not a dependent for purposes of Code Sec. 4980H.

> **COMMENT:** A child is a dependent for purposes of Code Sec. 4980H for the entire calendar month during which he or she attains age 26. An employer may rely on an employee's representation about the age(s) of his or her child(ren).

Additionally, a child otherwise qualifying as a dependent who is not a U.S. citizen or national is not a dependent unless the child is a resident of a country contiguous to the United States or is within the exception for adopted children under Code Sec. 152(b)(3)(B).

Transition Relief

The IRS has provided special transition relief related to employer coverage and dependents. Generally, an applicable large employer will not be subject to an assessable payment under Code Sec. 4980H solely on account of the employer's failure to offer coverage to dependents for the 2014 plan year. Additionally, applicable large employers may be eligible for transition relief for the 2015 plan year if dependent coverage is not offered, dependent coverage that does not constitute minimum essential coverage is offered, or dependent coverage is offered for some, but not all, dependents.

¶ 111 MAXIMUM 90-DAY WAITING PERIOD

Effective for plan years beginning on or after January 1, 2014, a group health plan or health insurance issuer offering group health insurance coverage may not apply any waiting period—the period of time that must pass before the individual is eligible for benefits—that exceeds 90 days. In 2014, the IRS along with HHS and DOL issued final regulations reiterating that a group health plan, and a health insurance issuer offering health insurance coverage, cannot apply a waiting period that exceeds 90 days. If, under the terms of the plan, an individual can elect coverage that becomes effective on a date that does not exceed 90 days, the coverage is treated as complying with the 90-day limitation.

> **COMMENT:** The plan or issuer will not be considered to have violated the limitation period merely because individuals may take additional time, beyond the 90-day period, to elect coverage, the agencies added.

Orientation Period

Code Sec. 4980H generally requires that health benefits begin by the first day of the fourth calendar month in which the qualified employee begins employment. After an individual is determined to be otherwise eligible for coverage, any waiting period may not extend beyond 90 days and all calendar days are counted beginning on the enrollment date, including weekends and holidays. However, a requirement to successfully complete a reasonable and bona fide employment-based orientation period may be imposed as a condition for eligibility. Under the regulations issued by the agencies, one month is the maximum length of any orientation period.

STUDY QUESTION

---

5. A _____ is considered a dependent under Code Sec. 4980H provisions.

   a. Spouse
   b. Foster child
   c. Son or daughter younger than age 26
   d. Stepchild

¶ 112 EMPLOYER MANDATE TRANSITION RELIEF FOR 2015

Employers with at least 50 but fewer than 100 full-time employees, including full-time equivalent employees, are eligible for transition relief for 2015 (Notice 2013-45). For employers with 100 or more full-time employees, including full-time equivalent employees, the employer mandate still becomes effective in 2015, but employers that qualify under new transition relief rules for that group will only be required to provide coverage to 70 percent, instead of 95 percent, of qualified employees in 2015. The transition relief is available for all of 2015, plus, in the case of any noncalendar plan that begins in 2015, the transition relief is available for the part of the 2015 plan year that falls in 2016. Employers that qualify for the transition relief will not be liable for an assessable payment under Code Sec. 4980H(a) or Code Sec. 4980H(b).

> **COMMENT:** At the time this course was prepared, HHS and the IRS indicated that transition relief would not be extended beyond 2015. It is possible, however, that the transition relief could be modified, expanded, or extended at a future date.

Requirements for Transition Relief

The IRS has imposed a number of requirements that employers must satisfy before they may be eligible for the transition relief:

- Limited workforce size;
- Maintenance of workforce;
- Maintenance of previously offered coverage; and
- Certification.

Limited workforce size. The qualified employer must employ on average at least 50 full-time employees, including full-time equivalent employees, but fewer than 100 full-time employees, including full-time equivalent employees, on business days during 2014.

> **EXAMPLE:** Brannock Co. sponsors a group health plan. As of February 9, 2014, 88 of its full-time employees (zero full-time equivalent employees) are offered coverage. Between February 9, 2014 and December 31, 2014, 2 full-time employees voluntarily leave employment, leaving a workforce of 86 employees. There are no further reductions in the number of full-time employees during the period February 9, 2014 and December 31, 2014. Brannock also makes no changes in the coverage offered to its employees during that relevant period. Three employees obtain coverage in the marketplace and are eligible for the Code Sec. 36B premium assistance tax credit. Brannock completes the required certification. Brannock is eligible for transition relief for 2015.

Maintenance of workforce. Beginning February 9, 2014, and ending on December 31, 2014, the transition relief requires that the employer make no reduction in the size of its workforce or the overall hours of service of its employees with the purpose of satisfying the workforce size requirement (discussed above). An employer may make changes to the size of its workforce or hours of service for bona fide business reasons.

> **COMMENT:** The IRS explained in the transition relief provisions that an example of a bona fide reduction would be a reduction made in response to changes in the economy and terminations of employees for poor performance. Reductions to take advantage of the transition relief by themselves are not bona fide reductions.

> **EXAMPLE:** Merrill Co. employees 112 full-time employees as of February 9, 2014. The company offers health coverage to its employees. No employee is receiving coverage through the marketplace as of February 9, 2014, and no employee is eligible for the Code Sec. 36B premium assistance tax credit as of February 9, 2014. On September 8, 2014, Merrill notifies 19 employees that their employment has been terminated effective the same day. Merrill made this decision for the sole purpose of reducing the number of full-time employees below 100 to take advantage of the transition relief. The company is not eligible for the transition relief because it failed to satisfy the maintenance of workforce requirement. The decision to end the employment of 19 employees was not based on a bona fide business reason but was made to take advantage of the transition relief.

Maintenance of previously offered coverage. Beginning February 9, 2014, and ending on December 31, 2014, for purposes of transition relief, the employer may not eliminate or materially reduce the health insurance as offered to employees on February 9, 2014. For employers with noncalendar year plans, the relevant period begins February 9, 2014, and ends on the last day of the plan year that begins in 2015.

Certification. The transition relief rules require that the employer certify it satisfies the eligibility requirements. At the time this course was prepared, the IRS had not yet posted a form on which employers would make this certification or provided any instructions. The IRS indicated that the certification will be part of Code Sec. 6056 reporting (discussed below).

New Employers

A new employer may be eligible for the transition relief. If the new employer comes into existence in 2015 and reasonably expects to employ and actually employs fewer than 100 full-time employees, including full-time equivalent employees, on business days during 2015, the employer may take advantage of the transition relief. The new employer must also provide the certification just described.

¶ 113 CODE SEC. 6056 REPORTING

The Affordable Care Act generally requires all applicable large employers to file an information return that reports the terms and conditions of the health care coverage provided to the employer's full-time employees for the year. This is known as *Code Sec. 6056 reporting,* whose purpose is to assist the IRS in the administration of the Code Sec. 36B premium assistance tax credit and Code Sec. 4980H, the employer mandate overall.

> **COMMENT:** The Affordable Care Act also requires every health insurance issuer, sponsor of a self-insured health plan, government agency that administers government-sponsored health insurance programs, and other entities that provide minimum essential coverage to file annual returns reporting information for each individual for whom such coverage is provided. This is known as *Code Sec. 6055 reporting.*

Reporting Requirements

An applicable large employer subject will generally be required to provide the following information to the IRS:

- The employer's name, address, and employer identification number;
- The calendar year for which information is being reported;
- A certification as to whether the employer offered to its full-time employees and their dependents the opportunity to enroll in minimum essential coverage under an employer-sponsored plan;
- The number, address and Social Security/taxpayer identification number of all full-time employees;
- The number of full-time employees eligible for coverage under the employer's plan; and
- The employee's share of the lowest cost monthly premium for self-only coverage providing minimum value offered to that full-time employee.

The IRS reported in 2013 that it intends to use indicator codes to simplify Code Sec. 6056 reporting. For example, an indicator code would be available to report whether an employer offered minimum essential coverage to the employee only, the employee and the employee's dependents only, the employee and the employee's spouse only, or the employee and the employee's spouse and dependents. At the time this course was prepared, the IRS was developing the requisite form for Code Sec. 6056 reporting. The IRS is requiring all Code Sec. 6056 information returns to be filed no later than February 28 (March 31 if filed electronically) of the year immediately following the calendar year to which the return relates.

> **COMMENT:** Generally, electronic filing is mandatory for employers filing 250 or more Code Sec. 6056 returns.

Employee Statements

Applicable large employers are also required to provide statements to each full-time employee describing the employer-sponsored coverage and some of the items reported to the IRS on the Code Sec. 6056 return. At the time this course was prepared, the IRS was developing additional guidance on the requirements for employee statements. Code Sec. 6056 employee statements will be provided annually to full-time employees on or before January 31 of the year immediately following the calendar year to which the employee statements relate.

Transition Relief

Under transition relief, Code Sec. 6056 reporting is optional for 2014. The IRS explained in Notice 2013-45 that additional time is needed for employers to prepare for Code Sec. 6056 reporting. The IRS encouraged employers to voluntarily comply with Code Sec. 6056 reporting for 2014.

> **COMMENT:** Under the transition relief, the first Code Sec. 6056 returns required to be filed are for the 2015 calendar year. These returns must be filed no later than March 1, 2016 (February 28, 2016, being a Sunday), or March 31, 2016, if filed electronically. The first employee statements must be provided to full-time employees no later than February 1, 2016 (January 31, 2016, is a Sunday).

STUDY QUESTION

6. Workforce and plan coverage requirements for Code Sec. 4980H transition relief apply to the period:

    a. Calendar year 2014

    b. February 9, 2014, through December 31, 2014

    c. February 9, 2014, through March 15, 2015

    d. Calendar year 2015

¶ 114 CONCLUSION

Since passage of the Affordable Care Act in 2010, the employer mandate provisions have been interpreted in final regulations and have been the subject of delay in transition relief. Large employers, especially very large employers, began to prepare for the employer mandate soon after passage of the Affordable Care Act. For midsize employers, the transition relief is particularly valuable. Midsize employers will have additional time to develop and implement the mechanics of gathering data and reporting information for the employer mandate. Small employers are and will continue to be exempt from the reach of the employer mandate.

MODULE 1: EMPLOYER/BUSINESS ISSUES—Chapter 2: Capitalization and Repairs—Compliance Rules

¶ 201 WELCOME

The deadline for complying with the final tangible property regulations (T.D. 9636, September 19, 2013), popularly known as the "repair regulations," is a taxpayer's first tax year beginning on or after January 1, 2014. Broadly speaking, the repair regulations provide rules for distinguishing between currently deductible repairs and capitalized improvements.

Compliance will typically require the filing of at least one Form 3115, *Application for Change in Accounting Method,* as well as the computation of a Code Sec. 481(a) adjustment for many of a taxpayer's current accounting methods that need to be changed to a method required under the final regulations.

¶ 202 LEARNING OBJECTIVES

Upon completion of the chapter you will be able to:

- Identify when to deduct materials and supplies;
- Recognize the significance of the *de minimis* safe harbor election, the small building-small taxpayer election, and book-capitalization election;
- Recognize the significance of the routine maintenance safe harbor;
- Identify expenditures that are capitalized as betterments, restorations, and adaptations and expenditures that are deductible as repairs; and
- Identify which accounting method changes need to be filed to comply with the repair regulations and special considerations in making those filings.

¶ 203 INTRODUCTION

The repair regulations were finalized by T.D. 9636, which was issued on September 19, 2013.

The final regulations primarily cover the following subject areas:

- Materials and supplies—Reg. § 1.162-3;
- *De minimis* safe harbor election—Reg. § 1.263(a)-1(f);
- Acquisitions of tangible property—Reg. § 1.263(a)-2; and
- Improvements to tangible property—Reg. § 1.263(a)-3.

The repair regulations will affect all taxpayers with depreciable assets, materials and supplies, or improvements or repairs to tangible assets.

¶ 204 FORM 3115 FILINGS

Effective Date of the Final Regulations

The final regulations are effective for tax years beginning on or after January 1, 2014. They may be applied to tax years that begin on or after January 1, 2012. Taxpayers are also allowed to apply the temporary repair regulations (T.D. 9564, December 27, 2011) that preceded and were replaced by the final regulations to tax years beginning on or after January 1, 2012, and before January 1, 2014. A taxpayer is not required to apply either the temporary or final regulations to tax years beginning on or after January 1, 2012, and before January 1, 2014.

A few of the provisions apply only to amounts paid or incurred in tax years beginning on or after January 1, 2014 (or, optionally, to amounts paid or incurred in tax years beginning on or after January 1, 2012). These provisions will be noted as covered in this course.

Accounting Method Changes

Most taxpayers will need to file one or more accounting method changes on Form 3115 to apply the repair regulations. For accounting method changes filed after January 24, 2014, accounting method procedures to change to a method in the final or temporary regulations are provided in Rev. Proc. 2014-16, 2014-19 IRB 606. Rev. Proc. 2014-16, superseded Rev. Proc. 2012-19, 2011-6 IRB 465, which provided procedures for changing to an accounting method in the temporary repair regulations for a tax year beginning on or after January 1, 2012.

Accounting method changes are discussed in detail later in this course.

¶ 205 MATERIALS AND SUPPLIES

The final regulations provide that a material or supply is deducted in the year used or consumed. However, incidental materials or supplies are deducted in the year of purchase (i.e., when the cost is paid or incurred). Materials and supplies are incidental if no record of their consumption is kept or if physical inventories at the beginning and end of the tax year are not taken (Reg. § 1.162-3(a)).

> **COMMENT:** If a taxpayer makes the *de minimis* safe harbor election described below, both nonincidental and incidental materials and supplies are deducted in the year of purchase.

A *material* or *supply* is defined as:

- A unit of property with an acquisition or production cost of less than $200;
- A unit of property that has an economic useful life of 12 months or less;
- A component, regardless of cost, used to repair or improve a unit of property;
- Fuel, lubricants, water, and similar items that are reasonably expected to be consumed in 12 months or less; or
- Any other tangible property identified in IRS guidance as a material or supply (Reg. § 1.162-3(c)(1)).

> **CAUTION:** Although the definition of a material or supply includes a component used to improve a unit of property, the regulations provide that the cost of such a material or supply must be capitalized (Reg. § 1.263(a)-3(c)(2)). However, the cost of such a material or supply may be deductible if the *de minimis* safe harbor is elected and its cost does not exceed the applicable $500 or $5,000 *de minimis* safe harbor per-item dollar limitation.

> **COMMENT:** In general, a *unit of property* is simply a group of functionally interdependent components, such as the components that compose a machine. In the case of a building, the entire building is a unit of property (Reg. § 1.263(a)-3(e)(3)).

Materials and supplies do not include inventory items or components of inventory items (Reg. § 1.162-3(c)(1)).

Rotable, Temporary, and Standby Emergency Parts

Special rules apply to rotable, temporary, and standby emergency spare parts. These parts are considered materials and supplies.

The cost of a rotable and temporary spare part, regardless of the amount, is deducted in the year of disposition unless the optional method of accounting is used or the election to capitalize and depreciate the part in the year acquired is made (Reg. § 1.162-3(a)(3)).

A *rotable spare part* is a component that is installed on a unit of property owned, leased, or serviced by the taxpayer, and that is later removed from the property, repaired or improved, and then either reinstalled on the same or other property or stored for later installation. *Temporary spare parts* are components that are used temporarily until a new or repaired part can be installed, and then are removed and stored for later installation (Reg. § 1.162-3(c)(2)).

The cost of a standby emergency spare part is deductible when installed (i.e., first used) unless an election is made to capitalize and depreciate the part in the tax year acquired.

A *standby emergency part* is a component of a particular item of machinery or equipment set aside for use as a replacement to avoid substantial operational time loss caused by emergencies due to failure of the replaced part. The part must be:

- Relatively expensive;
- Directly related to the machinery or equipment it services;
- Available only on special order (i.e., not readily available from a vendor or manufacturer); and
- Not subject to normal periodic replacement.

Generally, only one standby emergency part may be on hand for each piece of machinery or equipment (Reg. § 1.162-3(c)(3)).

> **COMMENT:** Prior to the final regulations, the IRS required a taxpayer to capitalize and depreciate standby emergency parts (Rev. Rul. 81-185, 1981-2 CB 59).

Optional method of accounting for rotable and temporary spare parts. Under the optional method, a taxpayer deducts the cost of a rotable or temporary spare part in the tax year the part is originally installed. When the part is removed, the fair market value (FMV) of the part is included in gross income, and the basis of the part ($0 because the cost was fully deducted) is increased by the FMV included in income plus the cost of removing the part, as well as any amount paid or incurred to repair, maintain, or improve the part after removal. When the part is reinstalled, the basis is deducted along with reinstallation costs. This cycle is followed for each reinstallation (Reg. § 1.162-3(e)).

The optional method is not an election and does not apply to standby emergency spare parts.

Election to capitalize and depreciate rotable, temporary, and standby parts. A taxpayer may elect to capitalize and depreciate rotable and temporary spare parts for which the optional method is not used and standby emergency spare parts (Reg. § 1.162-3(d)).

No special form or statement is required to make the election. The taxpayer simply claims a depreciation deduction for the affected spare parts on a timely filed original return (including extensions) for the tax year the asset is acquired. The election applies on a part-by-part basis and does not need to be made for all of a taxpayer's eligible rotable, temporary, or standby emergency parts (Reg. § 1.162-3(d)(3)).

Effective Date of Materials and Supplies Rules

The rules relating to materials and supplies apply to amounts paid or incurred in tax years beginning on or after January 1, 2014. However, the optional method of accounting for rotable and temporary spare parts applies to tax years beginning on or after January 1, 2014 (Reg. § 1.162-3(j)).

STUDY QUESTION

---

1. The optional method of accounting for spare parts does *not* apply to:
    a. Standby emergency spare parts
    b. Rotable spare parts
    c. Temporary spare parts
    d. The optional method applies to all three types of spare parts listed above

---

¶ 206 *DE MINIMIS* SAFE HARBOR ELECTION

The IRS has long allowed a business to expense noninventory units of property costing less than a specified dollar amount set by the taxpayer provided that the expensing policy does not materially distort taxable income. The final regulations provide formal rules regarding expensing policies in the form of a *de minimis* safe harbor election (Reg. § 1.263(a)-1(f)). If the election is made and the guidelines followed, the IRS will not challenge a taxpayer's expensing policy by arguing that taxable income is not clearly reflected.

Deduction Limits

The maximum safe-harbor deduction limit is $5,000 for each unit of property acquired or produced by a taxpayer if the taxpayer has an *applicable financial statement* (AFS) and $500 per unit of property for a taxpayer without an AFS. For example, an electing taxpayer may deduct the cost of a computer acquired or that it builds (i.e., produces) for its own use if the cost of buying or building the computer is less than the applicable $5,000 or $500 limit.

The taxpayer may set a dollar limit that is lower than the maximum limit if it desires.

In addition to units of property the safe harbor applies to materials and supplies that cost less than the applicable dollar limit, such as components used to repair or maintain or improve a unit of property.

A taxpayer may expense units of property or materials and supplies costing more than the applicable limit but the IRS will disallow those deductions if it determines in an audit that the deductions distort taxable income. No portion of such a deduction, including the cost of the unit of property that is less than the applicable $5,000 or $500 limit, is protected by the safe harbor.

An AFS includes a financial statement filed by a publicly traded company with the Securities and Exchange Commission (e.g., Form 10-K, *Annual Statement to Shareholders*), an audited financial statement certified by an independent certified public accountant, and financial statements required to be provided to a federal or state government or agency other than the SEC or IRS (Reg. § 1.263(a)-1(f)(4)).

Making the Election

A taxpayer with an AFS may make the election only if it has a *written* accounting procedure in place at the beginning of the election year that treats as an expense for nontax purposes amounts paid for property:

- Costing less than a specified dollar amount (not to exceed $5,000); or
- With an economic useful life of 12 months or less (Reg. § 1.263(a)-1(f)(1)(i)).

A taxpayer without an AFS must have a similar accounting procedure in effect (with a lower $500 limit) at the beginning of the year, but it does not need to be written (Reg. § 1.263(a)-1(f)(1)(ii)).

The safe harbor does not apply to inventory (including components of inventory) (Reg. § 1.263(a)-1(f)(2)).

> **CAUTION:** An amount that is otherwise deductible under the *de minimis* rule may need to be capitalized under the uniform capitalization (UNICAP) rules of Code Sec. 263A if it is a direct or allocable indirect cost of other property produced by the taxpayer or property acquired for resale (Reg. § 1.263(a)-1(f)(3)(v)).

The *de minimis* safe harbor is elected annually by the due date (including extensions) of the original income tax return. The election is irrevocable. A late election may be made on an amended return only with IRS consent (Reg. § 1.263(a)-1(f)(5)).

Effective Date of the *De Minimis* Safe Harbor

The safe harbor applies to amounts paid or incurred in tax years beginning on or after January 1, 2014, or, optionally, to amounts paid or incurred in tax years beginning on or after January 1, 2012 (Reg. § 1.263(a)-1(h)).

¶ 207 ROUTINE MAINTENANCE SAFE HARBOR

The costs of certain routine maintenance activities on a unit of property are currently deductible as repair expenses under a routine maintenance safe harbor (Reg. § 1.263(a)-3(i)).

Routine maintenance activities include the inspection, cleaning, and testing of the unit of property, and the replacement of damaged and worn parts with comparable and commercially available and reasonable replacement parts (Reg. § 1.263(a)-3(i)(1)(i) and (ii)). An expense that results in a betterment or adaptation is not covered. However, the cost of replacing a major component as part of routine maintenance is deductible even though the replacement of a major component would otherwise be considered a capitalized restoration cost.

The routine maintenance safe harbor is not elective.

Performance of Maintenance Activities

Under the safe harbor, an amount is currently deductible as a repair expense if it relates to ongoing activities performed to keep a unit of property in its ordinarily efficient operating condition. In the case of a building, the building structure and each building system is treated as a separate unit of property for purposes of the safe harbor (Reg. § 1.263(a)-3(i)(1)(i) and (ii)).

> **CAUTION:** The maintenance must be attributable to the taxpayer's use of the property. Thus, the safe harbor does not apply to scheduled maintenance performed shortly after purchasing a used machine or an existing building.

For property other than a building structure or system, the taxpayer must reasonably expect to perform the activities more than once during the class life of the unit of property. Class life is the same as the asset's depreciation period under the MACR alternative depreciation system (ADS) as set forth in Rev. Proc. 87-56, 1987-2 CB 674 (Reg. § 1.263(a)-3(i)(1)(ii)).

In the case of a building structure or building system, the taxpayer must expect to perform the activities more than once during the 10-year period beginning when the building structure or building system is placed in service by the taxpayer (Reg. § 1.263(a)-3(i)(1)(i)).

COMMENT: As long as the taxpayer reasonably expects to perform the maintenance at least twice during the class life or, for buildings, the 10-year period, the safe harbor applies even if it turns out that the maintenance is only performed once.

COMMENT: Betterment, restoration, and adaptation expenses are generally capitalized as improvements under the repair regulations. These types of expenses are covered in detail later in this course.

The safe harbor does not apply to the cost of replacing major or minor components if a retirement loss is claimed or a gain or loss is realized upon a sale of the replaced component (Reg. § 1.263(a)-3(i)(3)).

COMMENT: Whenever gain or loss is realized, the cost of replacing a major or minor component is a capitalized restoration expense.

The regulations provide numerous specific examples of routine maintenance, including aircraft engine shop visits performed every 4 years under a continuous maintenance program on an aircraft with a 10-year class life and maintenance expected to be performed every 4 years on a building's HVAC system (Reg. § 1.263(a)-3(i)(6)).

Effective Date of the Routine Maintenance Safe Harbor

The routine maintenance safe harbor is effective for tax years beginning on or after January 1, 2014, or optionally, for tax years beginning on or after January 1, 2012 (Reg. § 1.263(a)-3(r)).

STUDY QUESTION

2. The routine maintenance safe harbor applies to:
   a. Activities such as testing the unit of property and replacement of worn parts
   b. Activities performed at least once per year
   c. Capitalized betterment expenses
   d. Scheduled maintenance performed upon purchase of a used machine or existing building

¶ 208 BOOK CONFORMITY CAPITALIZATION ELECTION

A taxpayer may make an annual election to capitalize and depreciate repair and maintenance expenditures that are capitalized on the books and records it regularly uses to compute its trade or business income (Reg. § 1.263(a)-3(n)).

In effect, this election allows a taxpayer to sidestep the potentially complicated analysis of determining whether an expense is a repair or a capital expenditure and provides protection from the adverse audit consequences of incorrectly capitalizing a repair expense.

The election applies to all amounts paid for repair and maintenance of tangible property that are treated as capital expenditures on the taxpayer's books and records for the tax year that is covered by the election.

CAUTION: An amount that is deducted as a repair expense on the taxpayer's books and records is not deductible as a repair expense for tax purposes unless the amount is considered a repair expense under the regulations. Book treatment is irrelevant in this situation even if the election is made.

The election is made by attaching a statement to the taxpayer's timely filed original tax return (including extensions) for the tax year to which the election applies (Reg. § 1.263(a)-3(n)(2)).

Effective Date of the Book Conformity Capitalization Election

The election applies to amounts paid or incurred in tax years beginning on or after January 1, 2014, or, optionally, tax years beginning on or after January 1, 2012 (Reg. § 1.263(a)-3(r)).

¶ 209 SMALL BUILDING-SMALL TAXPAYER SAFE HARBOR ELECTION

Another elective safe harbor allows a taxpayer who owns a building with an unadjusted basis of $1 million or less to deduct otherwise capitalizable improvements to the building as repair expenses (Reg. § 1.263(a)-3(h)(3)).

Unadjusted basis is the building's cost unreduced by depreciation.

The taxpayer's average annual gross receipts during the three tax years preceding the year of election may not exceed $10 million (Reg. § 1.263(a)-3(h)(3)(iv)).

The safe harbor only applies if the total amount paid for repairs, maintenance, and improvements for the building during the tax year does not exceed the lesser of $10,000, or 2 percent of the unadjusted basis of the building.

COMMENT: Expenditures for property located outside of the building (e.g., landscaping) are not taken into account in determining whether the safe harbor applies. The treatment of such expenditures is determined without regard to the safe harbor. However, amounts deducted under the safe harbor for routine maintenance and the *de minimis* safe harbor are counted toward the $10,000 limit if they relate to the building (Reg. § 1.263(a)-3(h)(2)).

Deduction Limits

If the total of repairs, maintenance, and improvements for the building exceeds $10,000 or 2 percent of the unadjusted basis of the building, the safe harbor does not apply and the taxpayer may only claim a current deduction for its repair expenditures (Reg. § 1.263(a)-3(h)(8)).

EXAMPLE: Cody Riordan, a calendar-year taxpayer, owns two rental properties, each with an unadjusted basis of $300,000. Cody incurs $5,000 of repair and improvement expenses in 2014 on building A. Because $5,000 does not exceed the lesser of $10,000 or $6,000 ($300,000 unadjusted basis × 2 percent), Cody may elect to apply the safe harbor to building A and deduct $5,000. If Cody incurs $7,000 of repair and capital expenditures on building B, he may not make the election because $7,000 is greater than $6,000 (2 percent of building B's unadjusted basis). He deducts the expenditures that are repairs and capitalizes the expenditures that are improvements (Reg. § 1.263(a)-3(h)(10), Ex. 3).

A lessee of a building may also elect this safe harbor. For this purpose, the unadjusted basis of a leased building (or leased building space) is equal to the total amount of rent paid or expected to be paid over the entire lease term, including expected renewal periods (Reg. § 1.263(a)-3(h)(5)(ii)).

EXAMPLE: Cole Schroeder leases a building for 20 years. If the monthly rent is $4,000, the deemed unadjusted basis of the building is $960,000 ($4,000 × 12 months × 20 years). Cole may elect the safe harbor if his average annual gross receipts for the preceding 3 tax years are $10 million or less (Reg. § 1.263(a)-3(h)(10), Ex. 4).

The safe harbor is elected separately for each building that the taxpayer owns or leases.

The election is made annually by attaching an election statement on a timely filed (including extensions) original income tax return. The election is irrevocable (Reg. § 1.263(a)-3(h)(6)).

Effective Date of Small Building-Small Taxpayer Safe Harbor

The election applies to amounts paid or incurred in tax years beginning on or after January 1, 2014 or, optionally, tax years beginning on or after January 1, 2012 (Reg. § 1.263(a)-3(r)).

¶ 210 EXTENDED DUE DATE FOR ELECTIONS

Taxpayers who filed an original income tax return for a tax year beginning on or after January 1, 2012, and ending on or before September 19, 2013, are allowed an extension of time to make the election to capitalize rotable, temporary, and standby emergency parts, the *de minimis* safe harbor election, the small building-small taxpayer election, and the book-capitalization election. The election must be filed on an amended return within 180 days after the extended due date for the original return (whether or not the extension was filed). The time for making retroactive elections for a 2012 calendar year has passed; however, certain 2012-2013 fiscal year taxpayers may still qualify.

¶ 211 IMPROVEMENTS IN GENERAL

Amounts paid to "improve" a unit of tangible property are capitalized (Reg. § 1.263(a)-3(d)). There are three types of improvements:

- Betterments;
- Restorations; and
- Adaptations (Reg. § 1.263(a)-3(d)).

COMMENT: These categories of improvements are based on existing case law and generally require application of the "facts and circumstances" surrounding the particular expenditure. Consequently, it is safe to say that the repair regulations will not eliminate disputes between the IRS and taxpayers regarding the proper treatment of "borderline" expenses that share characteristics of repairs and improvements. However, the regulations formalize and illustrate with numerous examples the rules developed by case law and, in combination with the new bright line safe harbors, will provide more overall certainty than previously existed.

A taxpayer must capitalize all the direct costs of an improvement and all the indirect costs (including, for example, otherwise deductible repair costs) that directly benefit or are incurred by reason of an improvement (Reg. § 1.263(a)-3(g)(1)).

Expenditures paid or incurred prior to placing a property in service are capitalized even if they would be considered repair expenditures if paid or incurred after placing the property in service (Reg. § 1.263(a)-2(d)(1) and (d)(2), Ex. 10).

Unit of Property

The betterment, restoration, and adaptation tests are applied at the unit of property level. Generally, the larger or more costly a unit of property is the more likely expenditure can be classified as a repair rather than a betterment, restoration, or adaption that must be capitalized. For example, $100 spent on a $100 machine is more likely to be an improvement than $100 spent on a $100,000 machine.

For property other than a building, a unit of property is a group of functionally interdependent components. Components of property are functionally interdependent if the placing service of one component depends on the placing in service of the other component by the taxpayer (Reg. § 1.263(a)-3(e)(3)). For example, a car is a unit of property consisting of thousands of functionally interdependent components.

Although a *building,* including all of its structural components, is defined as a unit of property, the improvement rules requiring capitalization are applied separately to the following nine building "systems" (Reg. § 1.263(a)-3(e)(2):

- Heating, ventilation, and air conditioning (HVAC) systems (including motors, compressors, boilers, furnace, chillers, pipes, ducts, and radiators);

- Plumbing systems (including pipes, drains, valves, sinks, bathtubs, toilets, water and sanitary sewer collection equipment, and site utility equipment used to distribute water and waste to and from the property line and between buildings and other permanent structures);

- Electrical systems (including wiring, outlets, junction boxes, lighting fixtures and associated connectors, and site utility equipment used to distribute electricity from the property line to and between buildings and other permanent structures);

- All escalators;

- All elevators;

- Fire-protection and alarm systems (including sensing devices, computer controls, sprinkler heads, sprinkler mains, associated piping or plumbing, pumps, visual and audible alarms, alarm control panels, heat and smoke detection devices, fire escapes, fire doors, emergency exit lighting and signage, and firefighting equipment such as extinguishers and hoses);

- Security systems for the protection of the building and its occupants (including window and door locks, security cameras, recorders, monitors, motion detectors, security lighting, alarm systems, entry and access systems, related junction boxes, and associated wiring and conduits);

- Gas distribution systems (including associated pipes and equipment used to distribute gas to and from property line and between buildings or permanent structures); and

- Other structural components that are specifically designated as building systems in future published guidance.

Betterments

A *capitalized betterment* is an expenditure that:

- Ameliorates a material condition or defect that existed prior to the taxpayer's acquisition of the unit of property;

- Results in a material addition to a unit of property, such as a physical enlargement, expansion, extension, or addition of a new major component;

- Materially increases a unit of property's capacity, such as additional cubic or linear space; or

- Materially increases a unit of property's productivity, efficiency, strength, quality, or output (Reg. § 1.263(a)-3(j)(1)).

¶1211

The following descriptions, among many from the regulations, illustrate these various types of betterments.

The cost of remediating soil contaminated by a prior owner's leaking underground tank is the amelioration of a preexisting material condition or defect. Similarly, the amelioration of a preexisting material condition or defect includes the costs paid or incurred shortly after purchasing and placing a building in service to repair damaged drywall, repaint, rewallpaper, replace windows, repair and replace doors, replace and regrout tile, repair millwork, and repair and replace roofing materials (Reg. § 1.263(a)-3(j)(3), Exs. 1 and 5).

However, the cost of removing asbestos that begins to deteriorate after the purchase of a building is not the amelioration of a preexisting material condition or defect and may be currently deducted. Also, the cost of tuning up a machine shortly after purchase or performing scheduled maintenance is not the amelioration of a preexisting material condition or defect (Reg. § 1.263(a)-3(j)(3), Exs. 2, 3, and 4).

With respect to retail building "refresh" projects, the cost of making cosmetic and layout changes are currently deductible but the cost of a "refresh" that involves extensive remodeling must be capitalized (Reg. § 1.263(a)-3(j)(3), Exs. 6, 7, and 8).

The addition of expansion bolts that materially increases the strength of a building to protect it against earthquakes is a capitalized betterment (even if the addition was only made on account of state or local regulations) (Reg. § 1.263(a)-3(j)(3), Ex. 11). Likewise, the reinforcement of building columns to increase their ordinary load-bearing strength and replacement of a building's insulation with insulation that is significantly more energy efficient is a capitalized betterment (Reg. § 1.263(a)-3(j)(3), Exs. 14 and 21)).

COMMENT: If an expenditure is made to correct normal wear and tear that occurred to the unit of property after the taxpayer acquired it, the condition of the property after the expenditure is compared to the condition of the property after the taxpayer last corrected the effects of normal wear and tear. If the taxpayer has not previously corrected the effects of normal wear and tear, the condition of the property after the expenditure is compared to the condition of the property when placed in service by the taxpayer (Reg. § 1.263(a)-3(j)(2)(iv)(B)).

EXAMPLE: Elena Spada purchases a harbor with a channel that is 10 feet deep at the time of purchase. The cost of increasing the channel depth to 20 feet in order to handle larger boats is capitalized as a betterment because the 20-foot depth is a material increase in capacity as compared to the 10-foot depth of the harbor at the time of purchase. If the channel silts back to 10 feet, the cost the cost of redredging to 20 feet is a deductible repair because the channel's capacity is only restored to the 20-foot depth when the taxpayer last dredged (Reg. § 1.263(a)-3(j)(3), Exs. 14, 15, and 16).

Restorations

An amount is paid to restore a unit of property and, therefore is capitalized, if the expenditure (Reg. § 1.263(a)-3(k)(1)):

- Is for the replacement of a part or a combination of parts that compose a major component or a substantial structural part of a unit of property;
- Is for the replacement of a component of a unit of property and the taxpayer deducts a loss for that component;
- Is for the replacement of a component of a unit of property and the taxpayer realizes gain or loss by selling or exchanging the component;

- Returns a unit of property to its ordinary efficient operating condition after the property has deteriorated to a state of disrepair and is no longer functional for its intended use; or

- Rebuilds a unit of property to a like-new condition after the end of its class life.

Replacement of major component or substantial structural part. All facts and circumstances, including cost, size, and relative significance, are considered in determining whether a major component or substantial structural part of a unit of property is replaced (Reg. § 1.263(a)-3(k)(6)). A component may be both a major component and substantial structural part of a unit of property.

A *major component* is a nonincidental part or combination of parts that performs a discrete and critical function in the operation of the unit of property.

A substantial structural part is a part or combination of parts that composes a large portion of the physical structure of the unit of property.

In the case of a building, the replacement of a part or combination of parts that compose a major component or substantial structural part of the building structure or any one of the nine building systems is a capitalized restoration. In addition, in the case of a building structure or building system, the replacement of a significant portion of a major component of the building structure or a building system is a capitalized restoration (Reg. § 1.263(a)-3(k)(6)(ii)(A)).

EXAMPLE: The entire roof of a building is considered a major component of a building structure because the roof performs a discrete function. Alternatively, an entire roof is a major component because it is a substantial structural part of a building. Consequently, the replacement of an entire roof must be capitalized as a restoration. However, the replacement of a waterproof membrane or shingles that covers a roof's decking is not a restoration because neither the membrane nor shingles is a significant portion of the roof (i.e., a significant portion of a major component) or a substantial structural part of the building structure (Reg. § 1.263(a)-3(k)(7), Exs. 14 and 15)).

All of a building's windows in combination are treated as a single major component of the building structure that performs a discrete function. Similarly, all of the floors of a building constitute a single major component of the building structure that performs a discrete function.

EXAMPLE: A building has 300 windows that compose 25 percent of the building's surface area. The replacement of 100 windows is not the replacement of a significant portion of a major component or the replacement of a significant portion of the building structure. The replacement costs may be deducted. However, the replacement of 200 windows would constitute the replacement of a significant portion of a major component of the building structure and would have to be capitalized (Reg. § 1.263(a)-3(k)(7), Exs. 25 and 26).

EXAMPLE: The replacement of 100 of 300 of a building's windows that compose 90 percent of a building's surface area is the replacement of a substantial structural part of a building structure and must be capitalized (Reg. § 1.263(a)-3(k)(7), Ex. 27).

The regulations contain the following additional examples relating to replacements of major components (Reg. § 1.263(a)-3(k)(7)):

- A truck engine is a major component of a truck but not a substantial structural part of the truck (capitalization required) (Ex. 10);

- The cab of a truck is both a major component and a substantial structural part of the truck (capitalization required) (Ex. 10);

- A power switch assembly that controls the power supply to a drill press is an incidental component even though it is required to run the drill press (deduction allowed) (Ex. 13);
- A single furnace of an HVAC system composed of three furnaces, three air conditioning units, and duct work that runs throughout a building is not a major component or substantial structural part of the HVAC system (deduction allowed) (Ex. 16);
- Replacement of 10 percent of a hotel's entire wooden flooring is not the replacement of a significant portion of a major component or of a substantial structural part of building structure (deduction allowed) (Ex. 28);
- Replacement of 40 percent of the hotel's wooden flooring is a the replacement of a significant portion of a major component (capitalization required) (Ex. 29); and
- Replacement of one of four building elevators in the building's elevator system is not the replacement of a significant portion of a major component (all four elevators are treated as a single major component) or a substantial structural part of the building's elevator system (deduction allowed) (Ex. 30).

> **CAUTION:** As explained below, if a retirement loss is claimed on the remaining undepreciated basis of a replaced component, or portion of a replaced component, no repair deduction may be claimed.

Restoration of deteriorated units of property. If a taxpayer fails to perform regular maintenance and repair on a unit of property or a building structure or system and as a result it deteriorates to such a state that it is no longer fit for its intended use, the costs of restoring the property to a useable condition are capitalized (Reg. § 1.263(a)-3(k)(1)(iv)). The only specific example provided in the regulations requires the capitalization of the costs of shoring up the walls and replacing the siding of a deteriorated farm building that was unsafe to enter (Reg. § 1.263(a)-3(k)(7), Ex. 6).

> **COMMENT:** Although the replacement of the shingles or rubber membrane on a leaky roof is generally deductible, it appears capitalization is required if the leaks are so extensive that the building structure has become unusable.

Rebuilding to like-new condition. If a taxpayer rebuilds a unit of property to a like-new condition after the end of the unit of property's class life (i.e., the property's MACRS ADS recovery period), then all costs related to the rebuild must be capitalized (Reg. § 1.263(a)-3(k)(5)). If the rebuild occurs prior to the end of the class life, those portions of the expenditures, other than those related to the replacement of major components or substantial structural parts of the unit of property, may be deductible as repairs (Reg. § 1.263(a)-3(k)(7), Exs. 7 and 8, relating to rebuild of a railroad car).

Loss deduction results in capitalization. Although retirement of a structural component is outside the scope of this course, taxpayers are allowed to claim a retirement loss deduction on a structural component (or portion of a structural component) of a building or a component (or portion of a component) of Section 1245 property by making a partial disposition election under Reg. § 1.168(i)-8(d). However, if the taxpayer makes this election, the cost of replacing the component must be capitalized. The repair regulations specifically provide that the cost of replacing a component is a capitalized restoration if a loss on the replaced component is claimed (e.g., retirement or abandonment loss) or gain or loss is realized from the sale or exchange of the component (Reg. § 1.263(a)-3(k)(1)(i) and (ii)). If a retirement loss is claimed, removal costs are also deductible. Removal costs are discussed in detail below.

> **CAUTION:** A taxpayer should not claim a retirement loss on a replaced component (or portion of a component) unless the cost of replacement must otherwise be capitalized under the repair regulations. The repair deduction will

usually be larger than any foregone loss because the retirement loss is limited to the remaining undepreciated basis of the retired component. Generally, this means that a taxpayer should only claim a retirement loss on replaced major components because the cost of replacing a major component must be capitalized as a restoration. Note, however, that if the routine maintenance safe harbor applies, even the cost of replacing a major component is deductible and a taxpayer will also not want to claim a loss deduction on the replaced major component in this situation.

Effect of a casualty loss. A special rule applies if a casualty loss is claimed. A taxpayer that claims a casualty loss or receives an insurance reimbursement may deduct repair expenses only to the extent (if any) that the portion of the restoration expenditures that are repair expenses exceeds the adjusted basis of the property (prior to reduction by the casualty loss or insurance reimbursement) after reduction by restoration expenditures that are not capital expenses (Reg. § 1.263(a)-3(k)(4)(i)).

> **EXAMPLE:** A storm damages a building with an adjusted basis of $500,000. The cost of restoring the building is $750,000, consisting of a roof replacement ($350,000) and cleanup/repair costs ($400,000). The taxpayer claims a $500,000 casualty loss. The cost of the roof must be capitalized as a restoration/improvement because it is a major component and substantial structural part of the building structure. The remaining $400,000 cleanup/repair costs must be capitalized to the extent of the $150,000 excess of the building's adjusted basis ($500,000) over the capitalized cost of the roof ($350,000). The excess $250,000 of repair/cleanup costs ($400,000 - $150,000) are currently deductible (Reg. § 1.263(a)-3(k)(7), Exs. 3, 4, 5).

STUDY QUESTION

---

3. When a unit of property is rebuilt to like-new condition, the decision about capitalizing versus deducting costs depends on:

    a. Whether existing major components are reused when the property is rebuilt

    b. Whether the rebuild occurs during or after the property's class life

    c. Whether the taxpayer purchased the property during the same tax year it rebuilds the property

    d. Whether the taxpayer sells the property during the same tax year it rebuilds the property

---

Adaptations

An amount paid to adapt a unit of property to a use that is different from the use of the property when the taxpayer originally placed it in service must be capitalized as an improvement (Reg. § 1.263(a)-3(l)).

For example, capitalized adaptations include (Reg. § 1.263(a)-3(l)(3)):

- Conversion of a manufacturing building into a showroom;
- Regrading farmland to make it suitable for residential development; and
- Conversion of part of a retail drug store into an onsite medical clinic.

¶ 212 REMOVAL COSTS

The final repair regulations provide specific rules governing the treatment of costs for removing an asset or a component of an asset.

Removal costs are deducted as a repair expense if the taxpayer disposes of an entire asset or components of an asset and realizes gain or loss on the disposed of asset by reference to its adjusted basis. For example, removal costs are deductible if a taxpayer sells the replaced asset or has an abandonment or retirement loss, including a retirement loss claimed by making a partial disposition election under Reg. § 1.168(i)-8(d) for a component of an asset (Reg. § 1.263(a)-3(g)(2)(i)).

If a taxpayer disposes of a component of a unit of property, but the disposal of the component is not a disposition for federal tax purposes (e.g., no gain or loss is realized by making a partial disposition election), the removal costs:

- Are deductible if they directly benefit or are incurred by reason of a repair to the unit of property; and

- Must be capitalized if the removal costs directly benefit or are incurred by reason of an improvement to the unit of property (Reg. § 1.263(a)-3(g)(2)(i)).

EXAMPLE: Assume that Corbert Ellison replaces the columns in a building that support the second floor. The removal costs are deductible as a repair if:

- No loss is realized on the replaced columns by making a partial disposition election and the cost of the new columns is deductible as a repair expense because they are not stronger than the replaced columns; or

- A loss is realized on the replaced columns by making a partial disposition election whether or not the replacement columns are stronger.

The replacement costs must be capitalized if no loss is realized on the replaced columns and the new columns are stronger than the replaced columns (Reg. § 1.263(a)-3(g)(2)(ii), Exs. 1 and 2).

COMMENT: When an entire asset is replaced, the removal costs are deductible even if the asset is fully depreciated. The asset has been disposed of and the loss realized is considered $0. If a portion of a fully depreciated asset is replaced, it appears that the partial disposition election may be made to trigger a disposition event and the realization of a $0 loss in order to deduct the removal costs. The realization of a $0 loss should not trigger the rule requiring capitalization of replacement costs as a restoration expense if a loss is "deducted" because no loss is deducted.

CAUTION: Code Sec. 280B continues to require the capitalization of the costs of demolishing a building to the basis of the land. These costs include retirement losses and removal costs (Reg. § 1.168(i)-(d); Reg. § 1.263(a)-3(g)(2)(i)). For this purpose, demolitions include the removal of more than 25 percent of the existing external walls or internal structural framework (Rev. Proc. 95-27, 1995-1 CB 704). For assets other than buildings, demolition costs must be capitalized if the taxpayer acquires the property with an intent to demolish (Reg. § 1.165-3(a)).

¶ 213 ACCOUNTNG METHOD CHANGES

The final repair regulations are generally effective for tax years beginning on or after January 1, 2014. A taxpayer, however, is allowed to apply the final regulations (or the temporary repair regulations) in full or part to tax years beginning on or after January 1, 2012, and before January 1, 2014. A few of the provisions apply to amounts *paid or incurred* in tax years beginning on or after January 1, 2014 (or optionally, January 1, 2012).

Many taxpayers have not applied either the temporary or final regulations to a 2012 or 2013 tax year and are instead complying with the final regulations beginning in 2014.

COMMENT: Commentators have warned that filing a 2014 tax return that is not in compliance with the final regulations may be a violation of Circular 230, which governs practice before the IRS. Section 10.34 of Circular 230 allows the IRS to censure, suspend, or disbar a practitioner who willfully, recklessly, or through gross negligence signs a tax return that the practitioner knows or should know contains a position that lacks a reasonable basis.

It is critical to note that most portions of the repair regulations are *in effect* retroactive. As of the mandatory effective date—generally, for tax years beginning on or after January 1, 2014—the regulations are applied to expenses paid or incurred in prior years as if the repair regulations were in place in those tax years. On the other hand, the provisions that specifically apply to amounts paid or incurred in tax years beginning on or after January 1, 2014, are not retroactive.

The retroactive effect is achieved by requiring a taxpayer to file an accounting method change on Form 3115 for the 2014 tax year and to compute a Code Sec. 481(a) adjustment by applying the treatment (i.e., accounting method) required by the final regulations to a prior-year expenditure as if the final regulations were then in effect.

For example, assume a taxpayer claimed a deduction in a prior tax year for a repair expense that should be capitalized and depreciated under the rules of the final regulations. The taxpayer must file an accounting method change on Form 3115 to capitalize the repair expense and recapture, through a positive (unfavorable) Code Sec. 481(a) adjustment, the net benefit of the repair expense deduction. The Code Sec. 481(a) adjustment, however, does not need to be computed if the capitalized amount would have been fully depreciated prior to the year of change (i.e., the 2014 tax year if taxpayer implements the final regulations in 2014).

Conversely, if a previously capitalized amount is deductible as a repair expense under the final repair regulations, the taxpayer must file a Form 3115 to claim a deduction for the repair expense through a negative (favorable) Code Sec. 481(a) adjustment. However, the Code Sec. 481(a) adjustment is not necessary if the repair expense would have been fully depreciated prior to the 2014 tax year.

EXAMPLE: In 2010, Jessica Stewart capitalized and depreciated $500 of expenditures on major components of a blending machine, which under the routine maintenance safe harbor of the final repair regulations are deductible as repair expenses. She claimed $50 of depreciation in 2010, 2011, 2012, and 2013. In 2014, Jessica needs to file a Form 3115 and will compute a $300 negative (favorable) Section 481(a) adjustment ($500 - $200 depreciation from 2010 through 2013), which will reduce her 2014 taxable income.

EXAMPLE: Assume instead that Jessica claimed a $500 repair deduction in 2010 for an amount that is a capitalized betterment under the final repair regulations. The Form 3115 for 2014 would instead show a positive (unfavorable) Code Sec. 481(a) adjustment of $300 ($500 - $200 depreciation deemed allowed from 2010 through 2013) that is added to income. Jessica recovers the $300 adjustment over the remaining MACRS recovery period beginning in 2014.

COMMENT: If a repair expense that should have been capitalized is fully depreciated, it is not necessary to compute a Code Sec. 481(a) adjustment with respect to that expense. Nevertheless the taxpayer has adopted an impermissible accounting method by virtue of the manner in which the expense was previously treated and it is necessary to file a change in accounting method before this accounting method may be changed by applying the final regulations to similar future expenditures.

EXAMPLE: Assume that shingles originally replaced in 1990 and capitalized by Jessica are fully depreciated. If the shingles are replaced again in 2015, and are deductible as a repair expense under the final regulations, she may not claim a repair expense unless she files an accounting method change first.

Generally, a taxpayer who has adopted an accounting method that is inappropriate under the final repair regulations must file a Form 3115 before it can switch to the method that is required under the final repair regulations. Taxpayers may not change from an impermissible accounting method to a permissible accounting method without first obtaining IRS consent (Code Sec. 446(e) and Reg. § 1.446-1(e) (2) (i)).

COMMENT: A taxpayer has adopted an accounting method only if more than one income tax return using the improper treatment is filed (Reg. § 1.446-1(e) (2) (ii); Rev. Rul. 72-439, 1972-2 C.B. 104).

EXAMPLE: Jessica replaces the shingles of a roof in 2013 and capitalizes their cost even though they are deductible as a repair expense under the final regulations. These are the original shingles and she has never previously capitalized roof shingles on any other building that are deductible as a repair expense under the final regulations. Assuming Jessica has not filed her 2014 tax return, she must file an amended 2013 return to claim a repair deduction and may not file a Form 3115 because she has not yet adopted an accounting method by filing two incorrect returns.

STUDY QUESTION

4. In which situation is a Code Sec. 481(a) adjustment required if a taxpayer previously deducted a repair expense that should be capitalized under the final repair regulations?

    a. The repair expense would have been fully depreciated if the repair expense had been capitalized in the tax year it was claimed

    b. The repair expense was deducted in 2013 by a calendar year taxpayer and the current tax year is 2014

    c. The repair expense was claimed for the replacement of a major component which does not qualify for the routine maintenance safe harbor and must be capitalized under the repair regulations

    d. The provision requiring capitalization of the previously deducted repair expense applies to amounts paid or incurred in tax years beginning on or after January 1, 2014 and the cost in question was paid or incurred prior to that date

Elections Are Not Accounting Methods

The election to capitalize and depreciate rotable, temporary, and standby parts, the *de minimis* safe harbor election, book conformity capitalization election, and small building-small taxpayer election are not accounting methods and, therefore, making any of these elections does not require the filing of Form 3115 or a computation of a Code Sec. 481(a) adjustment. The elections may only be made on an income tax return by the prescribed deadlines previously discussed.

Revenue Procedure 2014-16

Most taxpayers will need to file one or more accounting method changes on Form 3115 to comply with the final repair regulations in their first tax year beginning on or after January 1, 2014. The repair regulations specifically provide that a taxpayer seeking to change to a method of accounting provided in the final tangible property regulations must secure IRS consent (Reg. §§ 1.162-3(i), 1.162-4(b), 1.263(a)-1(g), 1.263(a)-2(i), and 1.263(a)-3(q)).

The procedures for securing IRS consent to change to an accounting method permitted or required under the final repair regulations are provided in Rev. Proc. 2014-16, which supersedes Rev. Proc. 2012-19, effective January 24, 2014.

Rev. Proc. 2012-19 provided procedures for changes to comply with the temporary regulations for Forms 3115 filed on or before January 24, 2014.

Taxpayers who apply some or all of the temporary regulations to a tax year beginning in 2012 or 2013 are required to follow the procedures in Rev. Proc. 2014-16 if the Form 3115 is filed after January 24, 2014.

Rev. Proc. 2014-16 is an "automatic consent" procedure. Consequently, the general rules described in Rev. Proc. 2011-14 for automatic consent accounting method changes apply. Rev. Proc. 2014-16 modifies Rev. Proc. 2011-14 by adding the accounting method change procedures described in Rev. Proc. 2014-16 to the Appendix of Rev. Proc. 2011-14 and in some cases modifying existing automatic changes described in the appendix to conform to the rules in the repair regulations (e.g., the treatment of removal costs).

> **COMMENT:** The IRS does not charge a filing fee for automatic consent changes. Generally, a $7,000 filing fee applies to advance consent (nonautomatic) changes. Advance consent changes are made by following the procedures in Rev. Proc. 97-27, 1997-1 CB 680.

The accounting method change procedures that apply to the tangible property regulations are contained in Section 10.11 of the Appendix of Rev. Proc. 2011-14, as added by Rev. Proc. 2014-16. Further references to Section 10.11 refer to this appendix section.

Due date of Form 3115. Accounting method changes under Rev. Proc. 2014-16 are made by filing an original copy of Form 3115 with the taxpayer's income return no later than the extended due date of the taxpayer's income tax return for the year of change (Section 6.02 of Rev. Proc. 2011-14). A signed copy of the Form 3115 is filed with the IRS's Ogden, Utah, office in lieu of the national office, no sooner than the first day of the tax year of change and no later than the date the original copy is filed with the income tax return for the year of change (Section 10.11(7)).

This means that the deadline for filing a Form 3115 to comply with the final regulations for a 2014 calendar year individual taxpayer is October 15, 2015, assuming that the taxpayer obtains a six-month filing extension for the 2014 income tax return by filing Form 4868, *Application for Automatic Extension of Time to File U.S. Individual Income Tax Return*. The extended deadline for most business entities, however, is September 15, 2015.

> **CAUTION:** Practitioners will need to review each client's situation well in advance of the deadline in order to prepare a timely Form 3115. Form 3115 can be complicated, especially when Code Sec. 481(a) computations are required.

> **COMMENT:** The deadline for filing Form 3115 for the 2013 calendar tax year (September 15, 2014, for business entities, and October 15, 2014, for individuals) has already passed. However, taxpayers with a fiscal year beginning in 2013 may still have time to make changes for the 2013 tax year. Taxpayers who still have the opportunity to make method changes for their 2013 tax year will generally want to focus on particular changes that result in a negative (favorable) Code Sec. 481(a) adjustment and delay those changes that require a positive (unfavorable) adjustment.

COMMENT: Rev. Proc. 2014-16 was issued on January 24, 2014, which was too late for many taxpayers to use that procedure to change to a method in the final regulations for a 2012 tax year. The IRS offered no prior guidance for making such a change. A few taxpayers, however, may have used the advance consent procedure to change to a method in the final regulations in a 2012 tax year.

Concurrent filing on single Form 3115. A taxpayer should file a single Form 3115 to make all Section 10.11 accounting method changes. With the exception of certain method changes related to removal costs, Section 10.11 changes cover all of the changes described in the repair regulations.

CAUTION: Additional Form 3115s will likely need to be filed to come into compliance with MACRS regulations that were issued in connection with the repair regulations and are also effective for tax years beginning on or after January 1, 2014 (or optionally, for tax years beginning on or before January 1, 2012). For example, a taxpayer will need to file a Form 3115 to make a retroactive partial asset disposition election (Reg. § 1.168(i)-1(d)) if it wishes to claim retirement losses on partial dispositions of assets that took place before the 2012 tax year. A Form 3115 will also need to be filed to revoke retroactive general asset account elections made under the temporary regulations and to confirm the deduction of retirement losses that were claimed by filing a Form 3115 under the temporary regulations for a 2012 or 2013 tax year. Rev. Proc. 2014-54 is the automatic accounting method procedure for these and other changes under the MACRS regulations.

Summary of changes. The following chart from Rev. Proc. 2014-16 summarizes the Section 10.11 changes and provides the designated change number (DCN) and related regulation section for each type of method change.

Table 1. Designated Change Numbers for Section 10.11 Changes Definition		DCN Citation
A change to deducting amounts paid or incurred for repair and maintenance or a change to capitalizing amounts paid or incurred for improvements to tangible property and, if depreciable, to depreciating such property under Section 167 or Section 168. Includes a change, if any, in the method of identifying the unit of property, or in the case of a building, identifying the building structure or building systems for the purpose of making this change.	184	§§ 1.162-4, 1.263(a)-3
Change to the regulatory accounting method.	185	§ 1.263(a)-3(m)
Change to deducting nonincidental materials and supplies when used or consumed.	186	§§ 1.162-3(a)(1), (c)(1)
Change to deducting incidental materials and supplies when paid or incurred.	187	§§ 1.162-3(a)(2), (c)(1)
Change to deducting nonincidental rotable and temporary spare parts when disposed of.	188	§ 1.162-3(a)(3), (c)(2)
Change to the optional method for rotable and temporary spare parts.	189	§ 1.162-3(e)
Change by a dealer in property to deduct commissions and other transaction costs that facilitate the sale of property.	190	§ 1.263(a)-1(e)(2)
Change by a nondealer in property to capitalizing commissions and other costs that facilitate the sale of property.	191	§ 1.263(a)-1(e)(1)

Table 1. Designated Change Numbers for Section 10.11 Changes Definition		DCN Citation
Change to capitalizing acquisition or production costs and, if depreciable, to depreciating such property under Section 167 or Section 168.	192	§ 1.263(a)-2
Change to deducting certain costs for investigating or pursuing the acquisition of real property (whether and which).	193	§ 1.263(a)-2(f)(2)(iii)

COMMENT: The final tangible property regulations also include Reg. § 1.263(a)-2, which relates to the treatment of expenditures paid or incurred in connection with the acquisition or production of tangible property. These regulations are outside of the scope of this course but need to be reviewed and applied effective January 1, 2014, by filing accounting method changes also described in Section 10.11 on the same Form 3115 for all the method changes described in Section 10.11 relating to repairs, capitalization, units of property, materials and supplies, etc.

Scope limitations waived . The scope limitations for filing an automatic accounting method change described in Section 4.02 of Rev. Proc. 2011-14 do not apply to a taxpayer making one or more changes in method of accounting under Section 10.11 for a tax year beginning before January 1, 2015.

These scope limitations preclude a taxpayer from filing an automatic accounting method change if the taxpayer is under examination, terminating its existence, or ceasing to engage in the trade or business to which the change relates, or if during any of the five tax years ending with the year of change, the taxpayer changed its method of accounting for the same item (or attempted to change its method for the same item) (Section 4.02 of Rev. Proc. 2011-14).

One main consequence of waiver of the five-year scope limitation is that a taxpayer may file a method change for the 2013 tax year for only a portion of assets or transactions (e.g., for which data is available) and follow up with a second filing for the same method change in 2014 for the remaining assets or transactions. Taxpayers who wait to implement a particular method change until 2014 will need to gather all necessary information to make the change.

The scope limitations do not prevent a taxpayer from using the automatic consent procedure to make a method change for the 2015 tax year if the taxpayer did not file Form 3115 for the same method change for one of the five tax years ending with the year of change. However, if the IRS has begun an audit the scope limitations will preclude or limit the filing of a Form 3115.

STUDY QUESTION

5. The Rev. Proc. 2014-16 automatic consent procedure:

    a. Requires a $7,000 filing fee

    b. Applies to make method changes under the temporary regulations if filed on or before January 24, 2014

    c. Provides procedures for securing IRS permission to adopt an accounting method change under the final regulations if filed after January 24, 2014

    d. Waives the scope limitations for filing an accounting method change in a tax year beginning before January 1, 2016

Completing the Form 3115

A taxpayer must enter the designated accounting method change number for each method change on Part 1 line 1a of Form 3115 (Section 10.11(5)(a)).

For each separate accounting method change made on Form 3115, the taxpayer must provide a citation to the paragraph in the repair regulations that provides for the method to which the taxpayer is changing. For example, if a taxpayer is changing from capitalizing major components to deducting the cost by reason of the routine maintenance safe harbor, a citation to Reg. § 1.263(a)-3(i) is required (Section 10.11(4)(a)(i)).

Conversely, if a taxpayer is changing from claiming a repair deduction to capitalizing the deduction, a citation to Reg. § 1.263(a)-3(j) (betterments), (k) (restorations), (l) (adaptations), or some other controlling regulation is required (Section 10.11(4)(a)(i)).

Similarly, if a taxpayer makes a change relating to the identification of a unit of property or a building structure or building systems to which the improvement rules are applied, the unit of property, building structure, or building system used under the current taxpayer's method and the unit of property, building structure, or building system under the proposed method of accounting must be described in detail along with a citation to the paragraph in Reg. § 1.263(a)-3(e) that permits the unit of property changed to required (Section 10.11(4)(a)(i)).

The regulatory citation and, if applicable, identification of the unit of property, is provided with the information on the statement required by line 12 of Form 3115. This required statement consists of a detailed description of:

- The item being changed;
- The taxpayers' present method of accounting for the item; and
- The proposed method of accounting for the item.

Schedule E. A taxpayer who files an accounting method change to change from claiming a repair expense to capitalizing and depreciating the previously deducted amount must also complete Schedule E of Form 3115 for each item or class of depreciable property (Section 10.11(4)(iii)). Schedule E requests various specifics, including the depreciation period, method, and convention that apply to the asset and the reason for treating the asset as depreciable.

Reporting a Code Sec. 481(a) adjustment. A taxpayer changing to a method of accounting under Section 10.11 must include the total Section 481(a) adjustment for each change in method of accounting on Form 3115, Part IV line 25. The taxpayer must include on an attachment to Form 3115, the information required by line 25 for each change (i.e., a separate calculation of the Code Sec. 481(a) adjustment for each change), the information required by line 12 associated with each change (i.e., the item being changed and the taxpayer's proposed and present method), and a citation to the paragraph of the regulations that provides for the method change (Section 10.11(6)(c)).

In general a net negative Section 481(a) adjustment is taken into account in the year of change, and a positive adjustment is taken into account ratably over four years beginning in the year of change. A taxpayer may elect to take a net positive adjustment that is less than $25,000 entirely into account in the year of change (Sections 5.03 and 5.04 of Rev. Proc. 2011-14).

Statistical sampling may be used in determining the Code Sec. 481(a) adjustment for a Section 10.11 change unless the change requires a modified Section 481(a) adjustment (i.e., an adjustment that only takes into account amounts paid or incurred in tax years beginning on or after January 1, 2014).

¶213

COMMENT: It is not necessary to compute a Code Sec. 481(a) adjustment to adopt an accounting method that applies to amounts paid or incurred in tax years beginning on or after January 1, 2014, if the change is made for the first tax year beginning on or after January 1, 2014. However, a taxpayer making such an accounting method change is allowed (but not required) to compute a Code Sec. 481(a) adjustment by taking into account amounts paid or incurred in tax years beginning on or after January 1, 2012 (Section 10.11(6)(b)(i)). This option is desirable if the adjustment is negative, i.e., taxpayer favorable.

Reduced Filing Requirement for Small Taxpayers

A taxpayer with average annual gross receipts of $10 million or less in the three tax years preceding the year of change is not required to complete certain lines and sections of Form 3115 (Section 10.11(4)(b)). Although these time savings are somewhat helpful, the main burdens of filing the application are not affected. Explanatory statements, regulation citations, and Code Sec. 481(a) computations are still required.

Particular Method Changes

Change number 184. Method change number 184 includes all method changes described in Reg. § 1.263(a)-3, relating to improvements to tangible property (with the exception of certain removal costs). Each of these method changes, however, requires a separate computation of a Code Sec. 481(a) adjustment when applicable. Furthermore, it may be necessary to compute separate Code Sec. 481(a) adjustment for items involving the same type of method change. For example, a separate Code Sec. 481(a) adjustment needs to be computed for betterment expenditures on machine A that were improperly deducted and betterment expenditures on machine B that were improperly deducted in prior years.

Routine maintenance safe harbor. The routine maintenance safe harbor accounting method is mandatory (i.e., not elective). Many taxpayers may have capitalized costs that are deductible under the safe harbor (e.g., the cost of major components). A change in accounting method must be filed (change number 184) and a negative (favorable) Code Sec. 481(a) adjustment in the amount of the remaining undepreciated basis of the erroneously capitalized amounts computed.

If the taxpayer previously capitalized the cost of major components that were replaced in a previous year and those components are deductible under the routine maintenance safe harbor, the taxpayer must file Form 3115 before applying the routine maintenance safe harbor to deduct the cost of major components in the current tax year even if those capitalized costs are fully depreciated.

COMMENT: As a matter of precaution, commentators have advised taxpayers who expect to apply the routine maintenance safe harbor in any future year to file an accounting method change to protect against the possibility that the IRS later argues that the taxpayer has previously adopted a method inconsistent with the routine maintenance safe harbor.

Unit of property. Unit of property method changes (number 184) should be fairly common. One typical situation applies to a taxpayer that has previously filed an accounting method change on Form 3115 to treat an entire structure including its building systems as the unit of property for purposes of determining whether and expense was a repair or an improvement. Such a taxpayer needs to file an accounting method change indicating that the improvement rules will be applied separately to the building structural and its building systems. Another typical situation involves a taxpayer who inappropriately treats separate buildings in an apartment complex as a single unit of property, as evidenced on its depreciation schedule.

¶213

Unit of property method changes do not themselves require the computation of Code Sec. 481(a) adjustments. However, a change in the unit of property definition may require a change in method from previously deducting a cost as a repair to capitalizing that cost. For example, a taxpayer who erroneously treated an entire building a unit of property and deducted the cost of replacing an HVAC system or major component of an HVAC system must file a method change to redefine its unit of property and another method change to capitalize the prior repair deduction.

> **COMMENT:** Some commentators suggest that as a precautionary measure a taxpayer should identify its units of real and personal property and file a "protective" unit of property change. The change does not require a computation of a Section 481(a) adjustment, would demonstrate an intent to comply with the repair regulations, and would be made on a Form 3115 that needs to be filed anyhow.

Materials and supplies. Most taxpayers do not currently deduct nonincidental materials and supplies in the year used or consumed as required by the final regulations. The IRS has informally indicated that it expects most taxpayers with materials and supplies to file change number 186 to correct this situation. The IRS will pay particular attention to whether this method change was filed.

Because the effective date is for amounts paid or incurred in tax years beginning on or after January 1, 2014, this method change should not require the computation of a Section 481(a) adjustment if the method change is filed for 2014.

> **EXAMPLE:** Cortine Inc., a calendar-year taxpayer, has been deducting its nonincidental materials and supplies when paid or incurred rather than when used or consumed as required by the final regulations, effective for amounts paid or incurred on or after January 1, 2014. Cortine should file Form 3115 with its 2014 return to change its method to deducting post-2013 expenditures for nonincidental materials and supplies when the materials and supplies are used or consumed (change number 186). If Cortine fails to implement the final regulations in 2014 and continues to deduct materials and supplies that are paid or incurred on or after January 1, 2014, Cortine must file an accounting method change before it may begin deducting materials and supplies when used or consumed. The Code Sec. 481(a) adjustment, however, is only computed with respect to amounts paid or incurred for materials and supplies after January 1, 2014.

> **COMMENT:** Generally, any provision in the regulations that applies to amounts paid or incurred in tax years beginning on or after January 1, 2014, will not require the computation of a Code Sec. 481(a) adjustment unless the required method change is filed after 2014 or the taxpayer follows the exception in Section 10.11(6)(b)(i) and described above that permits a Code Sec. 481(a) adjustment with respect amounts paid or incurred in tax years beginning on or after January 1, 2012.

Most taxpayers currently deduct incidental materials and supplies when paid or incurred as required by the repair regulations, effective for amounts paid or incurred in tax years beginning on or after January 1, 2014. Consequently, method change (number 187) will be less common.

Uniform capitalization rules. A taxpayer may also make a change to comply with the uniform capitalization rules on the same Form 3115 as the changes to comply with the repair regulations (Section 10.11(5)(b)). It is not necessary to file a method change that is required under the UNICAP rules in order to file a related change under the tangible property regulations. These filings may be done separately in the future if necessary.

Removal costs. A change in accounting method for removal costs is filed using a separate Form 3115 in accordance with the automatic change procedure described in

Appendix Section 10.03(1) of Rev. Proc. 2011-14, as modified by Section 3.01(4) of Rev. Proc. 2014-16 (change number 21). However, a change involving removal costs paid or incurred in the disposal of a component of a unit of property that is not a disposition for federal tax purposes is a change described in Section 10.11 and is filed on the same Form 3115 as other Section 10.11 changes to comply with the repair regulations (Section 10.03(1) of Rev. Proc. 2011-14, as modified by Section 3.01(4) of Rev. Proc. 2014-16). In general, a disposal of a component of a unit of property is not a disposition for federal tax purposes only if the taxpayer does not make a partial disposition election to recognize gain or loss (Reg. § 1.168(i)-(d)(3)) or gain or loss on the component is not required to be recognized because the disposal does not involve a sale of the component, casualty event (Code Sec. 165), like-kind exchange (Code Sec. 1031), involuntary conversion (Code Sec. 1033), or step-in-the-shoes transaction (Code Sec. 168(i)(7)(B)) (Reg. § 1.168(i)-(d)(1)).

> **COMMENT:** Taxpayers who file an accounting method change to make a retroactive partial disposition election for a tax year beginning on or before January 1, 2012 (Sec. 6.33 of Rev. Proc. 2011-14, as modified by Rev. Proc. 2014-54), to claim retirement losses on the remaining adjusted basis of previously retired components (e.g., structural components of buildings) will also need to file a separate accounting method change (i.e., a separate Form 3115) to claim a deduction (through a Code Sec. 481(a) adjustment) for removal costs that were previously capitalized into the cost of the replacement component.

STUDY QUESTION

---

6. Schedule E of Form 3115 must be filed to:

   a. Use one of the safe harbor methods under the final repair regulations

   b. Comply with UNICAP rules

   c. Report a Code Sec. 481(a) adjustment

   d. Change from claiming a repair expense to capitalizing and depreciating that asset's deducted amount

---

¶ 214 CONCLUSION

In order to determine which accounting method changes are required, a tax practitioner will need to gather an assortment of information from the client such as repair and maintenance records and depreciation schedules from fixed asset software or spreadsheets. Depreciation schedules should be reviewed to find capitalized costs that qualify for repair expenditures under the repair regulations, such as major components that qualify as repair expenses under the routine maintenance safe harbor, capitalized removal costs, and retired components that are eligible for the partial disposition election.

The review of depreciation schedules may also reveal assets with erroneous depreciation periods and assets for which bonus depreciation was not claimed. Accounting method changes will need to be separately filed for such assets. These method changes are described in Section 6 of Rev. Proc. 2011-14.

The computation of Section 481(a) adjustments, which must be shown in detail on statements attached to Form 3115, will require particularly detailed information regarding the amount and timing of expenditures. Going forward, taxpayer must put recordkeeping systems in place that ensure all relevant data concerning expenditures is captured. Related documentation should be preserved.

A word of comfort is in order. The vast majority of automatic consent requests are not reviewed by the IRS. However, if a request is reviewed and the IRS determines that the application is not properly completed or if supplemental information is needed, the taxpayer will be given 30 days to provide any required information. An additional extension may be requested in writing (Section 10.02 of Rev. Proc. 2011-14). This means that taxpayers who make a good-faith attempt to properly complete a Form 3115 will likely have a second bite at the apple even if the application is reviewed and found deficient by the IRS. However, this protection only extends to the method changes that are reported on the form.

MODULE 1: EMPLOYER/BUSINESS ISSUES—Chapter 3: Passive Activity Rules for Passthrough Entities and Owners

¶ 301 WELCOME

The ability of partners and S corporation shareholders who are individuals, estates, trusts, closely held C corporations, and personal service corporations to deduct losses allocated to them by partnerships and S corporations, respectively, is limited by the passive loss rules. Partners and S corporation shareholders who are subject to the passive activity rules can only offset passive activity losses against passive activity income from other sources. Generally, a *passive activity* is one in which the taxpayer does not materially participate under one of several tests.

¶ 302 LEARNING OBJECTIVES

Upon completion of this chapter, you will be able to:

- Recognize the passive activity rules as they apply to rental activities conducted through passthrough entities;
- Identify the tests for material participation to partners and S corporation shareholders;
- Identify the character of items allocated to partners and shareholders by passthrough entities;
- Identify how activities conducted through passthrough entities are grouped for purposes of testing under the passive activity rules; and
- Recognize the tax consequences of disposing of passive activities conducted through passthrough entities.

¶ 303 INTRODUCTION

Under the passive activity rules, losses and expenses attributable to passive activities may only be deducted from income attributable to passive activities (Code Sec. 469). The effect is to prohibit the use of passive losses to offset nonpassive income. Similarly, tax credits attributable to passive activities may only be used to offset taxes attributable to income from passive activities. Taxpayers subject to the passive activity rules include individuals, trusts, estates, personal service corporations, and closely held C corporations. The rules do not apply to Subchapter S corporations and partnerships but do apply to their respective shareholders and partners. This chapter will focus on the application of the passive activity rules to individual partners and shareholders of partnerships and Subchapter S corporations. When an activity is conducted in a partnership or Subchapter S corporation, the passive activity rules are applied at the partner or shareholder level, rather than the entity level (Temp. Reg. § 1.469-1T(b)).

¶ 304 PASSIVE NETTING AND CARRYOVER RULES

A taxpayer's passive activity losses in excess of passive activity income are suspended and carried forward to succeeding tax years until the taxpayer has passive activity income to offset. The suspended passive activity loss for a year is allocated among all of the taxpayer's activities that produced the loss. The losses are generally treated as passive activity deductions from the activities in future tax years. A taxpayer who disposes of his or her entire interest in a passive activity or former passive activity in a fully taxable transaction may deduct the suspended passive activity losses allocable to that activity, including losses recognized on the disposition of the interest, against nonpassive income.

¶ 305 SCOPE OF PASSIVE ACTIVITIES

A passive activity is any activity that involves the conduct of a trade or business in which the taxpayer does not materially participate (Code Sec. 469(c); Temporary Reg. § 1.469-1T(e)). An individual taxpayer, including a partner or S shareholder, materially participates in a trade or business only if the taxpayer is involved in the operations of the activity on a regular, continuous, and substantial basis (Code Sec. 469(h)). This material participation requirement applies to the taxpayer regardless of whether the interest in the activity is owned directly as a proprietorship or indirectly through an entity such as a partnership or Subchapter S corporation. An interest in a limited partnership, however, is itself a passive activity because the taxpayer is presumed not to materially participate. In certain circumstances, the presumption of lack of material participation can be overcome. For example, when a limited partner is also a general partner, or when a limited partner participates in the partnership activity on a regular, continuous, and substantial basis, the interest in the limited partnership is not passive.

A passive activity does not include any working interest in an oil or gas property that the taxpayer holds directly or through an entity that does not limit the taxpayer's liability as to the interest. The degree of a taxpayer's participation in the activity is irrelevant. Trading personal property for the owner's account is not a passive activity regardless of whether the activity amounts to a trade or business.

STUDY QUESTION

1. The Code Sec. 469(c) rules for material participation do **not necessarily** include _____ involvement in the activity's operations.

    a. Substantial

    b. Managerial

    c. Continuous

    d. Regular

¶ 306 RENTAL ACTIVITIES

A rental activity is generally considered to be a passive activity, regardless of the extent of the taxpayer's participation in an activity (Code Sec. 469(c)(2) and (c)(4)). An activity is a rental activity for a taxpayer if:

- Tangible property, whether real estate or personal property, held in connection with the activity is used by customers or held for use by customers; and

- The gross income from the activity represents amounts paid, or to be paid, principally for the use of the property (Temp. Reg. § 1.469-1T(e)(3)).

This classification applies without regard to whether the use of property by customers is pursuant to a lease, service contract, or other arrangement that is not denominated as a lease.

EXAMPLE: A partnership with two partners, Amy Nystrom and Diana Bellamy, leases rental real estate to lessees for periods of one year. The partnership, Amy, and Diana all do not perform substantial services in connection with the rental activity. The rental activity is passive with respect to Amy and Diana. They can only deduct losses from the rental activity against passive activity income.

Exceptions to Rental Activities

A rental activity is generally considered a passive activity without regard to the material participation of the taxpayer in the activity (the so-called per se rule at Temp. Reg. § 1.469-1T(e)(3)). A taxpayer's rental real estate activity is not a passive activity, however, if the taxpayer, whether acting as an individual or as a partner or S shareholder, materially participates in the activity and is involved in a real property business as a real estate professional. In addition, passive loss rules do not apply when:

- The average period of customer use is seven days or less;
- The average period of customer use is 30 days or less, and significant personal services are provided by or on behalf of the owner of the property in connection with making the property available for use by customers;
- Extraordinary personal services are provided by or on behalf of the owner of the property in connection with making the property available for use by customers;
- The rental of the property is treated as incidental to a nonrental activity of the taxpayer;
- The taxpayer customarily makes the property available during defined business hours for nonexclusive use by various customers; or
- The taxpayer provides the property for use in an activity conducted by a partnership, Subchapter S corporation, or joint venture in which the taxpayer owns an interest.

The last exception is worthy of further explanation. The regulations provide that an activity involving the use of tangible property is not a rental activity for any tax year if the taxpayer provides the property for use in an activity conducted by a partnership, Subchapter S corporation, or joint venture in which the taxpayer owns an interest (Temp. Reg. § 1.469-1T(e)(3)(ii)(F)). The exception applies only if the entity is engaged in an activity other than a rental activity (Temp. Reg. § 1.469-1T(e)(3)(vii)).

EXAMPLE: Donald McNeal leased land and telecommunication towers to his wholly owned S corporation in exchange for a percentage of the corporation's revenues from its leases of tower access to third parties. The net income from the lease was passive activity rental income. Had the corporation used the towers in the conduct of a trade or business with the lease being a percentage of revenues from that trade or business, the rental income to Donald would not have been passive.

When an owner provides property for use by an entity, the owner's distributive share of the income from the entity is not treated as rental income for purposes of the passive loss rules. For example, if a partner contributes the use of property to a partnership, none of the partner's distributive share of partnership income is from a rental activity unless the partnership is engaged in a rental activity. In addition, when the entity is a partnership and the owner receives guaranteed payments for use of the property under Code Sec. 707(c), the guaranteed payments received are not treated as income from a rental activity. Whether the property used in the activity is provided by a taxpayer in the taxpayer's capacity as an owner of an interest in the entity is based on all the facts and circumstances.

¶306

Real Estate Professionals

The rental real estate activities of a real estate professional are not subject to the general rule that treats all rental activities as passive (Code Sec. 469(c)(7)). Specifically, a taxpayer's rental real estate activity is not a passive activity if the taxpayer materially participates in the rental activity and is involved in a real property business as a real estate professional. Each of a qualifying taxpayer's interests in rental real estate is treated as a separate activity, unless the taxpayer elects to treat all interests in rental real estate as a single activity.

Rental real estate for this purpose is any real property used by customers or held for use by customers in a rental activity. However, any rental real estate that the taxpayer grouped with a trade or business activity is not an interest in rental real estate for these purposes (Reg. § 1.469-9(b)(3)).

Requirements to qualify. To qualify as a real estate professional, a taxpayer must satisfy two tests:

- More than one-half of the personal services performed by the taxpayer in trades or businesses during the tax year must be performed in real property trades or businesses in which he or she materially participates; and
- The taxpayer must perform more than 750 hours of services during the tax year in real property trades or businesses in which the taxpayer materially participates (Code Sec. 469(e)(7)(B)).

In the case of married taxpayers who file a joint return, one spouse must satisfy these requirements separately for both to qualify for the real estate professional provision. However, spousal attribution is allowed for purposes of determining whether there has been material participation in real property trades or businesses (Reg. § 1.469-9(c)(4)).

Personal services performed as an employee are not considered services performed in a real property trade or business unless the taxpayer is a 5 percent owner in the business (Code Sec. 469(e)(7)(D)(ii). To be a 5 percent owner, a taxpayer must own at least 5 percent of:

- A corporation's' outstanding stock; or
- The total voting power of all the stock issued by the corporation; or
- Either the capital or the profit interest of a partnership (Code Sec. 416(i)(1)(B)).

If an employee is not a 5 percent owner in the business at all times during the tax year, only the personal services performed by the employee during the period the employee is a 5 percent owner is treated as performed in a real property trade or business (Reg. § 1.469-9(c)(5)). So, in order to qualify, a Subchapter S corporation employee-shareholder must own 5 percent of the Subchapter S corporation's stock. There is no minimum percentage for partners in a partnership, because partners are not employees.

Each interest of the taxpayer in rental real estate is treated as a separate activity unless the taxpayer makes the election described below to aggregate its rental real estate activities (Code Sec. 469(e)(7)(a)(ii)). A rental real estate activity may not be grouped with any other activity of the taxpayer, such as activities as a real estate agent or developer or construction activities (Reg. § 1.469-9(e)(3)). For example, a real estate agent who also owned rental property could not establish material participation in the rental activities by taking into account her activities as a real estate agent (*Gragg v. United States*, DC CA, 2014-1 ustc ¶ 50,245).

Election to aggregate real estate activities. Each of a real estate professional's interests in rental real estate is treated as a separate activity unless the taxpayer elects to treat all interests in rental real estate as a single activity (Code Sec. 469(c)(7)(A)). To make the election, the taxpayer must file a statement with the taxpayer's original income tax return for the tax year declaring that he or she is a qualified taxpayer for the tax year and is making the election (Reg. § 1.469-9(g)). Consistently aggregating rental income and expenses from rental properties on income tax returns does not constitute an election (***Kosonen v. Commissioner***, Dec. 53,821(M), TC Memo. 2000-107).

The election is binding for the tax year in which it is made and for all future years in which the taxpayer is a real estate professional, even if there are intervening years in which the taxpayer is not a real estate professional. To revoke the election, the taxpayer must file a statement with the taxpayer's original income tax return for the year of revocation.

EXAMPLE: Jeffrey Robertson is the sole general partner in two real estate partnerships that own and rent office buildings, and is not connected with any other business ventures. Jeffery is also a partner in an accounting firm and has significant ordinary income. Jeffrey can satisfy the material participation requirements for both partnerships, but to satisfy the 750-hour real estate professional requirement must be able to treat the two partnerships as a single entity. Accordingly, making the election allows Jeffrey to qualify as a real estate professional and set the losses off against his professional income.

In general, a real estate professional's interest in rental real estate held by a passthrough entity (a partnership or Subchapter S corporation) is treated as a single interest in rental real estate if the passthrough entity grouped its rental real estate as one rental activity under Reg. § 1.469-4(d)(5). If the passthrough entity grouped its rental real estate into separate rental activities, each rental real estate activity of the entity is treated as a separate interest. However, a qualifying taxpayer may elect to treat all interests in rental real estate, including the rental real estate interests held through passthrough entities, as a single rental real estate activity (Reg. § 1.469-9(h)(1)).

A partnership holding rental real estate should attach a schedule that lists the pertinent Schedule K-1 items on an activity-by-activity basis. It is then up to each individual partner to determine whether he or she meets the material participation test when combined with other rental real estate activities. Thus, the aggregation rule does not permit a limited partner to bootstrap him- or herself into being considered as materially participating in a limited partnership.

A real estate professional may not group a rental real estate activity with any other activity of the taxpayer (Reg. § 1.469-9(e)(3)(i)). For example, if a qualifying taxpayer develops real property, constructs buildings, and owns an interest in rental real estate, the taxpayer's interest in rental real estate may not be grouped with the taxpayer's development activity or construction activity.

EXAMPLE: Savannah Roberts is the sole general partner in two real estate partnerships. Her Cannoga partnership owns and rents office buildings. Her Springfield partnership develops and rents office buildings. Savannah performs 700 hours of services for each partnership during the partnerships' tax year and performs no services for any other business. She can meet the material participation requirement in either partnership only under the 500-hour test (described below). Both partnerships operate at a loss. Unless Savannah performs at least 500 hours of her services at the Springfield partnership in connection with its rental activities, the losses incurred by both partnerships are classified as passive losses because she:

- Fails the material participation test for that partnership;
- Is therefore not permitted to combine its rental activities with the Cannoga partnership; and
- Does not meet the professional real estate test for that partnership.

A special rule applies if a real estate professional holds a 50-percent-or-greater interest in a passthrough entity. Under this rule, if a qualifying taxpayer owns, directly or indirectly, a 50-percent-or-greater interest in the capital, profits, or losses of a passthrough entity for a tax year, each interest in rental real estate held by the passthrough entity is treated as a separate interest in rental real estate of the real estate professional, regardless of how the passthrough entity' groups activities (Reg. § 1.469-9(h)(2)).

> **COMMENT:** If a passthrough entity owns a 50-percent-or-greater interest in the capital, profits, or losses of another passthrough entity for a tax year, each interest in rental real estate held by the lower-tier entity is treated as a separate interest in rental real estate of the upper-tier entity, regardless of the lower-tier entity's grouping of activities (Reg. § 1.469-9(h)(3)). However, a qualifying taxpayer may elect to treat all interests in rental real estate—including the rental real estate interests held through passthrough entities—as a single rental real estate activity (Reg. § 1.469-9(h)(2)).

In general, if a taxpayer elects to treat all rental real estate interests as a single rental real estate activity, and the taxpayer holds at least one interest in rental real estate as a limited partner interest in a limited partnership, the combined rental real estate activity is treated as a limited partner interest in a limited partnership for purposes of determining material participation. Accordingly, the taxpayer is not treated as materially participating in the combined rental real estate activity unless the taxpayer materially participates under the tests applicable to limited partners.

Under a *de minimis* exception, the general rule does not apply if the taxpayer elects to treat all interests in rental real estate as a single activity and the taxpayer's share of gross rental income from all the taxpayer's limited partnership interests in rental real estate is less than 10 percent of the taxpayer's share of gross rental income from all of the taxpayer's interests in rental real estate for the tax year. In such case, the taxpayer may use any of the material participation tests to establish material participation (Reg. § 1.469-9(f)(2)).

STUDY QUESTION

2. A real estate professional may elect to aggregate all interests in rental real estate by:
    a. Consistently aggregating rental income and expenses on his or her tax returns
    b. Filing a Schedule K-1 listing the activities
    c. Filing a statement of election with his or her tax return
    d. Grouping rental income with that from other real estate activities, such as construction

¶ 307 MATERIAL PARTICIPATION

An activity is generally a passive activity if it involves the conduct of any trade or business in which the taxpayer does not materially participate (Code Sec. 469(c)(1)). Material participation in an activity requires that a taxpayer is involved in the operations of the activity on a regular, continuous, and substantial basis (Code Sec. 469(h)(1)). Participation in an activity means any work done in connection with an activity by an owner of an interest in the activity, without regard to the capacity in which the individual does the work (Reg. § 1.469-5(f)(1)).

The extent of a taxpayer's participation in an activity may be established by any reasonable means. Contemporaneous daily time reports, logs, or similar documents are not required if the extent of the taxpayer's participation may be established by other reasonable means. For these purposes, reasonable means include, but are not limited to, the identification of services performed over a period of time and the approximate number of hours spent performing the services during that period, based on appointment books, calendars, or narrative summaries (Temp. Reg. § 1.469-5T(f)(4)).

Tests for Material Participation

In general, an individual is treated as materially participating in a trade or business for purposes of the passive activity rules during the tax year only if any one of these seven tests is met:

- The individual participates in the activity for more than 500 hours during the year;
- The individual's participation constitutes all of the participation in the activity by all individuals for the year;
- The individual participates in the activity for more than 100 hours during the tax year and his or her participation in the activity is not less than the participation in the activity of any other individual for the year;
- The activity is a significant participation activity for the individual for the tax year, and his or her aggregate participation in all significant participation activities exceeds 500 hours for the year;
- The individual materially participated in the activity for any 5 tax years (which do not need to be consecutive) during the 10 tax years that immediately precede the current tax year;
- The activity is a personal service activity, and the individual materially participated in the activity for any three tax years (need not be consecutive) preceding the current tax year; or
- The individual does not satisfy any of the other tests but, based on all of the facts and circumstances, the individual participates in the activity on a regular, continuous, and substantial basis for the tax year (Temp. Reg. § 1.469-5T(a)).

EXAMPLE: Gary Hastings and Bob McKell are partners in a snow shoveling business. In 2014, Gary and Bob each spent 305 hours in the partnership's business activities. Because each of them participates more than 100 hours and the number of hours they spend is not less than any other person, both Gary and Bob qualify under the 100-hours test.

In contrast, although a taxpayer's status as a real estate professional is based on participation in real property trades or businesses, the taxpayer still must "materially participate" in the individual rental real estate activity (as determined under Reg. § 1.469-5T(a)) to avoid passive activity loss treatment for his or her rental real estate activities (CCA 201427016). Chief Counsel determined that the taxpayer satisfied the requirements for being a real estate professional, it was still necessary to determine whether the taxpayer materially participates in an individual activity.

Material Participation in Passthrough Entities

For a partnership or a Subchapter S corporation, material participation is determined at the partner or shareholder level. The participation of each partner or shareholder must be examined as to each of the activities conducted by the entity. Participation is determined for the entity's tax year, not the tax year of the partner or shareholder (Temp. Reg. § 1.469-2T(e)(1)).

¶307

EXAMPLE: Henry Jameson, a calendar year taxpayer, is a partner in a partnership with a tax year ending January 31. During its tax year ending on January 31, 2014, the partnership engages in a single activity: programming apps for phones. For the period from February 1, 2013, through January 31, 2014, Henry does not materially participate in the activity. On Henry's calendar year 2014 return, his distributive share of the partnership's gross income and deductions from the activity must be treated as passive, regardless of any participation by him in the period of February 1, 2014, through January 31, 2015.

Treatment of limited partners. A taxpayer who owns an interest in a limited partnership as a limited partner generally for purposes of the passive activity rules is not treated as materially participating in the limited partnership's activities (Code Sec. 469(h)(2); Temp. Reg. § 1.469-5T(e); Prop. Reg. § 1.469-5(e)). A limited partner's distributive share of the income, gain, loss, deductions, or credits from an activity in which he or she owns a limited partnership interest, and any gain or loss recognized from the sale or exchange of the partnership interest, are presumed to be passive. A limited partner may nevertheless be treated as materially participating in a partnership if he or she satisfies the 500-hour participation test, the 5-of-10-preceding-years participation test, or the personal service activity participation test.

A partnership interest is treated as a limited partnership interest if it is limited in liability for partnership obligations under applicable state law to a determinable fixed amount (Temp. Reg. § 1.469-5T(e)(3)(i)). For example, a partner is a limited partner if his or her liability is limited to the sum of capital contributions to the partnership plus any additional amount that the partner is required to contribute under the terms of the partnership agreement.

A partner's interest is also treated as a limited partnership interest if is it designated as a limited partnership interest in the partnership agreement or certificate of limited partnership. This characterization applies regardless of whether the liability of the partner is in fact limited under applicable state law. Thus, if an individual who is designated as a limited partner participates in the affairs of the partnership to a degree that his or her liability as to the partnership is no longer limited, the individual is nevertheless still considered a limited partner for purposes of the passive activity rules.

In certain circumstances, a partner who is both a general partner and a limited partner in a partnership is not treated as a limited partner if he or she satisfies any of the seven material participation tests (Temp. Reg. § 1.469-5T(e)(3)(ii)). For this exception to apply, however, the individual must be a general partner in the partnership at all times during the partnership's tax year ending with or within his or her tax year. If a general partner is also a limited partner but for only part of the partnership's tax year, he or she must be a general partner during that portion of the partnership's tax year that he or she directly or indirectly owns the limited partnership interest.

Limited liability company members. The Tax Court has ruled that an individual who is a member in a limited liability company (LLC) or limited liability partnership (LLP) will be treated as a general, rather than a limited, partner if the individual is allowed by state law to participate in the management of the entity (***Garnett v. Commissioner***, Dec. 57,875, 132 TC 368). For example, a taxpayer who held a managing member interest in a California LLC that was classified as a partnership was a general partner because members of a California LLC can participate directly in management (***Newell v. Commissioner***, Dec. 58,127(M), TC Memo 2010-23). The Federal Claims Court has also ruled that an individual's interest in an LLC is not a limited partnership interest if the individual may participate in management of the entity (***Thompson v. United States***, FedCl, 2009-2 ustc ¶ 50,501, 87 FedCl 728, acq. in result only, 2010-15 IRB np).

Temporary and proposed regulations. Under the temporary regulations currently in force, a partnership interest is treated as a limited partnership interest if the interest is designated a limited partnership interest in the limited partnership agreement or the certificate of limited partnership, or the partner's liability is limited under state law. When a limited partner also holds a general partnership interest in the same partnership, the limited partnership interest is not treated as a limited partnership interest (Temp. Reg. § 1.469-5T(e)(3)).

Proposed regulations, which will be effective after finalized, eliminate the reliance on an individual's limited liability as a limited partner under state law or as designated in the partnership agreement in determining whether in interest is a limited partnership interest (Prop. Reg. § 1.469-5(e)(3)(i)). Instead, whether an individual is a limited partner in an entity depends upon the individual's right to participate in the management of the entity, whether it is a partnership or LLC. Thus, an individual's interest in an entity is treated as an interest in a limited partnership if:

- The entity is classified as a partnership for federal income tax purposes under the check-the-box regulations; and
- The holder of the interest does not have any rights to manage the entity at any time during the entity's tax year under the applicable state law or under the operating agreement of the entity.

The general partnership exception continues to apply under the proposed regulations. Thus, an individual is not treated as holding a limited partnership interest in a limited partnership if he or she also holds a general partnership at all times during the partnership's tax year ending with or within the individual's tax year (Prop. Reg. § 1.469-5(e)(3)(ii)).

STUDY QUESTION

3. The proposed regulations state that determining that an individual is a limited partner will depend solely on:

- **a.** State law
- **b.** The partnership agreement
- **c.** The right to participate in the entity's management
- **d.** The percentage of distributive income and losses allocable to him or her

¶ 308 CALCULATING PASSIVE ACTIVITY INCOME AND DEDUCTIONS

After a taxpayer has examined all of his or her activities, enterprises, investments, etc., for a tax year and has decided which are passive activities, he or she can calculate passive activity income or loss for the tax year. In general, passive income or loss is determined by aggregating passive activity gross income and deductions from all passive activities during the year (Temp. Reg. § 1.469-2T).

EXAMPLE: Jessie Page is a limited partner in two partnerships. One allocates him $10,000 in net losses in 2014; the other allocates him $4,000 in net income. Because Jessie is a limited partner, these amounts are passive activity losses and passive activity income, respectively. He has no other passive activities. Jessie can net $4,000 of passive activity losses for 2014 against passive activity income. The remaining $6,000 in losses may not be taken in 2014 but must be carried forward to 2015.

Separate Reporting

Certain types of income and deductions from a passive activity, however, are subject to special rules and must be excluded and reported separately as nonpassive income or deductions, including:

- Portfolio income and deductions;
- Self-charged interest and expenses;
- Personal service income;
- Gain or loss from the disposition of property used in a passive activity;
- Casualty and theft losses;
- Discharge of debt income;
- Recharacterization of passive income;
- Income from a taxpayer's working interest in an oil and gas activity when the taxpayer's liability is not limited;
- Other specific exclusions from passive activity gross income; and
- Other specified deductions that are not treated as passive activity deductions.

Self-charged Interest Income and Expenses

Special rules apply when partners or Subchapter S corporation shareholders loan their entities money. Generally, the self-charged interest rules recharacterize self-charged interest income as passive activity gross income, treat interest expenses allocable to this income as passive activity deductions, and allocate the resulting passive activity income and deductions among the taxpayer's trade, business, or income-producing activities (Reg. § 1.469-7).

These rules apply to interest expense that is allocated under the tracing rules of Temp. Reg. § 1.163-8T to an expenditure that is either properly chargeable to a capital account with respect to the investment producing the interest income or may reasonably be taken into account as a cost of producing the interest income. In general, an interest expense is properly allocable to interest income if the proceeds of the borrowing giving rise to the expense were used to make the loan giving rise to the income.

EXAMPLE: Meg Castile and Mary French each own a 50 percent interest in the capital and profits of M & M, a calendar year partnership. M & M is engaged in a single rental real estate activity. Meg lends M & M $10,000 of her own money and receives $1,000 of interest income from this loan. Mary borrows $20,000 from a bank and pays $1,800 of interest on this loan. Mary lends this $20,000 to M & M and receives $2,000 of interest income from the loan. M & M uses all of the proceeds of both loans in the rental real estate activity. Meg and Mary are each allocated $1,500 (50 percent × $3,000) of interest expense as their distributive shares of M & M's interest expense for the tax year. The self-charged interest rules apply because:

- M & M has self-charged interest deductions for the tax year;
- Meg and Mary each own direct interests in M & M and have gross income from interest charged to M & M; and
- Meg's and Mary's shares of M & M's self-charged interest deductions include passive activity deductions.

These rules apply to both loans to a passthrough entity (i.e., a partnership or Subchapter S corporation) by its owners and loans by a passthrough entity to its owners. The self-charged interest rules also apply to lending transactions between passthrough entities if each owner of the borrowing entity has the same proportionate ownership interest in the lending entity. Guaranteed payments to a partner for the use of capital are covered under the rules as well because they are treated as interest payments.

A passthrough entity may elect out of the self-charged interest rules by attaching a written statement to that effect to its return or amended return (Reg. § 1.469-7(g)). The statement must include the name, address, and taxpayer identification number of the passthrough entity, and a declaration that the election is being made. The election applies to all lending transactions between the entity and its owners and is effective for the year in which it is made and all subsequent years, until revoked. The election may be revoked only with the consent of the IRS.

> **COMMENT:** An entity's partners and shareholders who have large investment interest expenses or who can claim a net operating loss (NOL) may benefit by electing out of the self-charged interest rules. It allows them to absorb more of their investment interest as well to claim more business deductions, which for the NOL deduction are limited to their investment income.

Taxpayer loans to a passthrough entity. The self-charged interest rules apply to a loan from a taxpayer to a passthrough entity if, for the tax year:

- The borrowing entity has self-charged interest deductions;
- The taxpayer owns a direct or indirect interest in the borrowing entity and has gross income from interest charged to the borrowing entity (or a passthrough entity through which the taxpayer holds an interest in the borrowing entity); and
- The taxpayer's share of the borrowing entity's self-charged interest deductions includes passive activity deductions (Reg. § 1.469-7(c)).

If the self-charged interest rules apply to a loan from an owner to a passthrough entity, a percentage of the owner's interest income from the loan is recharacterized as passive activity gross income instead of portfolio income. The percentage is computed by dividing the owner's allocable share of the borrowing entity's deduction for self-charged interest that is a passive activity deduction by the greater of the owner's interest income from the entity or his share of all of the entity's deduction for self-charged interest (whether or not treated as passive activity deductions). The percentage to be recharacterized must be computed separately for each activity if the entity conducts more than one activity.

When the rules apply to loans between entities, to the extent an owner shares in interest income from the loan, the owner is treated as having made the loan to the borrowing passthrough entity and the percentage of income recharacterized is computed under the general rules (Reg. § 1.469-7(e)(2)).

Passthrough entity loans to a taxpayer. The self-charged interest rules apply to a loan from a passthrough entity to its owners (including persons who own an indirect interest) if, for the tax year:

- The lending entity has gross income from interest charged to its owners;
- The owner has deductions for interest charged by the lending entity to the taxpayer (or a passthrough entity through which the taxpayer holds an interest in the lending entity); and
- The owner's self-charged interest deductions include passive activity deductions (Reg. § 1.469-7(d)).

If the self-charged interest rules apply to a loan from a lending entity to its owner, the percentage *(applicable percentage)* of the owner's share for the tax year of each item of the entity's self-charged interest income that is recharacterized is treated as passive activity gross income. The applicable percentage is computed by dividing the owner's deductions for the tax year for interest charged by the lending entity to the owner (or intermediary entities), to the extent treated as passive activity deductions, by the greater of the owner's deductions for interest charged by the lending entity (whether or not treated as passive deductions from the activity), or the owner's distributive share of the entity's self-charged interest income. The percentage must be computed separately for each activity if the entity conducts more than one activity.

EXAMPLE: Siblings Amy and Bob Allingham each own 50 percent of the stock of an S corporation. Amy borrows $300,000 from the corporation at 10 percent interest. Accordingly, in the current tax year, she pays the corporation $30,000 of interest. Amy uses $150,000 of the loan proceeds to make a personal expenditure and uses $150,000 of loan proceeds to purchase a limited partnership interest. Her involvement with the partnership is treated as a passive activity. Amy and Bob are each allocated $15,000 as their pro-rata share of the corporation's interest income from the loan for the taxable year.

The corporation has gross income for the year from interest charged to Amy. Amy has interest deductions for the year, some of which are passive activity deductions. The applicable percentage of Amy's share of the corporation's self-charged interest income is recharacterized as passive activity gross income from the activity. The applicable percentage is obtained by dividing Amy's deductions for the taxable year for interest charged by the corporation, to the extent treated as passive activity deductions from the activity ($15,000), by the greater of Amy's deductions for the taxable year for interest charged by the corporation, regardless of whether those deductions are treated as passive activity deductions ($30,000), or Amy's share for the taxable year of the corporation's self-charged interest income ($15,000). Thus, Amy's applicable percentage is 50 percent ($15,000 ÷ $30,000), and $7500 (50 percent × $15,000) of Amy's share of the corporation's self-charged interest income is treated as passive activity gross income.

Taxpayer and passthrough entity with different tax years. The self-charged rules apply only to self-charged items recognized in the same tax year. If an owner and the entity have different tax years or different methods of accounting, the owner may recognize an income item and a related expense item from the same transaction involving self-charged interest in different tax years. The self-charged interest rules apply by reference to the taxpayer's tax year and the tax year of the entity for which the entity reports items that are taken into account in the taxpayer's tax year (Reg. § 1.469-7(b)(4)).

Passive income from self-rented property. A rental activity is considered to be a passive activity and any income from the activity is generally passive income. Net rental income for the tax year from an "item of property" is recharacterized as nonpassive income, however, if the property is rented for use in a trade or business in which the taxpayer materially participates (Reg. § 1.469-2(f)(6); *Dirico v. Commissioner*, Dec. 59,253, 139 TC No. 16). This *self-rental rule* only applies to net rental income from the item of property, not net losses from an item of property. Material participation for the self-rental rule is determined without the restrictions applicable to material participation in a limited partnership.

EXAMPLE: Tim Jefferson is a CPA who is a shareholder in a personal service corporation that conducts an accounting practice and has made a Subchapter S corporation election. Tim materially participates in the operation of the personal service corporation on a regular, continuous, and substantial basis. In his individual capacity, Tim owns and rents a building to the corporation that it uses for its offices. Because Tim materially participates in the trade or business activity and rents property to that activity, his net rental income from the building is recharacterized as nonpassive income.

The self-rental rule does not apply to property rented incidental to a development activity that may be recharacterized as a nonpassive activity. The rule also does not apply to any rental income attributable to the rental of property pursuant to a written binding contract entered into before February 19, 1988 (Reg. § 1.469-11(c)(1)(ii)).

STUDY QUESTION

---

4. The self-charged interest rules:

   a. Apply only to loans to, by, and between passthrough entities

   b. Apply only to loans by owners to their passthrough entities

   c. Apply only to loans by entities to their owners

   d. Apply only to lending transactions between passthrough entities with owner interests in common

---

¶ 309 GROUPING

In applying the passive activity rules, one of the most important determinations that must be made is the scope of a particular business or professional activity. For example, if two or more activities of a partner or shareholder are treated as one activity, the taxpayer need only establish material participation with respect to the activity as a whole. If two or more activities are separate activities, the taxpayer must establish material participation separately for each one.

In addition, knowing the scope of the activity is critical to determining whether the taxpayer has disposed of his or her interest, triggering the recognition of suspended losses. When there is a disposition of a substantial part of an activity, the taxpayer may treat the interest disposed of as a separate activity (Reg. § 1.469-4(g)). This allows him or her to claim suspended passive losses even though the taxpayer has not disposed of the entire interest in an activity. In order to take advantage of the partial disposition rule, the taxpayer must be able to establish with reasonable certainty the amount of gross income, deductions, and credits allocable to that part of the activity for the tax year (including suspended amounts carried forward from prior tax years). Grouping activities is an especially important issue for partners and Subchapter S corporation shareholders who conduct their businesses through more than one entity.

One or more trade or business activities of a taxpayer may be treated as a single activity if the activities constitute an appropriate economic unit (Reg. § 1.469-4(c)). Whether activities may be grouped as a single activity depends upon relevant facts and circumstances, and the taxpayer may use any reasonable method for grouping activities. Once activities are grouped or kept separate, the taxpayer generally must be consistent in the treatment of these activities from year to year. Thus, subject to certain exceptions, a taxpayer is generally prohibited from regrouping activities in subsequent tax years. A taxpayer is required to disclose his or her grouping of activities for purposes of the passive activity rules, as well as the addition of specific activities within the current grouping of activities.

The following five factors are to be given the greatest weight in determining whether activities constitute an appropriate economic unit, and taxpayers can apply these factors to come up with different results:

- Similarities or differences in the types of businesses;
- The extent of common control;
- The extent of common ownership;
- Geographical location; and
- Interdependence of the activities (for example, the extent to which the activities purchase or sell goods among themselves, involve products or services that normally are provided together, have the same customers, have the same employees, or are accounted for with a single set of books and records).

There are limitations on grouping certain activities for purposes of the passive activity rules, including:

- Grouping rental activities with nonrental activities;
- Grouping real property rentals and personal property rentals;
- Certain activities of limited partners and limited entrepreneurs; and
- Grouping activities conducted through entities.

Certain Activities of Limited Partners and Limited Entrepreneurs

A limited partner (or other limited entrepreneur) is generally prohibited from grouping the following activities, engaged in as a trade or business or for the production of income, with any other activity:

- Holding, producing, or distributing motion picture films or video tapes;
- Farming;
- Leasing any Code Sec. 1245 property;
- Exploring for, or exploiting, oil and gas resources; and
- Exploring for, or exploiting, geothermal deposits (Reg. § 1.469-4(d)(3)).

A taxpayer that owns an interest as a limited partner (or limited entrepreneur) in any of these activities may group that activity with another activity in the same type of business if the grouping is appropriate. A *limited entrepreneur* is a person who has an interest in an enterprise other than as a limited partner but does not actively participate in its management (Code Sec. 464(e)(2)).

Grouping Activities Conducted Through Entities

A Subchapter S corporation or a partnership must also group activities. Once the entity has grouped its activities, a shareholder or partner may group those activities with each other, with activities conducted directly by the individual and with other activities conducted through other entities. A shareholder or partner may not treat activities grouped together by an entity as separate activities (Reg. § 1.469-4(d)(5)). An activity that a shareholder conducts through a C corporation subject to the passive activity loss rules may be grouped with another activity of the taxpayer, but only for purposes of determining whether the taxpayer materially participates in the other activity. Items attributable to interests in publicly traded partnerships, however, must be treated as separate activities (Code Sec. 469(k)). This rule applies to a regulated investment company or mutual fund holding an interest in a qualified publicly traded partnership with respect to items attributable to the interest.

Regrouping

A taxpayer that has grouped activities for purposes of the passive activity loss rules generally cannot regroup them in subsequent tax years. However, an individual, estate, or trust may make a one-time regrouping in the first tax year in which the taxpayer satisfies the eligibility criteria for the net investment income (NII) tax (Reg. § 1.469-11(b)(3)(iv)). Thus, an individual, trust, or estate can make a one-time regrouping in the first year in which the taxpayer both has modified adjusted gross income (MAGI) that exceeds the applicable NII tax threshold and has net investment income. The determination of whether the taxpayer satisfies these criteria is made without regard to the regrouping. The regrouping applies to the tax year in which it is made and all subsequent tax years.

STUDY QUESTION

---

5. Which of the following activities may be grouped with another activity for income generation by a limited partner?

    a. Exploring for or exploiting oil and geothermal resources

    b. Producing and distributing motion picture films and video tapes

    c. Conducting real property rentals and personal property rentals

    d. Holding interest in publicly traded and privately owned partnerships

---

¶ 310 CHARACTER OF ITEMS RECEIVED FROM PASSTHROUGH ENTITIES

The determination of whether items of income or deduction allocated to a partner or a Subchapter S corporation shareholder are passive or not passive is made at the partner or shareholder level. In any case in which participation is relevant, the determination is made by reference to the extent of the partner or shareholder's participation in the activity (or activities) that generated the items of income or deduction. Participation is determined for the tax year of the entity (and not the tax year of the partner or shareholder) (Temp. Reg. § 1.469-2T(e)(1)). LLC members generally are treated like partners for this purpose.

If the activity of the passthrough entity is subject to the passive activity rules, each passive activity and each partner's or shareholder's share of each passive activity must be accounted for in a manner that permits the partners or shareholders to determine their share of the income or loss from the activity, in order to make the necessary calculations to determine the passive activity loss for the tax year. The partnership or the Subchapter S corporation must provide this separate information either on the Schedule K-1 or as an attachment to the Schedule K-1, which must provide the following information:

- A statement that the information is the breakdown by activity of the passive activity amounts reported on the Schedule K-1;

- The identity of each specified activity and type of passive activity by the following categories: trade or business, rental real estate, or other rental activities;

- The amount of income, loss, deduction, or credit from the activity and the line on the Schedule K-1 at which the amount is included;

- The date on which the activity was either started or acquired; and

- If applicable, a statement that the partnership or Subchapter S corporation disposed of its interest in an activity in a fully taxable disposition to an unrelated party.

Transactions Between Partner and Partnership Involved in a Passive Activity

Any item of gross income or deduction attributable to a transaction between a partnership and a partner acting in a capacity other than as a partner is treated for passive activity purposes in a manner consistent with its treatment under Code Sec. 707(a) (Temp. Reg. § 1.469-2T(e)(2)(i)). In general, Code Sec. 707(a) transactions include a partner selling property to the partnership, leasing property to the partnership, lending money to the partnership, or performing services for the partnership.

Under this rule, if a partner is performing services for the partnership, the allocation of income to the partner is for the performance of services and is not passive activity income. If a partner lends money to the partnership, income received by the partner is interest, treated as portfolio income. If the partner sells or exchanges property to the partnership, any income is treated as arising from a sale or exchange; the character is passive or nonpassive depending on the nature of the asset sold or exchanged.

Sale or Exchange of Interest in a Passthrough Entity Involved in a Passive Activity

In the case of the sale, exchange, or other disposition of an interest in a partnership or a Subchapter S corporation, a taxpayer's gain or loss is allocated for purposes of the passive activity rules among the activities conducted by the entity based on a hypothetical disposition of each of those activities by the entity (Temp. Reg. § 1.469-2T(e)(3)). That is, a ratable portion of the taxpayer's gain or loss from the disposition is treated as gain or loss from the disposition of an interest in each trade or business, rental, and investment activity in which the entity owns an interest on the applicable valuation date.

If the taxpayer recognizes a gain on the disposition of his or her interest in the entity, the gain is allocated among those activities that would have generated gains in the deemed disposition. Likewise, if the taxpayer recognizes a loss on the disposition, this loss is allocated among those activities that would have generated a loss in the deemed disposition.

Any adjustment to the basis of partnership property under Code Sec. 743(b) made with respect to the taxpayer is taken into account in computing the net gain or net loss that would have been allocated to him or her if the partnership had sold its entire interest in an activity (Temp. Reg. § 1.469-2T(e)(3)(ii)(D)(2)).

¶ 311 DISPOSITIONS OF PASSIVE ACTIVITIES

A taxpayer who disposes of his or her entire interest in a current or former passive activity in a fully taxable transaction may deduct the suspended passive activity losses allocable to that activity from the current and prior tax years, including losses recognized on the disposition of the interest, against nonpassive income (Code Sec. 469(g)). A disposition of a taxpayer's entire interest involves a disposition of the taxpayer's interest in all entities that are engaged in the activity and, to the extent the activity is held in the form of a sole proprietorship, of all the assets used or created in the activity. A fully taxable transaction includes a sale of the transferred property to a third party at arm's length for a price equal to fair market value. In a transfer by death, the deductible amount of suspended losses must be reduced by any step-up in the transferee's basis in the acquired activity. For gifts and dispositions by an estate or trust, the disallowed losses are added to the donee's basis in an activity.

Upon the disposition of an entire interest in a passive activity, suspended losses (plus any loss from the activity for the tax year of the disposition, if any) are offset against any net income or gain for the tax year from all passive activities. Any excess loss remaining is treated as a nonpassive loss and may offset nonpassive income. The recognition of suspended losses, however, may be restricted by the limitations on capital losses.

EXAMPLE: George Thompson owns interests in two passive activities, Permaflux LLC and Mercurial Partners, in which he has never materially participated. During the tax year, George disposes of his entire interest in Permaflux and recognizes a $15,000 gain. With respect to activity Permaflux, he has $20,000 of suspended losses from prior years and has a current operating loss of $8,000. Mercurial has no losses carried forward from prior years and generates passive income of $6,000 during the year. The $28,000 of suspended and current losses from Permaflux is first deducted against the $15,000 gain from disposition. The remaining $13,000 of losses is deducted against the $6,000 of current year passive income from Mercurial. The remaining $7,000 is treated as a loss from an activity that is not a passive activity and can be deducted against any income.

Disallowed passive activity credits are not triggered when a taxpayer disposes of his or her entire interest in a passive activity. They are carried forward unless the taxpayer elects to increase the property's basis by any disallowed credits that reduced the basis when the credit was taken.

Disposition of an Entire Interest in a Passive Activity

A taxpayer must generally dispose of his or her entire interest in a passive activity to trigger suspended passive activity losses. A disposition of a taxpayer's entire interest includes the taxpayer's interest in all entities that are engaged in the activity such as a partnership or Subchapter S corporation (Senate Committee Report to P.L. 99-514 (1986), S. Rep. 99-313; Conference Committee Report to P.L. 99-514 (1986), H.R. Conf. Rep. No. 99-841, at 725 (1986)). If a partnership or Subchapter S corporation conducts two or more separate activities and the entity disposes of all the assets used or created in one activity, such disposition constitutes a disposition of the entire interest of the partner or shareholder in the activity.

Disposition of a Passive Activity in a Fully Taxable Transaction

A fully taxable transaction generally involves a sale of the transferred property to a third party at arm's length for a price equal to fair market value (Senate Committee Report to P.L. 99-514 (1986), S. Rep. 99-313). In addition to outright sales, however, other types of dispositions can trigger the recognition of suspended losses including dispositions by death and by gift. The complete abandonment of an interest in a passive activity is also a disposition that triggers suspended passive activity losses (Conference Committee Report to P.L. 99-514 (1986), H.R. Conf. Rep. No. 99-841). Similarly, when the worthlessness of security is treated as a sale or exchange, it is treated as a disposition triggering suspended passive activity losses.

Not triggering suspended losses is:

- An exchange of a taxpayer's interest in a passive activity in a nonrecognition transaction such as a transfer of property to a corporation under Code Sec. 351;
- A transfer of property to a partnership under Code Sec. 721; or
- A like-kind exchange under Code Sec. 1031 in which no gain or loss is recognized.

Suspended losses that are not recognized in a tax-free transaction continue to be treated as passive activity losses of the taxpayer. In some circumstances, however, they may be deducted against income from the property received in the exchange that is attributable to the original activity (but not income attributable to other activities). For example, if a passive activity conducted by a general partnership is contributed to a Subchapter S corporation, followed by the dissolution of the partnership, subsequent income from the activity may be offset by suspended losses from the activity of a shareholder who was formerly the passive general partner. The suspended losses may nonetheless not be applied against income from property that is attributable to an activity that is different from the one that the taxpayer exchanged. Therefore, unless the taxpayer can show that income against which suspended losses are offset is clearly from the passive activity, no such offset is permitted.

> **EXAMPLE:** Valerie Scott owns property that she transfers to a partnership in exchange for an interest in the partnership that is tax-free under Code Sec. 721. At the time of the exchange, Valerie has $22,000 of previously suspended passive activity losses from the operation of the property. The income or loss of the partnership from its interest in the property passes through as income or loss from a passive activity to Valerie, as a partner. Her $22,000 suspended loss may be deducted against any income from the property that is passed through to her. However, the suspended loss is not allowed against any portfolio income of the partnership passed through to Valerie.

STUDY QUESTION

6. Which of the following dispositions involving a taxpayer's entire interest does **not** trigger recognition of suspended losses for the passive activity?

- **a.** Disposition following the taxpayer's death
- **b.** Abandonment of the interest
- **c.** A Code Sec. 351 or Code Sec. 721 transfer
- **d.** Worthless securities treated as a sale or exchange

¶ 312 CONCLUSION

Taxpayers need to take account of the passive activity loss rules when planning investments in limited partnerships, limited liability companies, and S corporations. The rules can prevent the taxpayers from taking advantage of the tax benefits associated with losses allocated to them by those entities. The rules in this area continue to evolve, particularly with respect to the definition of a "limited partner." Accordingly, tax professionals with clients who invest in passthrough entities need to pay constant attention to this area and keep up to date on the changes.

MODULE 2: FINANCIAL ISSUES: CURRENCY, INTERNATIONAL ACCOUNTS—Chapter 4: Virtual Currency

¶ 401 WELCOME

As virtual currencies, such as Bitcoin, rise in prominence and begin to become part of an increasing number of everyday transactions, the IRS has for the first time described how virtual currency will be treated for tax purposes. The agency's conclusion appears in Notice 2014-21: Bitcoin and other virtual currencies are not currency, but property. This chapter explores some of the questions that have arisen from Notice 2014-21, as well as concerns about the retroactive impact of the IRS's position on the current tax filing season.

¶ 402 LEARNING OBJECTIVES

Upon completion of this chapter, you will be able to:

- Recognize the role of virtual currency;
- Identify the benefits and risks of using Bitcoins;
- Recognize the U.S. tax treatment of virtual currency; and
- Identify the penalties and penalty relief that may be involved for failure to comply with tax laws in virtual currency transactions.

¶ 403 INTRODUCTION

Actual (or "real") *currency* is commonly defined as a system of money in general use in a particular country. The U.S. dollar is an example of actual currency. A single definition of "virtual currency," on the other hand, has not yet achieved widespread acceptance. *Virtual currency* (sometimes referred to as "*crypto-currency*") is a medium of exchange that operates like actual currency under some circumstances. Although a digital representation of value that functions as a medium of exchange, a unit of account, or a store of value, virtual currency does not function exactly like actual currency. In fact, virtual currency does not have legal tender status in any jurisdiction.

Virtual currency that has an equivalent value in real currency or that acts as a substitute for real currency is referred to as "convertible" virtual currency. Currently, the most prominent example of a convertible virtual currency is Bitcoin, which can be digitally traded between users and can be purchased for, or exchanged into, U.S. dollars, euros, and other real currencies. The Government Accountability Office, in a 2013 report, applied the term "open-flow" virtual currencies to those that can be used to purchase goods and services in the real economy and can be converted into real, government-issued currencies through virtual currency exchanges. This contrasts with "closed-flow" virtual currencies," which can only be used in particular environments, such as in an online role-playing game. "Hybrid" virtual currencies" are those that can be used to buy real goods and services but are not exchangeable for government-issued currencies.

The current real-time value of a Bitcoin on various Bitcoin exchanges is available on a number of websites.

¶ 404 VIRTUAL CURRENCY TRANSACTIONS

Bitcoin is the first implementation of the "crypto-currency concept," which was first described in 1998 by Wei Dai on the Cypherpunks mailing list, suggesting the idea of a new form of money that uses cryptography to control its creation and transactions, rather than a central issuing authority. The first Bitcoin specification and proof of concept was published in 2009 in a cryptography mailing list by Satoshi Nakamoto. Satoshi left the project in late 2010. The community has since grown exponentially, with many developers working on Bitcoin. The Bitcoin protocol and software are published openly, and any developer around the world can review the code or make his or her own modified version of the Bitcoin software. Just like current developers, Satoshi's influence was limited to the changes he made being adopted by others and therefore, he did not control Bitcoin.

Bitcoin is defined as an open source, peer-to-peer electronic money and payment network. One reason for the appeal of Bitcoin is the fact that there is no central bank to control the supply.

Steps for Using Virtual Currency

A transaction using Bitcoin or other similar virtual currency consists of several steps. Using Bitcoin as an example, an individual who wants to engage in a Bitcoin transaction downloads and installs the Bitcoin software (the "client") on his or her computer. This application uses public key cryptography to generate a "Bitcoin address" where the user can receive payments. This address consists of a randomly generated, 36-character-long sequence of letters and numbers. A user can create as many Bitcoin addresses as desired to receive payments. A user can use a new address for every transaction the user receives. The address is stored in the user's digital "wallet" on the user's local computer.

> **COMMENT:** A digital *wallet* is software with which an individual or business can enter into transactions using virtual currency. A wallet includes a private key and a public key. The public key identifies the wallet and is used to make payments to the wallet. It is visible on the block chain. The owner of the wallet is not identified in the public key. The private key is held by the owner and is used to access and make payments from the wallet. A person who has both the public key and the private key can control the wallet, including removing its contents, virtual currency. There is no way to reverse a virtual currency transaction. Therefore, maintaining security over one's wallet is critical.

> **COMMENT:** A *transaction* is a section of data that has been electronically signed and sent to the Bitcoin network, where it is collected into *blocks*. The transaction will usually reference previous transactions. It dedicates a certain number of Bitcoins to one or more public keys (the *Bitcoin address*).

> **COMMENT:** Bitcoin transactions are recorded on the *block chain*, a computer file that acts as a public ledger that anyone can examine. Specifically, the block chain is a transaction database shared by all nodes participating in a system based on the Bitcoin protocol. A virtual currency's block chain contains information on every transaction ever executed in the currency. A user can learn how much value belonged to each address at any point in history. A conventional ledger records the transfer of actual bills or notes. Bitcoins, however, are simply entries on the block chain and do not exist outside of it.

> **COMMENT:** A *block chain browser* is a website where every transaction included in the block can be viewed. The viewer can see the technical details of the transaction and can use this for payment verification purposes. To send Bitcoins, the user inputs the address to which he or she wants to send Bitcoins and an

amount to be transferred. The user's computer then digitally signs the transaction. The information is sent to the Bitcoin network. This network verifies that the person who is sending the Bitcoins is the owner of those Bitcoins. This precaution is intended to prevent a malicious user from spending the same Bitcoins multiple times. Once the transaction has been validated by the Bitcoin network, the Bitcoin recipient is able to spend them.

When the buyer in a transaction sends Bitcoins to the seller as payment, the transaction includes three pieces of information:

- The first piece is the *input,* which is a record of the address from which the Bitcoins were sent to the buyer. The input refers to the output of a different transaction. A transaction will often list multiple inputs. The values of the referenced outputs from these other transactions are added up, and the total can be used in the current transaction;
- The second piece of information that is part of the Bitcoin transaction is the *amount* of Bitcoins that the buyer is sending to the seller; and
- The third piece of information is the *output,* or the seller's address.

The buyer will have a Bitcoin address. This is analogous to possessing a safe deposit box, but one for which the contents are known by all parties. The buyer will also have a private key—another sequence of numbers—which is known only to the buyer. The buyer will send a message to the seller, signed with his or her private key. The message will contain the input, the amount, and the output. By doing so, the buyer sends the Bitcoins to the seller from his or her Bitcoin wallet to the Bitcoin network. Bitcoin *miners* then verify the transaction and put it into a transaction block. It may take some time for the miners to solve (or mine) the transaction, so the buyer may have to wait until that is done—usually within 10 minutes, which is the time set for mining a block. In the case of low-value transactions, the merchant may not require a purchaser to wait for verification, because the risk of fraud is not significant in such transactions.

Making Change

The transactions that were undertaken to send the buyer the Bitcoins in the first place are not combined and remain separate transactions in the buyer's wallet. When the buyer wishes to send an amount of Bitcoins, his or her wallet will try to use different transactions that add up to the amount being sent. Frequently, the existing transactions will not add up to the correct amount. Therefore, a larger number of Bitcoins is sent, and the buyer will receive change in his or her wallet. The wallet will automatically send the correct amount to the seller and the change to a newly created address, which was created to hold change from the transaction.

EXAMPLE: Moira Seline wishes to buy a computer from CompSeller, a computer retailer. Moira first goes to a website to find out the value of a Bitcoin today. The website that hosts her wallet has that information, and she establishes that a Bitcoin is worth $570. She goes to CompSeller's website, where she obtains CompSeller's Bitcoin address and learns that the computer she wants is available for purchase and costs $1,995. That means it will cost 3 1/2 Bitcoins. Moira's Bitcoin wallet contains "unspent outputs" from other transactions, including one unspent output for 4 Bitcoins. Moira instructs the wallet to split her transaction, a feature that is supported by Bitcoin. She splits the 4-Bitcoin unspent output into one output for 3 1/2 Bitcoins, which she transfers to CompSeller's Bitcoin address. The other half a Bitcoin is transferred to a newly created change account.

Some merchants charge transaction fees, but currently most do not. This may change in the future as the Bitcoin protocols are amended. Any amount that is not picked up by the seller or returned to the buyer as change is considered a transaction fee and may be considered a reward to the miner who solved the transaction block.

¶404

Bitcoins are divisible into *satoshis,* which are a hundredth of a millionth of a Bitcoin. If a Bitcoin were worth $1,000, then a satoshi would be worth one-thousandth of a penny. If necessary in the future, further divisions may be made possible.

A Bitcoin is abbreviated "BTC." A *millibitcoin* (mBTC) is one-thousandth of a Bitcoin, or 100,000 satoshis. A *microbitcoin* (µBTC), where "µ" stands for the Greek letter mu, is 100 satoshis.

COMMENT: A Bitcoin is created, or "mined," electronically according to a purely mathematical process. A complex computer algorithm is applied. As more and more Bitcoins are mined, the difficulty of doing so will increase, as it becomes computationally more difficult to create them. This process was designed to mimic the production rate of a commodity such as gold. Once a Bitcoin is mined or acquired, it is stored as a numerical balance at a Bitcoin address.

COMMENT: Companies like BitPay or Coinbase act as intermediaries in Bitcoin transactions. According to the director of Business Development and Sales at Coinbase, more than a million customers use Coinbase as their Bitcoin wallet, allowing Coinbase to accept Bitcoin payments on their behalf using its payment tools. More than 28,000 merchants participate in Bitcoin use.

Price Comparisons

Blockchain.info allows downloads of pricing data, as well as comparison of prices among various exchanges. One can find out, for example, the total number of Bitcoin transactions that occurred on a given day, double-spends that have been detected, or the total number of Bitcoins in circulation (almost 13 million Bitcoins as of July 2014). One can also create a free Bitcoin wallet at that website.

COMMENT: *Double-spending* is the result of successfully spending money more than once. Bitcoin protects against double-spending by verifying each transaction added to the block chain to ensure that the inputs for the transaction had not previously already been spent. Other electronic systems prevent double-spending by having a master authoritative source that follows business rules for authorizing each transaction. Bitcoin uses a decentralized system, where a consensus among nodes following the same protocol is substituted for a central authority. Bitcoin has some exposure to fraudulent double-spending when a transaction is first made, with less and less risk as a transaction gains confirmations.

COMMENT: The finite limit of 21 million has been set on the number of Bitcoins in existence. Currently, more than 12 million are in circulation. That means that fewer than 9 million Bitcoins are waiting to be discovered. At the current rate of creation, the final Bitcoin will be mined in the year 2140. However, that date is based on technical factors that may not be true at that time, such as the software's ability to divide up Bitcoins into fractional amounts. (Just as a dollar can be divided into 100 cents, a Bitcoin can be divided into 100 million "satoshis"). It is possible that changes in technology will mean that a final limit will never be reached.

STUDY QUESTION

1. Which of the following is true about a Bitcoin wallet?
    a. The wallet's public key is invisible on the block chain
    b. The user pays a fee to create and use it
    c. Its private key is used to access it and make payments
    d. Reversals of virtual currency transactions are credited to the wallet

¶ 405 CHARACTERISTICS OF BITCOINS

Bitcoin transactions are decentralized. This means that there is no central bank or other institution holding the value of a Bitcoin. The Bitcoin network is not controlled by a single individual or entity. Each machine that mines Bitcoins and processes transactions is part of the network.

Following are the key features and benefits of virtual currencies such as Bitcoin:

- A Bitcoin transaction is *easy to initiate*. It is possible to create a Bitcoin address in seconds. There are no fees payable and no one asks any questions about the transaction;

- A Bitcoin transaction is *anonymous but transparent*. This means that information regarding the transaction is available to all, but the information is not tied to a particular individual. There is no link to names, addresses, or other identifying information. A person looking at a particular Bitcoin address can tell how many Bitcoins are there but not who owns them;

- A Bitcoin transaction has *few, if any, transaction fees*. This may change, but at the moment most merchants do not charge transaction fees or only charge a very small amount;

- A Bitcoin transaction is *fast*. Transactions anywhere in the world take only a few minutes, just long enough for the Bitcoin network to process them; and

- A Bitcoin transaction is *final*. It cannot be repudiated, so any Bitcoins lost cannot be recovered unless the seller sends them back to the buyer.

¶ 406 ASSOCIATION WITH ILLEGAL ACTIVITIES

In April of 2012 the FBI issued a report that analyzed the likelihood and consequences of different types of illegal activity involving Bitcoin. This includes money laundering, theft of Bitcoins (such as at Mt. Gox), and theft of services for purposes of mining Bitcoins (using software to take over computers and make them mine Bitcoins).

One problem with Bitcoin's reputation and general public image is that the virtual currency has been associated with various illegal transactions. Drug dealers using the now-defunct Silk Road website made Bitcoins their favored currency. When a group of law enforcement agencies (including the FBI, DEA, and IRS, among others) shut down the Silk Road in 2013, they confiscated 174,000 Bitcoins, worth $34 million at the time of the seizure.

Bitcoin is vulnerable to hacking. Mt. Gox, a Japanese Bitcoin exchange, collapsed recently due to theft by hackers of more than $500 million in Bitcoins. The exchange has filed for bankruptcy. This followed other problems for Mt. Gox: In 2013, law enforcement agencies seized the accounts of a U.S.-based subsidiary of Mt. Gox for operating an unlicensed money services business. Mt. Gox was accused of moving funds into numerous online black markets, most of which were associated with illegal drugs, firearms, and child pornography.

Bitcoins have also been used as a way to evade taxes and facilitate financial crime.

EXAMPLE: A two-island country in the West Indies, St. Kitts and Nevis, does not tax its citizens and has a citizenship by investment program through which people can essentially buy a citizenship. The citizenship costs from $250,000 to

$400,000 that people can buy with Bitcoins. China, for example, has government limits on money transfers that would make it very difficult for wealthy Chinese to purchase the citizenship, but Bitcoins allow people to circumvent that restriction. An individual in China can purchase Bitcoins in his or her home through one of the numerous exchanges available, and using a smartphone, transfer the Bitcoins to St. Kitts without the Chinese government being aware of it. In 2013, close to 3,000 U.S. citizens renounced their U.S. citizenships and some became citizens of St. Kitts and Nevis reportedly to avoid complying with the *Foreign Account Tax Compliance Act* (FATCA) and paying taxes on foreign accounts.

Financial regulators have become involved with certain activities involving virtual currencies.

EXAMPLE: In July 2013 the Securities and Exchange Commission (SEC) charged Bitcoin entrepreneur Erik Voorhees, along with his business, with defrauding investors through a Bitcoin-based investment scheme. In June 2014, Erik Voorhees agreed to pay more than $50,000 to settle allegations that two websites he co-owned publicly offered shares without registering them with the SEC.

The SEC has also issued related investor alerts and has started reviewing a registration statement from an entity that wants to offer virtual-currency-related securities. The SEC is also monitoring for potential securities law violations related to virtual currencies.

Other actions involving Bitcoin have been taken by various agencies to combat money laundering, narcotics trafficking, and other illicit activities. Events like this have resulted in mistrust among many people with regard to virtual currencies.

Another illegal technique that has recently been observed is "ransomware," which is a computer virus that locks the user's files and will not release them until a payment in Bitcoins has been made to a particular address. A version of this virus targets mobile phones.

STUDY QUESTION

---

2. All of the following are illegal activities associated here with using virtual currency *except:*

    a. Tax avoidance

    b. Money laundering

    c. Ransomware

    d. Exorbitant conversion fees

¶ 407 VIRTUAL CURRENCY USED IN ONLINE GAMES

Virtual currencies are comparable in some ways to currencies used in large-scale online games, also known as "massive multiplayer online role-playing games" (MMORPGs). Some of these games, such as Second Life, have created a large virtual world in which large numbers of individuals participate via their computers. Part of this participation includes the use of virtual money to purchase items for use in the games.

Second Life was developed by Linden Lab, and virtual currency called the Linden Dollar is used in the game. In some cases, this virtual money has been used to facilitate transactions outside of the games themselves. There is a "vibrant" market for virtual goods that exists outside of the game, in which individuals sell or auction virtual land and other property in exchange for actual currency such as dollars. Linden Lab runs one currency exchange, LindeX Market. On that market, Linden Dollars trade for real dollars, with the current rate being approximately 248 Linden Dollars per U.S. dollar. These games generate significant revenue for their developers: The gross domestic product of Second life has recently been estimated at $64 million. Also, about 3,000 individuals earned more than $20,000 in income, in U.S. dollars, each year from their activities in Second Life. As a result, the use of virtual currency in this context should be looked at as at least analogous to the use of virtual currency such as Bitcoins, and the tax consequences that eventually apply to one may also be applicable to the other. Another similarity between game currency and other types of virtual currency is its potential use in criminal activity. The FBI has noted that organized criminal groups have been using an online roleplaying game to facilitate the laundering of money. The criminal purchases virtual currency used in the game with criminal activity proceeds. This virtual currency is then used to purchase in-game virtual items that can be sold to other players for "clean money."

¶ 408 ALTERNATIVES TO BITCOIN: HOUSE HEARING

The U.S. House Committee on Small Business held a hearing on April 2, 2014, "Bitcoin: Examining the Benefits and Risk for Small Business," Jerry Brito, senior research fellow at the Mercatus Center at George Mason University, explained that "because there is no central intermediary in Bitcoin transactions, fees associated with those transactions are relatively small." This contrasts with the much higher fees charged to businesses accepting credit cards, which include a fee per swipe of the card plus 2 to 4 percent of the total transaction. Businesses that use a merchant processor pay fees of 1 percent or less for Bitcoin transactions. "If you are a small-margin business," according to Brito, "that difference could mean doubling your profits."

> **COMMENT:** The most obvious risk one faces in using virtual currency is the volatility of the currency. The value of a Bitcoin went from pennies to $1,200 in a five-year period and then back down to around $600 in 2014. According to Brito, the volatility of Bitcoin exists because it is new and thinly traded, and should even out over time, especially as the number of people and businesses using it expands.

¶ 409 U.S. TAX TREATMENT

The IRS acknowledged that virtual currency may be used to pay for goods or services, or held for investment. The IRS issued guidance providing answers to frequently asked questions (FAQs) about virtual currency, offering Bitcoin as "one example" of convertible virtual currency (Notice 2014-21). Those FAQs provided only basic information on the tax implications of transactions in, or using, virtual currency. Practitioners hope that IRS refinement of these rules will be forthcoming, particularly in connection with *de minimis* transactions and other reporting situations.

> **COMMENT:** The lack of an exception to reporting gain above a *de minimis* amount has been raised as a serious problem. The typical scenario described to illustrate this issue involves the person who buys a cup of coffee with a Bitcoin, resulting in gain of a few cents or fractions of a cent for the merchant. This is not a problem with foreign currency but is a problem with virtual currency. Some have suggested that the IRS does not have the resources to police this kind of requirement, but that situation does not resolve the issue. Exempting *de minimis* Bitcoin transactions would probably require an act of Congress and would not be resolvable under the terms of the existing Internal Revenue Code. One possible solution is software that provides "instant conversion" tools, which would enable a person to buy Bitcoins at the moment needed for a transaction; thus effectively eliminating taxable gain or loss.

Property

Notice 2014-21 treats virtual currency as property for U.S. federal tax purposes. As such, it is governed by the same general principles that apply to property transactions generally. The sale or exchange of convertible virtual currency such as Bitcoin, or its use to pay for goods or services in a real-world economic transaction, has immediate tax consequences that may not apply if it were considered pure "legal tender." Virtual currency is also not treated as currency that could generate foreign currency gain or loss.

Conversion Required

A taxpayer who receives virtual currency in payment for goods or services is required to include the fair market value of the virtual currency in computing the taxpayer's gross income. This value must be measured in U.S. dollars as of the date the virtual currency was received.

If a virtual currency is listed on an exchange and the exchange rate is established by market supply and demand, the fair market value of the virtual currency is determined by converting the virtual currency into U.S. dollars (or into another real currency that in turn can be converted into U.S. dollars) at the exchange rate, in a reasonable manner that is consistently applied. The basis in virtual currency, for example, used to determine any gain or loss on its future use, is its fair market value in U.S. dollars on the date of receipt. Because convertible virtual currency such as Bitcoin has an established marketplace, the value and therefore basis is determined by reference to that exchange. In transactions with other types of virtual currency, it is unclear whether the value of the goods or services given in exchange for such currency can set the value for the virtual currency for purposes of setting basis.

Capital Gain or Ordinary Income

A taxpayer has gain or loss upon an exchange of virtual currency for other property. If the fair market value of property received in exchange for virtual currency exceeds the taxpayer's adjusted basis of the virtual currency, the taxpayer has taxable gain. The taxpayer has a loss if the fair market value of the property received is less than the adjusted basis of the virtual currency.

The character of gain or loss from the sale of virtual currency or its exchange for other property or services depends on whether the virtual currency is a capital asset in the hands of the taxpayer. A *capital asset* generally is an asset held for investment purposes, such as stocks, bonds, or other investment property. Property held as inventory or other property mainly for sale to customers in a trade or business is not considered a capital asset. If the virtual currency is held as an investment, gain or loss on its disposition will be capital gain or loss. If the virtual currency is held as inventory for sale to customers in a trade or business, gain or loss on its disposition will be ordinary gain or loss.

Unlike capital assets, gain or loss from the sale or exchange of foreign currencies is treated as ordinary gain or loss.

> **COMMENT:** It remains unclear whether Bitcoins will be treated as "coins" for purposes of the 28 percent capital gains rate on collectibles or will be considered a permitted investment within individual retirement accounts or in other, similar circumstances.

Virtual currency miners. Taxpayers who create or mine virtual currency are treated as financial services providers rather than prospectors and realize gross income on receipt of the virtual currency resulting from that activity. The fair market value of the virtual currency as of that date is includible in gross income. Prospectors, on the other hand, would not have income until the sale of the discovered treasure. Notice 2014-21 presumes that the income from mining would be ordinary, and if mining constitutes trade or business and is not undertaken as an employee, any net earnings (generally, gross income less allowable deductions) constitute self-employment income subject to the self-employment tax.

Information reporting and backup withholding. A payment made using virtual currency is subject to information reporting and backup withholding to the same extent as any other payment made in property. Thus, a person who in the course of a trade or business makes a payment of fixed and determinable income using virtual currency with a value in excess of $600 to a U.S. nonexempt recipient is required to report the payment to the IRS and to the payee. This includes payment of rent, salaries, wages, premiums, annuities, and compensation.

Wages paid to employees using virtual currency are taxable to the employee, must be reported by an employer on a Form W-2, and are subject to federal income tax withholding. Also, payments using virtual currency made to independent contractors and other service providers are taxable, and self-employment tax rules generally apply to such payments. Payers using virtual currency must normally issue Form 1099-MISC, *Miscellaneous Income,* to the payee.

Payors making reportable payments using virtual currency must solicit a taxpayer identification number (TIN) from the payee. The payor must backup withhold from the payment if a TIN is not obtained prior to payment or if the payor receives notification from the IRS that backup withholding is required.

Third-party settlement organizations. The information reporting rules currently applicable to third-party settlement organizations (TPSOs) apply to payment processors that settle transactions in virtual currency. In general, a third party that contracts with a substantial number of unrelated merchants to settle payments between the merchants and their customers is a TPSO. The most common example of a TPSO is an online auction-payment facilitator, which operates merely as an intermediary between buyer and seller by transferring funds between accounts in settlement of an auction/purchase. A TPSO is required to report payments made to a merchant on Form 1099-K, *Payment Card and Third Party Network Transactions,* if, for the calendar year, both the number of transactions settled for the merchant exceeds 200 and the gross amount of payments made to the merchant exceeds US$20,000. The dollar value of payments denominated in virtual currency is based on the fair market value of the virtual currency on the payment date.

The banking industry. Janet Yellen, chairwoman of the Federal Reserve, stated during a recent Senate Banking Committee hearing that the use of virtual currency is "entirely outside the banking industry." The central bank, according to Yellen, does not have the authority to regulate Bitcoins.

STUDY QUESTION

---

3. Taxpayers who mine virtual currencies are treated as _____ for federal tax purposes.

    a. Currency traders

    b. Investment counselors

    c. Financial services providers

    d. Prospectors

¶ 410 PENALTIES LOOM

Taxpayers may be subject to penalties for failure to comply with tax laws for past tax years. Underpayments attributable to virtual currency transactions may be subject to penalties, such as accuracy-related penalties under Code Sec. 6662. In addition, failure to timely or correctly report required virtual currency transactions may trigger information reporting penalties under Code Secs. 6721 and 6722. However, penalty relief may be available to taxpayers and persons required to file an information return who are able to establish that the underpayment or failure to properly file information returns is due to reasonable cause.

The IRS made it a point to underscore that it was issuing Notice 2014-21 on March 25, 2014, to provide taxpayers adequate time to address the treatment of virtual currency on 2013 tax year returns. Some practitioners, however, maintain that to apply Notice 2014-21 retroactively to 2013 transactions imposes an undue retroactive record-keeping burden and penalty exposure to taxpayers who had acted on a good-faith misinterpretation of the rules during 2013.

At the April 2, 2014, House Committee's Bitcoin hearing, L. Michael Couvillion, a professor at Plymouth State University in New Hampshire, pointed out that taxpayers who treated virtual currencies inconsistently with IRS Notice 2014-21 before it was issued will not receive penalty relief unless they can establish that their underpayment or failure to properly file information returns was due to reasonable cause. This will require many businesses and individuals to go back and determine the existence of gain or loss on transactions that occurred in the past—perhaps several years in the past.

Some commentators argue that, in light of the fact that the IRS released Notice 2014-21 three weeks before the due date for 2013 individual income tax returns, all taxpayers should be considered to have satisfied the "reasonable cause" exception for penalty relief for the 2013 tax year. Professor Couvillion noted that this "creates a huge paperwork burden. Technology can help, but especially this year, many people think it's simply unfair to expect taxpayers to amend their returns at this late date because the IRS just issued this ruling."

> **COMMENT:** Others, on the other hand, believe that the compliance costs would not be severe because most people subject to the Notice have a sophisticated knowledge of business, have most likely already obtained, or will obtain, extensions to file, and are able to obtain the necessary information to amend their returns.

¶ 411 TREATMENT BY STATE GOVERNMENTS

The State of California has expressed its own views on Bitcoin and other virtual currency. In June 2014 Assembly member Roger Dickinson's (D-Sacramento) Assembly Bill 129 (AB 129) was signed into law, lifting a ban on using currencies besides the U.S. dollar. This change in law is meant to accommodate the increasing use of alternative methods of payment, including virtual currencies like Bitcoin. Section 107 of California's Corporations Code 'had prohibited corporations or individuals from issuing money other than U.S. dollars. People using digital currencies, community currencies, and reward points were in violation of the law but were not penalized. The new law affects exchange media such as Amazon's Coins and Starbucks' Stars, as well as Bitcoin. In each case, the state legislature deemed it inappropriate to ignore the growing use of cash alternatives. One likely effect will be an increase in the confidence surrounding the use of Bitcoin.

In July 2014, The New York State Department of Financial Services issued a proposed "BitLicense" regulatory framework for New York virtual currency businesses.

The proposed framework—the first on a statewide basis in the country—will require licensees to have strong compliance and supervisory policies and procedures. The Texas Department of Banking has stated that Bitcoin transmissions are permitted but are not technically "currency" transmissions.

A number of states, including Massachusetts, Wisconsin, and Florida, have stated that crypto-currency is a volatile investment with an unusually high risk compared to normal investments.

A group of state banking regulators from around the nation established a task force in February 2014 to investigate digital currencies, including Bitcoin.

Two of four known Bitcoin ATMs (also known as Bitcoin kiosks) are located in Massachusetts, whereas two others are located in New Mexico and Texas. These machines allow users to deposit cash and get Bitcoins, which are stored in a digital wallet. The transactions are managed by thousands of computers linked in an international network. In Massachusetts, the state government is in the process of trying to determine whether these machines are similar enough to traditional ATMs that they must be approved and licensed by the state, as ATMs are.

¶ 412 FinCEN

Under the regulations from the Financial Crimes Enforcement Network (FinCEN), with the U.S. Treasury Department, a person or entity that is engaged in certain types of activity is considered a "money services business." Dealers in foreign exchange, providers and sellers of prepaid access, and money transmitters are included in the definition of *"money services business."* Money transmitters are subject to the *Bank Secrecy Act* (BSA), as implemented by FinCEN regulations. It is a criminal offense under the *Uniting and Strengthening America by Providing Appropriate Tools Required to Intercept and Obstruct Terrorism Act of 2001* (Patriot Act) to operate an unlicensed money-transmission business. Licensing such businesses is primarily for the purpose of consumer protection. Money services businesses are subject to certain requirements under the regulations, including an obligation to maintain an antimoney-laundering program, as well as registration, reporting, and recordkeeping requirements.

FinCEN issued guidance on March 18, 2013, on the use of virtual currency, including Bitcoin. FinCEN regulations distinguish between currency of a state, or "real currency," and "virtual currency." FinCEN defines *virtual currency* as "a medium of exchange that operates like a currency in some environments but does not have all the attributes of real currency." In particular, convertible virtual currency has an equivalent value in real currency, or acts as a substitute for real currency. FinCEN regulations also conclude that "administrators" (which are engaged in the business of issuing and redeeming virtual currencies) and "exchangers" (which are engaged in the business of exchanging virtual currency for real currency, funds, or other virtual currency) of convertible virtual currency are money transmitters, and therefore money services businesses, whereas "users" of convertible virtual currency are not money services businesses. As of December 2013, about 40 virtual currency exchangers had registered with FinCEN.

FinCEN Form 114, *Report of Foreign Bank and Financial Accounts* (known as FBAR), must be filed by U.S. persons with an interest in foreign accounts if the aggregate value of the accounts exceeds $10,000. A business that transfers virtual currencies or that exchanges virtual currencies for real currencies is considered a money transmitter and is treated as a financial institution for FBAR purposes. A U.S. individual who stores Bitcoins with any of the Bitcoin exchanges located in foreign countries (as most are) is arguably subject to FBAR reporting if the value of the person's Bitcoin holdings was more than $10,000 at any time during the year, according to the American Institute of Certified Public Accountants (AICPA). However, an IRS official has stated that Bitcoins are not reportable on the FBAR, at least for the 2014 filing season. Thus, this issue has not been definitively resolved as of the publishing date of this course.

An online wallet stores copies of private keys for accessing Bitcoin addresses and does not have control or custody over the Bitcoins. Therefore, an online wallet service should not be considered a money transmitter, and a person who uses a foreign online wallet does not appear to be subject to FBAR reporting requirements.

STUDY QUESTION

4. None of the state governments summarized here treats Bitcoin transactions as:
- **a.** Currency transmissions
- **b.** Cash alternatives
- **c.** Investment exchanges
- **d.** High-risk investments

¶ 413 FATCA

Foreign financial institutions (FFIs) are required under FATCA to report to the IRS information on financial accounts held by U.S. taxpayers, or by foreign entities controlled by U.S. taxpayers. Individuals with at least $50,000 in foreign financial assets must file Form 8938, *Statement of Specified Foreign Financial Assets*. Foreign assets that are subject to FATCA reporting requirements include accounts with any FFI.

Bitcoin exchanges accept deposits in the ordinary course of business and therefore may be considered financial institutions for FATCA purposes, although the law on this subject is undeveloped at this time. The AICPA recommends that Bitcoin deposit accounts be reported in the summary information on Part I of Form 8938. Specific information should be given in Part V. However, online wallets do not need to be reported for FATCA purposes. Because Form 8938 is attached to the taxpayer's return, persons not required to file a return need not file Form 8938.

STUDY QUESTION

5. FATCA rules for reporting Bitcoins do *not* apply to:
- **a.** Bitcoin exchanges
- **b.** Online wallets
- **c.** Foreign Bitcoin entities controlled by U.S. taxpayers
- **d.** Bitcoin deposit accounts

¶ 414 TREATMENT BY OTHER NATIONS

Other countries had already bowed to pressure to clarify the tax treatment of Bitcoin. Germany, beginning in 2013, declared Bitcoin to be a "unit of account." This is not the same thing as currency, but Germany is treating Bitcoin as "private money." The HM Revenue & Customs (HMRC, United Kingdom tax authority), under the proposed new rules, will change its classification of Bitcoin and other virtual currency from a tradable

73

voucher to private currency. The HMRC' has clarified that exchanging or mining Bitcoins will be exempt from the value-added tax (VAT) in the United Kingdom, but accepting Bitcoins for goods and services is subject to the VAT. Those changes closely mirror similar tax guidance issued recently in Singapore, which announced plans to treat Bitcoins like a product subject to its goods and services tax (i.e., like neither currency nor pure capital gains).

China has tried to discourage the use of virtual currency such as Bitcoin. Its largest e-commerce website, Alibaba Group Holding, Ltd, has banned the sale of Bitcoin and other virtual currencies. This ban includes mining software and hardware for virtual currency. None of Alibaba's platforms has accepted Bitcoin as a payment method, and the company's payment affiliate, Alipay, does not support websites that use Bitcoin. These rules come as a result of recent regulations from China's central bank, enacted in response to concerns about Bitcoin's volatility. Many third-party payment systems have stopped processing transactions for Bitcoin purchases.

Taiwan's Financial Supervisory Commission recently banned Bitcoin ATMs, calling Bitcoin a "false currency."

Bitcoin use is growing in Argentina, a nation with a history of periods of high inflation. Many Argentinians consider Bitcoins a safer investment than the official currency. As a consequence, Argentina may ban digital currency.

Other nations such as Taiwan, Japan, Iceland, India, and Vietnam have banned or restricted Bitcoin transactions, but the extent of these restrictions is not yet settled due to a lack of applicable laws on the subject of virtual currency.

¶ 415 DERIVATIVE MARKET

A Dublin-based market in 2013 announced the creation of Bitcoin Options Spreads, enabling both long-and short-term positions to be created on the virtual currency. Since then, other entrepreneurs have joined the fray, dealing in options involving virtual currency. For example, in March 2014, a derivative exchange announced that it would start handling Bitcoin derivatives swap agreements, which would give investors a way to hedge against the extreme variation in prices for Bitcoins.

Bitcoins are subject to different market dynamics than actual currencies. They can be difficult to hedge against because there is a lack of traditional financial instruments that can be used to mitigate the risk. The fact that Bitcoin transactions are anonymous makes it hard to track down market manipulation. The volume of the virtual currency derivatives market is currently very low.

¶ 416 TAX ISSUES

The following tax issues with respect to virtual currencies have been raised after issuance of Notice 2014-21 and have not yet been resolved by the IRS.

PFIC and CFC Implications

It is not clear whether virtual currencies should constitute passive assets for purposes of the 50 percent asset test applicable to passive foreign investment companies (PFICs). However, income from the sale or exchange of virtual currencies should constitute passive income for purposes of the 75 percent gross income test applicable to PFICs. This is because virtual currencies do not give rise to any income; income from the sale or exchange of virtual currencies should be includible as subpart F income for purposes of the rules applicable to controlled foreign corporations (CFCs).

Hedging and Notional Contracts Considerations

A taxpayer hedging the risk of fluctuation in the value of virtual currency that it holds is not guaranteed ordinary income treatment under the specialized tax rules applicable to hedging transactions. It is also not clear whether the tax rules applicable to "notional principal contracts" would apply to swaps or other derivatives the payments on which are calculated by reference to published virtual currency exchange rates because it is not clear whether they would be considered a "specified index" under the rules.

Like-Kind Exchanges

The like-kind exchange rules exclude certain property from qualifying for deferral of recognition. This property includes stocks, bonds, notes, or other securities or evidences of indebtedness, partnership interests, certificates of trust or beneficial interests, choses in action, and foreign currencies. It is not clear whether virtual currencies would be excluded from such treatment. However, virtual currencies are not expressly included in the list of excluded items.

IRS regulations on like-kind exchanges do not provide much information regarding intangible personal property such as virtual currency. The regulation states that nonrecognition is available in the case of an exchange of intangible personal property only if the exchanged properties are of like kind. No like classes are given by the regulation for these properties. The question of whether intangible personal property is of a like kind with other such property depends in general on the nature or the character of the rights involved. Examples given are patent and copyright. Also relevant is the nature of the underlying property to which the intangible personal property relates. This regulation was clearly drafted with more traditional intangibles such as copyright in mind, and its application to exchanges involving virtual currency is unclear.

There are other varieties of virtual currency besides Bitcoin. A website, Altcoins.com, maintains a list of alternatives to Bitcoin. The term *altcoin* is used to designate such alternative virtual currencies. Some of these altcoins, such as Namecoin, Peercoin, Freicoin, and Deutsche eMark, use the same algorithm as Bitcoin. Other altcoins, such as Litecoin, Digitalcoin, Quark, and Pandacoins, use a different algorithm. There are about 190 virtual currencies traded in the marketplace today, totaling more than $6 billion in stated value (Bitcoin represents about 92 percent of this value). The existence of such alternatives becomes relevant to the issue of like-kind exchanges because it seems likely that exchanging a Bitcoin for an altcoin of some other type could possibly qualify as such an exchange of similar property. However, the IRS has not yet addressed this issue.

Mark-to-Market Rules of Code Secs. 465 and 1256

It is not clear whether a taxpayer who deals or trades in virtual currencies would be able to take advantage of the elective mark-to-market rules that exist for dealers in commodities and traders in securities and commodities. Additionally, because a derivative contract with respect to a virtual currency would not be considered a "Section 1256 contract" it would not need to be marked-to-market either.

Treatment of Mining Pools as Entities

Miners who engage in pooled mining might be treated as a partnership or other entity for U.S. federal tax purposes. Special tax rules apply to entities, including ongoing reporting obligations.

Potential Exclusions from Specified Foreign Financial Asset Reporting

The rules applicable to the reporting of "specified foreign financial assets" do not appear to contemplate property such as virtual currencies and appear outside of the scope of the reporting obligations by U.S. individuals.

¶416

Charitable Contributions of Virtual Currencies

Though the notice indicates virtual currency is property, it is not clear that such treatment also applies in the context of charitable contributions. Cash is regarded as intangible personal property for purposes of the charitable deduction rules, and money of a bullion or numismatic nature has been ruled in other tax contexts to be tangible personal property and has been treated as such for the charitable tax rules.

Foreign Tax Credit Implications

It is not clear whether the gains from the sale or exchange of virtual currency will be sourced under the rules applicable to personal property sales and treated the same for purposes of determining their fraction of a taxpayer's foreign tax credit limitation.

Constructive Sales and Straddles

The rules applicable to constructive sales do not contemplate monetization transactions with respect to virtual currencies. It is also not clear whether the rules applicable to straddles apply equally to virtual currencies and that virtual currency constitutes personal property of a type that is "actively traded."

Barter Transactions

In the 1970s, "barter clubs" were formed as a means of avoiding income tax obligations arising from the exchange of goods or services. These clubs allowed their members to sell their services or goods in exchange for the goods or services of another, thus avoiding receiving cash. Members of the club earned "trade units" by offering their own services, which could be exchanged for other goods and services listed by the club in a directory available to its members. The IRS took the position that such transactions became taxable when the trade units were received, rather than later, when the trade units were redeemed for services or goods. In other words, a member of a barter club received income for his or her services on receipt of trade units. The rationale of the IRS was that the receipt of trade units constituted the receipt of valuable property because those trade units could be redeemed for goods or services at any time. This made the receipt of trade units a taxable event.

If virtual currency is treated as property, as the IRS has now held, then the exchange of units of such virtual currency for other property looks much like the exchange of two pieces of property for each other, or barter. This is consistent with the IRS position in its most recent notice that a taxpayer receiving virtual currency in an exchange must include the value of that currency in income. However, the IRS has not expressly compared the exchange of virtual currency to barter exchanges at this time. However, concepts underlying the IRS's policy on barter, such as the actual receipt doctrine and the constructive receipt doctrine, could be applied to virtual currency. It remains unclear exactly how much of the law that has developed around barter exchanges (such as an analysis of a trade unit's liquidity or nonassignability, that is, of substantial limitations or restrictions on the use of the units) would apply to virtual currency transactions.

STUDY QUESTION

6. Tax issues regarding treatment of virtual currencies remain unclear *except* for:

    a. Subpart F income for controlled foreign corporations

    b. Like-kind exchanges

    c. Charitable contributions

    d. Notional principal contracts

¶ 417 CONCLUSION

The IRS has joined several other jurisdictions in publishing guidance regarding the income tax consequences of convertible virtual currency transactions. Notice 2014-21 clarifies that existing general tax principles apply to transactions using convertible virtual currency and that virtual currency should be treated as "property" rather than "currency" for U.S. federal income tax purposes. The IRS has also indicated that penalties may apply to taxpayers that have taken return positions that are inconsistent with its position in the notice or that have failed to file the appropriate information returns. Although the immediate implications of the notice are apparent, the long-term consequences are still being considered. As virtual currencies grow in popularity, federal regulators will continue to refine and revise their approaches to virtual currencies and their users. Persons that are engaged in "mining" activities, investments, or any other use of virtual currencies should closely monitor the activities of federal regulators to stay abreast of this rapidly developing area of law.

MODULE 2: FINANCIAL ISSUES: CURRENCY, INTERNATIONAL—Chapter 5: International Tax Reporting

¶ 501 WELCOME

In their ongoing effort to close the *tax gap,* or the taxable amounts underreported on tax returns, Congress and the Internal Revenue Service continue to extend the information reporting requirements for taxpayers and financial institutions domestically and abroad. With the ability to locate and collect excess monies already owed, Congress can, in effect, increase revenues without having to increase taxes. At the same time, information reporting is extremely useful to the IRS because collecting this data enables the agency to verify a taxpayer's income by matching what is reported by one taxpayer with that provided by another and then act upon discrepancies. As a result, these matching efforts are likely to expand even further. In keeping with this trend, this chapter examines the reporting requirements for foreign assets and financial interests imposed by the *Foreign Account Tax Compliance Act* (FATCA) and the FinCEN Form 114, *Report of Foreign Bank and Financial Accounts* (FBAR), and discusses how certain taxpayers may decide to use the Offshore Voluntary Disclosure Program (OVDP) developed by the IRS.

¶ 502 LEARNING OBJECTIVES

Upon completion of this chapter, you will be able to:

- Recognize the differences between the FBAR and FATCA reporting requirements;
- Recognize the civil and criminal penalties associated with noncompliance with the FATCA and FBAR requirements;
- Identify how the Offshore Voluntary Disclosure Program may be used; and
- Recognize the differences between the 2014 OVDP and the Streamlined Compliance Process.

¶ 503 INTRODUCTION

U.S. persons with foreign financial interests may be subject to various information reporting requirements. A *U.S. person* includes:

- A citizen or resident of the United States;
- A domestic partnership;
- A domestic corporation;
- Any estate (other than a foreign estate); and
- Any trust, if

  - A court within the United States is able to exercise primary supervision over the administration of the trust, and

  - One or more U.S. persons have the authority to control all substantial decisions of the trust (Code Sec. 7701(a)(30) and Reg. § 1.1471-1(b)(132)).

First, under FATCA, U.S. citizens, resident aliens, and certain nonresident aliens must file information returns using Form 8938, *Statement of Specified Foreign Financial Assets,* with their annual income tax returns for any year in which their interests in specified foreign assets exceed the applicable reporting threshold.

Second, a U.S. person with financial interests in or signature authority over foreign financial accounts generally must file FinCEN Form 114, *Report of Foreign Bank and Financial Accounts* (FBAR) if, at any point during the calendar year, the aggregate value of the accounts exceeds the reporting threshold.

These reporting requirements may often overlap, but they apply separately. Thus, a person who satisfies both the FATCA and the FBAR filing requirements must file both Form 8938 and FinCEN Form 114. Filing one of the forms does not satisfy the filing requirement for the other form.

Different policy considerations apply to Form 8938 and FinCEN Form 114. In addition to tax administration, FBAR reporting is also used for law enforcement purposes. These differences are reflected in the different categories of persons required to file each form, the different filing thresholds, and the different assets and accompanying information required on each form.

¶ 504 FATCA REQUIREMENTS

As discussed above, FATCA mandates that for some taxpayers a report of foreign financial assets be made. Accordingly, *specified persons* who hold an interest in a "specified foreign financial asset" during the tax year must attach to their tax returns a Form 8938, *Statement of Specified Foreign Financial Assets,* to report certain information for each asset if the total value of all such assets exceeds an applicable reporting threshold amount.

This requirement applies to any U.S. citizen and any individual who is resident alien for any part of the tax year. A nonresident alien who makes the election to be treated as a resident alien for purposes of filing a joint return for the tax year must also file Form 8938, as must a nonresident alien who is a bona fide resident of American Samoa or Puerto Rico.

Form 8938 must also be filed by any domestic entity formed or availed for purposes of holding, directly or indirectly, specified foreign financial assets, in the same manner as if the entity were an individual.

> **COMMENT:** Proposed regulations (Proposed Reg. § 1.6038D-6(a)) have designated specified domestic entities subject to the reporting requirement. They include certain closely held domestic corporations or partnerships, as well as certain domestic trusts. Reporting by specified domestic entities, however, will not be required before the date provided in final regulations.

Interests

A specified person has an interest in a specified foreign financial asset if any income, gains, losses, deductions, credits, gross proceeds, or distributions from holding or disposing of the asset are or would be required to be reported, included, or otherwise reflected on the specified person's income tax return. The interest exists even if there are no income, gains, losses, deductions, credits, gross proceeds, or distributions from holding or disposing of the asset included or reflected on the taxpayer's income tax return for that tax year.

> **COMMENT:** Therefore, a specified person must file a Form 8938 despite the fact that none of the specified foreign financial assets that must be reported affects his or her tax liability for the year.

STUDY QUESTION

1. Which of the following is *not* a U.S. person potentially subject to FATCA and/or FBAR requirements?

    a. A foreign estate

    b. A domestic corporation

    c. A domestic trust

    d. A holding company for specified foreign financial assets

Specified Foreign Financial Assets

Specified foreign financial assets include:

- Any financial account maintained by a foreign financial institution; and
- Any of the following assets that are not held in an account maintained by a financial institution

    - Any stock or security issued by a person other than a U.S. person (as defined above),

    - Any financial instrument or contract held for investment that has an issuer or counterparty which is other than a United States person, and

    - Interest in a foreign entity.

Financial accounts. The primary type of specified foreign assets is financial accounts maintained by foreign financial institutions. "Financial account" and "foreign financial institution" are generally defined by reference to the Code Sec. 1471 FATCA rules that require withholding from payments to foreign financial institutions. Thus, a *financial account* is any depository or custodial account maintained by a foreign financial institution, as well as any equity or debt interest in a foreign financial institution (other than interests that are regularly traded on an established securities market). A *foreign financial institution* (FFI) is generally any financial institution (other than a U.S. entity) that:

- Accepts deposits in the ordinary course of a banking or similar business;
- Holds financial assets for the account of others as a substantial part of its business; or
- Is engaged (or holds itself out as being engaged) primarily in the business of investing, reinvesting, or trading in securities, partnership interests, commodities, or any interest (including a futures or forward contract or option) in such securities, partnership interests, or commodities.

However, for purposes of the FATCA reporting requirements for specified persons, a specified foreign financial asset also includes a financial account maintained by a financial institution organized under the laws of a U.S. territory. As a result, such an account is subject to FATCA unless it is owned by a bona fide resident of the relevant U.S. territory.

FATCA also imposes complex reporting requirements for foreign financial institutions. Under Code Sec. 1471, FFIs are required to report to the IRS certain information about financial accounts held by U.S. taxpayers or by foreign entities in which U.S. taxpayers hold substantial ownership interests. If an FFI fails to meet the FATCA requirements, a U.S. withholding agent must deduct and withhold a tax equal to 30 percent on any "withholdable payment" made to the FFI after June 30, 2014, unless the withholding agent can reasonably rely on documentation that the payment is exempt from withholding. No withholding is required, however, if an FFI enters into an agreement with the IRS to provide the required information (participating FFI). An FFI may also be deemed to meet the requirements of the agreement (deemed-compliant FFI). These agreements encourage reporting by U.S. taxpayers. If the taxpayers fail to comply with the reporting requirements themselves, the FFIs will provide the required information directly to the IRS, which can then use that information to target the noncompliant taxpayer.

> **COMMENT:** The FATCA rules apply to the foreign financial account itself. The assets held in the account do not have to be separately reported on Form 8938, because their value is included in the determination of the account's maximum value.

> **COMMENT:** Foreign deposit and custodial accounts are reported on Part I of Form 8938.

Other assets. The following items are also specified foreign assets if they are held for investment, even if they are not held in an account maintained by a foreign financial institution:

- Any stock or security issued by a person other than a U.S. person;
- Any financial instrument or contract held for investment that has an issuer or counterparty that is not a U.S. person; and
- Any interest in a foreign entity.

> **COMMENT:** The other assets categories are broad and may sometimes overlap, so a single asset may fall into more than one category, for example, stock issued by a foreign corporation is stock that is issued by a person other than a U.S. person and is also an interest in a foreign entity.

> **COMMENT:** The IRS has stated that an interest in a social security, social insurance, or other similar program of a foreign government is not a specified foreign financial asset.

Examples of assets other than financial accounts that may be considered *other specified foreign financial assets* include, but are not limited to:

- Stock issued by a foreign corporation;
- A capital or profits interest in a foreign partnership;
- A note, bond, debenture, or other form of indebtedness issued by a foreign person;
- An interest in a foreign trust;
- An interest rate swap, currency swap, basis swap, interest rate cap, interest rate floor, commodity swap, equity swap, equity index swap, credit default swap, or similar agreement with a foreign counterparty; and
- Any option or other derivative instrument with respect to any of the items listed as examples in this paragraph or with respect to any currency or commodity that is entered into with a foreign counterparty or issuer.

> **COMMENT:** Specified foreign financial assets that are not held in deposit and custodial accounts are reported on Part II of Form 8938.

Exceptions. Exceptions to the reporting requirements apply to particular types of foreign financial assets, as well as assets subject to duplicative reporting, assets held by certain types of trusts, and assets held by certain bona fide residents of U.S. possessions.

¶504

The following types of assets are not specified foreign financial assets and, therefore, do not have to be reported on Form 8938:

- A financial account (including the assets held in it) that is maintained by a U.S. payer, such as a domestic financial institution. In general, a U.S. payer also includes a domestic branch of a foreign bank or foreign insurance company and a foreign branch or foreign subsidiary of a U.S. financial institution;

- A financial account (including the assets held in it) that is maintained by a dealer or trader in securities or commodities, if all of the holdings in the account are subject to the mark-to-market accounting rules for dealers in securities, or a mark-to-market election is made for all of the holdings in the account; and

- Any other financial asset, if the asset is subject to the mark-to-market accounting rules for dealers in securities or commodities or a mark-to-market election is made for the asset.

The rules intend to limit duplicative reporting and provide that specified foreign financial assets do not have to be reported on Form 8938 if they are properly reported on any of the following timely filed forms for the same tax year:

- Form 3520, *Annual Return to Report Transactions with Foreign Trusts and Receipt of Certain Foreign Gifts;*

- Form 5471, *Information Return of U.S. Persons with Respect to Certain Foreign Corporations;*

- Form 8621, *Information Return by a Shareholder of a Passive Foreign Investment Company or Qualified Electing Fund;*

- Form 8865, *Return of U.S. Persons with Respect to Certain Foreign Partnerships;* and

- Form 8891, *U.S. Information Return for Beneficiaries of Certain Canadian Registered Retirement Plans.*

COMMENT: The specified person's Form 8938 must identify these other form(s) that reported the specified foreign financial asset and report how many of these forms were filed.

COMMENT: The value of assets reported on these duplicative forms must be included in determining whether the specified person satisfies the application reporting threshold.

If the grantor trust rules treat a specified person as the owner of one of these trusts or a portion of the trust for income tax purposes, the following assets held by trust (or the owned portion) do not have to be reported on the specified person's Form 8938:

- A domestic trust that is a widely held fixed investment trust;

- A domestic trust that is a liquidating trust created under a court order in a chapter 7 bankruptcy; or

- A foreign trust, if

  - The specified person reports the trust on a Form 3520 timely filed with the IRS for the tax year,

  - The trust timely files Form 3520-A, *Annual Information Return of Foreign Trust With a U.S. Owner, with the IRS,* and

  - The specified person's Form 8938 reports the filing of the Form 3520 and Form 3520-A.

¶504

Additionally, bona fide residents of U.S. possessions (American Samoa, Guam, the Northern Mariana Islands, Puerto Rico, or the U.S. Virgin Islands) who must file Form 8938 do not have to report the following specified foreign financial assets:

- A financial account maintained by a financial institution organized under the laws of the U.S. possession where the specified person is a bona fide resident;
- A financial account maintained by a branch of a financial institution not organized under the laws of the U.S. possession where the specified person is a bona fide resident, if the branch is subject to the same tax and information reporting requirements that apply to a financial institution organized under the laws of the U.S. possession;
- Stock or securities issued by an entity organized under the laws of the U.S. possession where the specified person is a bona fide resident;
- An interest in an entity organized under the laws of the U.S. possession where the specified person is a bona fide resident;
- A financial instrument or contract held for investment, provided each issuer or counterparty that is not a U.S. person either is an entity organized under the laws of the U.S. possession where the specified person is a bona fide resident or is a bona fide resident of that U.S. possession.

STUDY QUESTION

2. Which of the following is *not* a reportable specified foreign financial asset?
   a. A financial account maintained by a financial institution organized under U.S. territorial law
   b. A currency swap with a foreign counterparty
   c. Stock issued by an entity under the laws of Guam owned by a bona fide resident there
   d. Any interest in a foreign entity

Reporting Threshold

The FATCA requirements apply when:

- A specified person is required to file an annual return; and
- The aggregate value of the specified person's specified foreign assets exceeds the applicable threshold.

The applicable reporting thresholds for specified foreign financial assets are shown in Table 1.

Table 1. Reporting Thresholds for Application of FATCA Requirements

Taxpayer Type	Threshold Amount on Last Day of Year Exceeding	or	Threshold Amount at Any Time During the Year Exceeding
Unmarried and living in United States	$ 50,000		$ 75,000
Joint filers living in United States	$100,000		$150,000
Single filers living abroad	$200,000		$300,000
Joint filers living abroad	$400,000		$600,000

These thresholds are not adjusted for inflation.

¶504

> **COMMENT:** The statute requires reporting only when an individual's specified foreign financial assets exceed the threshold dollar amounts (for example $50,000 on the last day of the tax year for unmarried taxpayers). However, the IRS can prescribe a higher dollar amount for the reporting threshold, which was done in T.D. 9567, which increased the reporting threshold for specified individuals who are qualified individuals under Code Sec. 911(d).

> **COMMENT:** Taxpayers generally must include the value of all of their specified foreign financial assets, even if they are also reported on another form.

Valuation. Once the reporting threshold is triggered, specified persons must report the maximum value during the tax year of each specified foreign financial asset reported on Form 8938. Account assets are generally valued at their fair market value (FMV). Thus, the maximum value of a specified foreign financial asset is generally equal to a reasonable estimate of the asset's highest FMV during the tax year. If this amount is less than zero, such as in the case of a foreign mortgage, the value of the asset is treated as zero for the purposes of determining the aggregate value and the maximum value of the specified person's specified foreign financial assets. All values must be determined and reported in U.S. dollars.

Financial accounts. The value of assets held in a financial account maintained by an FFI is included in determining the value of that financial account. A specified person may rely upon periodic account statements provided at least annually to determine a financial account's maximum value, unless the specified person has actual knowledge or reason to know (based on readily accessible information) that the statements do not reflect a reasonable estimate of the maximum account value during the tax year.

> **COMMENT:** The value of particular assets held in a financial account does not have to be separately reported on Form 8938 because that value is included in the value of the account itself.

Other assets. The maximum value of a specified foreign asset that is not held in a financial account maintained by an FFI is generally equal to the value of the asset as of the last day of the tax year. However, this general rule does not apply to a specified person with actual knowledge or reason to know, based on readily accessible information, that the FMV determined as of the last day of the tax year does not reflect a reasonable estimate of the maximum value of the asset during the year—for example, because there is a reason to know that the asset's value declined significantly during the year.

An interest in a foreign pension or deferred compensation plan is reported if the value of the specified foreign financial assets is greater than the reporting threshold that applies. In general, the value of an interest in the foreign pension plan or deferred compensation plan is the FMV of the taxpayer's beneficial interest in the plan on the last day of the year. However, if the taxpayer does not know or have reason to know based on readily accessible information the FMV of his or her beneficial interest in the pension or deferred compensation plan on the last day of the year, the maximum value is the value of the cash and/or other property distributed to the taxpayer during the year. This same value is used in determining whether the reporting threshold has been met.

> **EXAMPLE:** James Chatley, an individual taxpayer, has publicly traded foreign stock not held in a financial account, with a fair market value as of the last day of the tax year of $100,000. However, based on daily price information that is readily available, the 52-week high trading price for the stock results in a maximum value of the stock during the tax year of $150,000. If James satisfies the applicable

reporting threshold, he must report the maximum value of the foreign stock as $150,000, based on readily available information of the stock's maximum value during the tax year.

Trusts. If the specified person is a beneficiary of a foreign trust, the maximum value of the specified person's interest in the trust is the sum of the FMV, determined as of the last day of the tax year, of all of the currency or other property distributed from the foreign trust during the tax year to the specified person as a beneficiary; plus the value as of the last day of the tax year of the specified person's right as a beneficiary to receive mandatory distributions from the foreign trust. This amount is also used to determine the aggregate value of the specified person's specified foreign financial assets, if the specified person does not know or have reason to know based on readily accessible information the FMV of his or her interest in a foreign trust during the tax year.

Estates, pension plans, and deferred compensation plans. The maximum value of a specified person's interest in a foreign estate, foreign pension plan, or a foreign deferred compensation plan is the FMV, determined as of the last day of the tax year, of the specified person's beneficial interest in the assets of the estate, pension plan, or deferred compensation plan. If the specified person does not know or have reason to know (based on readily accessible information) that value, then the maximum value to be reported, and the value to be included in determining the aggregate value of the specified foreign financial assets, is the FMV, determined as of the last day of the tax year, of the currency and other property distributed during the tax year to the specified person as a beneficiary or participant. If the specified person received no distributions during the tax year and does not know or have reason to know (based on readily accessible information) the FMV of the interest as of the last day of the tax year, the maximum value of the asset is zero.

Jointly owned interests. The treatment of jointly owned interests depends on the specified person's relationship to the other owner. If the owners are married to each other and one spouse is not a specified person, each spouse includes the entire value of the jointly owned asset to determine the total value of his or her specified foreign financial assets.

If both owners are spouses who file jointly (and, therefore, file a single Form 8938), the total value of the jointly owned asset is taken into account only once in determining the total value of the couple's specified foreign financial assets. If the spouses also file Form 8814, *Parents' Election to Report Child's Interest and Dividends,* to include a child's unearned income on their own return, they also must include the maximum value of the child's specified foreign financial assets in the calculation of their own specified foreign financial assets.

If both owners are spouses who do not file jointly, each includes one-half of the value of the jointly owned assets in his or her own specified foreign financial assets. A spouse who files Form 8814, *Parents Election to Report Child's Interest and Dividends*, to include a child's unearned income on his or her own return must include the maximum value of the child's specified foreign financial assets in his or her own specified foreign financial assets.

If the owners are not married to each other, each owner includes the entire value of the jointly owned asset to determine the total value of his or her specified foreign financial assets.

Foreign currency. As mentioned above, all values must be determined and reported in U.S. dollars. The value of a specified foreign financial asset that is denominated in a foreign currency is first determined in the foreign currency prior to conversion into U.S. dollars (that is, independently of exchange rate fluctuations during the year). The asset's foreign currency value is then converted into U.S. dollars at the tax year-end spot rate for converting the foreign currency into U.S. dollars (that is, the rate to purchase U.S. dollars). The U.S. Treasury Department's Financial Management Service foreign currency exchange rate is used to convert the value of a specified foreign financial asset into U.S. dollars. If no such rate is available, another publicly available foreign currency exchange rate may be used to determine an asset's maximum value, but the use of such rate must be disclosed on Form 8938.

STUDY QUESTION

3. Co-owners of a jointly owned interest should list the entire value of the interest on Form 8938 unless they are:

    a. Married filing separately

    b. Owners not married to each other

    c. Co-owners who are a parent and minor child using Form 8814

    d. Married owners when one spouse is not a specified person

Penalties

Failure to disclose. A $10,000 penalty applies to any failure to properly furnish the required information. If the failure is not corrected within 90 days after the IRS mails notice of it to the taxpayer, an additional $10,000 penalty applies for each 30-day period (or portion thereof) in which the failure continues after that 90-day period expires. This additional penalty with respect to any failure is limited to $50,000. Married taxpayers who file a joint return are treated as one taxpayer for purposes of the penalty, and their liability for the penalty is joint and several.

For purposes of assessing the penalty, if an individual with multiple financial assets does not provide sufficient information to determine their aggregate value, the IRS presumes that the aggregate value exceeds the reporting threshold. In other words, the IRS presumes that the individual was required to file Form 8938 and, therefore, is liable for penalties for failing to do so.

The penalty is not imposed on any specified person that can show that the failure is due to reasonable cause and not willful neglect. The determination of whether a failure to disclose a specified foreign financial asset on Form 8938 was due to reasonable cause and not due to willful neglect is made on a case-by-case basis, taking into account all pertinent facts and circumstances. The specified person must make an affirmative showing of all the facts alleged as reasonable cause for the failure to disclose.

Accuracy-related penalty. A 40 percent accuracy-related penalty applies to underpayments attributable to transactions involving undisclosed foreign financial assets. *Undisclosed foreign financial assets* are foreign financial assets that are subject to information reporting under various provisions, but for which the required information was not provided by the taxpayer.

Limitations. Reporting failures can also affect the limitations period for assessments. The statute of limitations on tax assessment does not begin to run until the taxpayer provides the required information. In addition, although the IRS normally has a *maximum* of three years to assess tax, it has a *minimum* of three years to assess tax arising from improperly reported specified foreign financial assets. These rules generally apply to the taxpayer's entire tax liability; however, if the taxpayer has reasonable cause for the reporting failures, these rules apply only to items related to the unreported specified foreign financial assets.

¶504

Finally, the normal three-year limitations period for assessments is extended to six years for any substantial omission of gross income in excess of $5,000 that is attributable to a specified foreign financial asset. This extension applies even if the taxpayer's specified foreign financial assets:

- Are properly reported;
- Fall below the reporting threshold; or
- Are included in classes of assets that the IRS has excepted from the reporting requirements.

STUDY QUESTION

4. The IRS statute of limitations for assessments may **not** be extended if:
   a. The assets that increase gross income more than $5,000 fall in the classes of excepted assets
   b. The specified foreign financial assets with values of more than $5,000 are properly reported
   c. The omitted income amount in question is less than $5,000
   d. The value of the specified foreign financial assets that increase gross income by more than $5,000 falls below the reporting threshold

¶ 505 FBAR REQUIREMENTS

Under the terms of the FBAR requirements, a U.S. person with financial interests in or signature authority over foreign financial accounts generally must file FinCEN Form 114, *Report of Foreign Bank and Financial Accounts* (FBAR) if, at any point during the calendar year, the aggregate value of the accounts exceeds the reporting threshold of $10,000. Under terms of the *Bank Secrecy Act* (BSA), FBARs must be electronically filed through the BSA e-filing system for each calendar year on or before June 30 of the succeeding year. The June 30 deadline may not be extended.

Those subject to FBAR reporting are:

- U.S. citizens;
- Resident aliens; and
- Entities created, organized, or formed under U.S. laws, including, but not limited to
  - Domestic corporations,
  - Partnerships,
  - Limited liability companies (LLCs),
  - Trusts, and
  - Estates.

The federal tax treatment of a person or entity does not determine whether an FBAR filing is required.

   COMMENT: An entity disregarded for federal tax purposes must still file an FBAR if filing is otherwise required.

   EXAMPLE: FBARs are required under Title 31 and not under any provisions of the Internal Revenue Code. Thus, a single-member LLC, which is a disregarded entity for U.S. tax purposes, must file an FBAR if one is otherwise required.

Interest

A U.S. person can have a financial interest in a foreign account in three situations.

Owner of record or the holder of legal title. A U.S. person has a financial interest in each bank, securities, or other financial account in a foreign country for which that person is the owner of record or holds legal title, regardless of whether the account is maintained for that person's own benefit or for the benefit of others. If an account is maintained in the name of more than one person, each U.S. person in whose name the account is maintained has a financial interest in that account.

Constructive owner. A U.S. person has a financial interest in each bank, securities, or other financial account in a foreign country if the owner of record or holder of legal title is a person acting on behalf of the U.S. person, such as an attorney, agent, or nominee with respect to the account.

Deemed owner. A U.S. person is deemed to have a financial interest in a bank, securities, or other financial account in a foreign country if the owner of record or holder of legal title is:

- A corporation in which the U.S. person owns, directly or indirectly, more than 50 percent of the voting power or the total value of the shares;
- A partnership in which the U.S. person owns, directly or indirectly, more than 50 percent of the profits or capital interest;
- Any other entity, other than a trust, in which the U.S. person owns, directly or indirectly, more than 50 percent of the voting power, total value of the equity interest or assets, or profits interest;
- A trust, if the U.S. person is the trust grantor and has an ownership interest for U.S. federal tax purposes; or
- A trust, if the U.S. person
  - Has a present beneficial interest in more than 50 percent of the assets, or
  - Receives more than 50 percent of the trust's current income.

However, a U.S. person does not have a financial interest in a discretionary trust merely because of the person's status as a discretionary beneficiary. Similarly, a remainder interest in a trust is not a present beneficial interest in the trust.

Signature Authority

Qualification of an individual. An individual has *signature or other authority* over an account if the individual has the authority, alone or in conjunction with another, to control the disposition of money, funds, or other assets held in a financial account by direct communication, written or otherwise, to the person with whom the financial account is maintained. An individual also has signature or other authority over an account if the FFI will act upon a direct communication from that individual regarding the disposition of assets in that account. Additionally, an individual has signature or other authority in conjunction with another if the FFI requires a direct communication from more than one individual regarding the disposition of assets in the account.

Exceptions. Exceptions to the FBAR requirements apply to officers and employees of financial institutions that have a federal functional regulator, certain entities that are publicly traded on a U.S. national securities exchange, and certain entities that are otherwise required to register their equity securities with the Securities and Exchange Commission (SEC). These exceptions apply, however, only when the officer or employee has no financial interest in the reportable account.

¶505

The exceptions to the FBAR requirements include:

- Bank officers and employees need not report that they have signature or other authority over a foreign financial account if
  - The account is owned or maintained by the bank,
  - The officer or employee has no financial interest in the account, and
  - The bank is examined by the Office of the Comptroller of the Currency, the Board of Governors of the Federal Reserve System, the Federal Deposit Insurance Corporation, the Office of Thrift Supervision, or the National Credit Union Administration;
- Officers and employees of a financial institution that is registered with and examined by the SEC or Commodity Futures Trading Commission (CFTC) need not report that they have signature or other authority over a foreign financial account if
  - The account is owned or maintained by the financial institution, and
  - The officer or employee has no financial interest in the account;
- Officers and employees of an authorized service provider (ASP) need not report that they have signature or other authority over a foreign financial account if
  - The account is owned or maintained by an investment company that is registered with the SEC, and
  - The officer or employee has no financial interest in the account. An ASP is an SEC-registered entity that provides services to a regulated investment company (RIC). Because mutual funds do not have employees of their own, they can use ASPs, such as investment advisors, to conduct their day-to-day operations. Thus, this exception can apply to persons who do not qualify for the exception for RICs, discussed above, but it is limited to the reportable accounts of RICs that are managed by the ASP;
- Officers and employees of an entity with a class of equity securities (or American depository receipts) listed on any U.S. national securities exchange need not report their signature or other authority over the entity's foreign financial accounts if the officer or employee has no financial interest in the accounts. This exception also applies if the American depository receipts are listed on the designated offshore market. In addition, if the entity is a U.S. entity, the officers and employees of any U.S. subsidiary need not report that they have signature or other authority over a foreign financial account of the subsidiary if
  - The officer or employee has no financial interest in the account, and
  - The U.S. subsidiary is named in a consolidated FBAR filed by the parent; and
- Officers and employees of an entity that has a class of equity securities (or American depository receipts in respect of equity securities) registered under Section 12(g) of the *Securities Exchange Act* need not report their signature or other authority over the entity's foreign financial accounts if the officer or employee has no financial interest in the accounts. This exception applies when corporations must register their stock with the SEC and comply with related reporting requirements because of their size in terms of assets and shareholders (currently more than $10 million in assets and more than 500 shareholders of record).

Accounts

An *account* is a formal relationship with a person to provide regular services, dealings, and other financial transactions. The length of the time the service is provided does not affect the fact that a formal account relationship has been established. For example, an escrow arrangement can qualify as an account, even if it exists for only a short period of time. However, an account is not established simply by conducting transactions like wiring money or purchasing a money order.

Bank accounts, securities accounts, and other financial accounts are all reportable accounts. *Bank accounts* include savings deposit, demand deposit, checking, and other accounts maintained with persons engaged in a banking business. This includes time deposits such as certificate of deposit accounts (CDs) that allow individuals to deposit funds with a banking institution and redeem the initial amount (along with interest earned) after a prescribed period of time. *Securities accounts* are accounts with persons engaged in the business of buying, selling, holding, or trading stock or other securities.

Other financial accounts include:

- Accounts with persons in the business of accepting deposits as a financial agency;
- Insurance or annuity policies with cash value;
- Accounts with persons who act as brokers or dealers for futures or options transactions in commodities that are on or subject to the rules of a commodity exchange or association;
- Accounts with mutual funds or similar pooled funds that issue shares that are available to the general public and have a regular net asset value determination and regular redemptions; and
- Other investment funds.

> **COMMENT:** The inclusion of "accounts with persons in the business of accepting deposits as a financial agency" is intended to ensure that deposit accounts and similar arrangements are covered by the reporting requirements, despite international differences in terminology, financial institution operations, and legal frameworks.

> **COMMENT:** When a reportable account is an insurance policy with cash value, the owner of the policy, not the beneficiary, is responsible for filing the FBAR.

> **COMMENT:** A federal district court (*U.S. v. J.C. Hom,* DC Calif., 2014-1 ustc ¶ 50,307) has held that because foreign poker websites functioned for a U.S. poker player as banks, his online accounts with them were reportable.

Exceptions. Certain accounts are specifically exempted from the reporting requirements. For example, no reporting is required with respect to correspondent accounts that are maintained by banks and used solely for bank-to-bank settlements.

Several other types of accounts are excluded from the reporting requirements based on the governmental status and functions of the entities and agencies involved.

The reporting requirements do not apply to:

- Accounts of an international financial institution that includes the United States as a member;
- Accounts in a U.S. military banking facility or U.S. military finance facility operated by a U.S. financial institution designated by the U.S. government to serve U.S. government installations abroad;
- Accounts of a department or agency of the United States, an Indian tribe, or any state or its political subdivisions, or a wholly owned entity, agency or instrumentality of any of the foregoing, including

- An employee retirement or welfare benefit plan of a governmental entity, and

- A college or university that is an agency of, an instrumentality of, owned by, or operated by a governmental entity; and

- Accounts of an entity that is established under the laws of, and exercises governmental authority on behalf of, the United States, an Indian tribe, any state or its political subdivision, or any intergovernmental compact among states and/or Indian tribes. An entity generally exercises governmental authority only if it has taxing, police, and/or eminent domain powers

Foreign accounts. A *foreign country* is any area outside the geographical boundaries of the United States; and a *foreign financial account* is a reportable account located outside the United States. For instance, an account with a U.S. bank is a foreign financial account if it is maintained in a branch of the bank that is physically located outside the United States. Conversely, an account with a foreign bank is not a foreign account if it is maintained in a bank branch that is physically located in the United States. The mere fact that an account may contain holdings or assets of foreign entities does not mean the account is foreign, as long as the account is maintained with a financial institution in the United States.

> **EXAMPLE:** Joshua Bloom, a U.S. citizen, has an account with a securities broker located in New York. He occasionally uses this account to purchase securities of foreign companies. Because Joshua maintains his securities account with a financial institution in the United States, the account is not a foreign account even though it contains foreign securities.

> **COMMENT:** A federal district court (*U.S, v. J.C. Hom*, DC Calif., 2014-1 ustc ¶ 50,307) has held that digital online accounts with poker websites were located in the foreign countries where the websites that created and managed the accounts were located, not the geographic location of the funds. Thus, it was irrelevant where the poker websites opened their own accounts.

In an omnibus account, a U.S. institution acts as the global custodian for a U.S. person's foreign assets, and creates pooled cash and securities accounts in the non-U.S. market to hold assets for multiple investors. The omnibus account is in the name of the global custodian. When the U.S. person has no legal right to the account and cannot directly reach the foreign assets in it, the U.S. person is treated as maintaining an account with a financial institution located in the United States.

An omnibus account with a financial institution located in the United States is not a reportable foreign account if the U.S. person:

- Does not have any legal right to the account; and
- Can access foreign holdings in the account only through the U.S. institution.

> **COMMENT:** A custodial arrangement that permits the U.S. person to have direct access to foreign assets maintained at a foreign institution is a reportable foreign financial account.

Valuation

An account's maximum value is a reasonable approximation of the greatest value of currency or nonmonetary assets in the account during the year. Periodic account statements can establish the maximum value of an account, as long as the statements fairly reflect that value during the calendar year. This includes a statement that provides the account value at the end of the statement period, as long as it is a bona fide statement prepared in the ordinary course of business.

Account value is determined in the currency of the account. Any value stated in foreign currency must be translated into U.S. currency by using the Treasury's Financial Management Service Rate from the last day of the calendar year. If no such rate is available, the FBAR filer must use another verifiable exchange rate and identify its source. If the currency is of a country that uses multiple exchange rates, the filer must use the one that would apply if the currency in the account were converted into U.S. dollars on the last day of the calendar year.

Penalties

The civil penalty for *willfully* failing to file an FBAR may be as high as the greater of $100,000 or 50 percent of the total balance of the foreign account per violation. *Nonwillful* violations that the IRS determines were not due to reasonable cause are subject to a $10,000 penalty per violation.

The criminal penalties are also harsh. For example, a person who fails to file a tax return is subject to a prison term of up to one year and a fine of up to $100,000. Willfully failing to file an FBAR and willfully filing a false FBAR are both violations that are subject to criminal penalties under U.S. tax law.

Possible criminal charges related to tax matters include tax evasion (Code Sec. 7201), filing a false return (Code Sec. 7206(1)), and failure to file an income tax return (Code Sec. 7203). Willfully failing to file an FBAR and willfully filing a false FBAR are both violations that are subject to criminal penalties under 31 U.S.C. § 5322. Additional possible criminal charges include conspiracy to defraud the government with respect to claims (18 U.S.C. § 286) and conspiracy to commit offense or to defraud the United States (18 U.S.C. § 371).

Table 2 summarizes penalties associated with the criminal charges under FBAR requirements.

Table 2. Comparative Prison Terms and Fines for Violating Tax Laws and FBAR Requirements

Violation	Maximum Prison Term	Maximum Fine
Tax evasion	5 years	$250,000
Filing false return	3 years	$250,000
Failing to file an FBAR	10 years	$500,000
Conspiracy to defraud government for claims	10 years	$250,000
Defrauding government	5 years	$250,000

STUDY QUESTION

5. Which individual violation of the tax reporting laws potentially carries the highest maximum fine?

   a. Tax evasion

   b. Filing a false return

   c. Failing to file an FBAR

   d. Defrauding the government

¶ 506 OFFSHORE VOLUNTARY DISCLOSURE PROGRAM

Taxpayers who have failed to previously to report their taxable income—including failing to disclose their interests in foreign accounts (and failing to file the applicable FBARs)—but who have not been contacted by the IRS may consider filing delinquent or amended income tax returns or otherwise notifying the IRS of the reason for their noncompliance.

Historically, voluntary disclosure programs were put in place by the IRS in order to give those taxpayers who had not been fully compliant a method of coming forward without fear of criminal prosecution. The theory behind the voluntary disclosure programs makes sense as it would be impossible for the IRS to catch every taxpayer who is noncompliant; the better approach is to entice them to come forward voluntarily. Their incentive, as stated, is no criminal prosecution and perhaps a promise of reduced taxes and related penalties/interest if the noncompliant taxpayer agrees to come forward and file all delinquent returns.

2014 Offshore Voluntary Disclosure Program

For 2014, the IRS is again offering an Offshore Voluntary Disclosure Program (OVDP). The objective remains the same as the with previous OVDPs from 2009, 2010, and 2012, which is to bring taxpayers that have used undisclosed foreign accounts and undisclosed foreign entities to avoid or evade tax into compliance with the U.S. tax laws. The 2012 OVDP established a procedure to encourage U.S. taxpayers to come forward and avoid criminal prosecution while agreeing to provide detailed information about their offshore assets and activities; file corrected tax forms; and pay tax, interest, and penalties under a specified framework. The 2014 OVDP is a continuation of that program. The IRS has disclosed that since the launch of the first program more than 45,000 taxpayers have become compliant voluntarily, paying about $6.5 billion in taxes, interest, and penalties.

Because the purpose of the 2014 OVDP is to provide a way for taxpayers who did not report taxable income in the past to come forward voluntarily and resolve their tax matters, a taxpayer who has properly reported all of his or her taxable income but not filed FBARs is not eligible for the 2014 OVDP. These taxpayers should consider making a quiet disclosure by filing their FBARS and may follow the delinquent FBAR submission procedures provided by the IRS on its website. The IRS will not impose a penalty for the failure to file the delinquent FBARs if the taxpayer properly reported on U.S. tax returns, and paid all tax on, the income from the foreign financial accounts reported on the delinquent FBARs, and the taxpayer had not previously been contacted regarding an income tax examination or a request for delinquent returns for the years for which the delinquent FBARs are submitted.

Voluntary disclosure is required to be complete, accurate, and truthful. Consequently, in addition to disclosing all items relating to foreign financial accounts, OVDP submissions must correct any previously unreported income from domestic sources; inappropriate deductions or credits claimed; or other incomplete, inaccurate, or untruthful items on the originally filed returns. The offshore penalty structure only resolves liabilities and penalties related to offshore noncompliance. Domestic portions of a voluntary disclosure are subject to examination.

The 2014 OVDP penalty framework requires participants to:

- Provide all required documents;
- File both amended returns (or original tax returns if delinquent) and FBARs for the past eight years;
- Pay the appropriate tax and interest;
- Pay a 20 percent accuracy-related penalty on such tax;
- Cooperate in the voluntary disclosure process, including
  - Providing information on foreign accounts and assets, institutions, and facilitators, and

- Assigning agreements to extend the period of time for assessing Title 26 liabilities and FBAR penalties;

- Pay a failure-to-file penalty and/or failure-to-pay penalty, if applicable; and

- Pay, in lieu of all other penalties that may apply to the undisclosed foreign accounts, assets and entities, including FBAR and offshore-related information return penalties and tax liabilities for years prior to the voluntary disclosure period, a miscellaneous Title 26 offshore penalty equal to 27.5 percent (or 50 percent in some circumstances) of the highest aggregate value of OVDP assets as defined in FAQ 35 during the period covered by the voluntary disclosure.

Beginning on August 4, 2014, the 27.5 percent offshore penalty percentage has been increased to 50 percent if, before the taxpayer's OVDP preclearance request is submitted, it becomes public that a financial institution where the taxpayer holds an account or another party facilitating the taxpayer's offshore arrangement is under investigation by the IRS or the Department of Justice (DOJ).

In fact, the IRS has pointed out that, balanced against the modified OVDP program, the government change will bolster its continued effort to combat the misuse of offshore assets. Working closely with the DOJ, the IRS will continue to investigate FFIs that may have assisted US taxpayers in avoiding their tax filing and payment obligations, whereas, on July 1, the new information reporting regime resulting from FATCA went into effect, and FFIs will begin to report to the IRS the foreign accounts held by U.S. persons.

Streamlined Procedure. Effective as of September 1, 2012, a special procedure for U.S. citizens living abroad was put into place, known as "Streamlined Procedure." The procedure was launched with the objective of bringing U.S. citizens living overseas into compliance with tax obligations. This procedure was only applicable to U.S. taxpayers living abroad who represent a low risk of tax evasion ($1,500 liability threshold) and who have not filed tax returns since 2009.

In 2014, the streamlined filing compliance procedures were expanded to include U.S. taxpayers whose failure to disclose their offshore assets was "nonwillful." To participate in the Streamlined Procedure, taxpayers must now certify that previous failures to comply were due to nonwillful conduct. The low-risk threshold, as well as the $1,500 liability threshold, is no longer required.

The expanded streamlined procedures are available to a greater number of U.S. taxpayers living outside the United States who have unreported foreign financial accounts and, for the first time, to certain American taxpayers residing in the United States. Taxpayers who choose the Streamlined Procedure must file information returns for the last three years (and six years of FBARs) as well as the payment of income tax and interest for each such tax year.

For eligible American taxpayers residing outside the United States, all penalties are to be waived. For eligible U.S. taxpayers residing in the United States, the only penalty will be a miscellaneous offshore penalty equal to 5 percent of the foreign financial assets that gave rise to the tax compliance issue.

STUDY QUESTION

6. A change in the Streamlined Procedure for tax compliance in 2014 was:

   a. Eliminating all penalties for U.S. taxpayers currently living in the United States

   b. Replacing the "low risk" of tax evasion requirement with "nonwillful" failure to disclose offshore assets

   c. Narrowing the scope of the procedure so it applies to fewer taxpayers

   d. Raising the amount of liability threshold for eligibility

¶ 507 CONCLUSION

As Congress and the IRS continue to focus on the reporting of income and assets held abroad, taxpayers must carefully examine the different reporting requirements set forth above to determine whether the rules apply to the taxpayers' foreign assets and financial interests and then take the necessary steps to comply in order to avoid the penalties.

FATCA generally requires certain U.S. taxpayers (specified individuals) holding foreign financial assets with an aggregate value exceeding $50,000 to report certain information about those assets on a Form 8938. This form must be attached to the taxpayer's annual tax return. Reporting applies for assets held in taxable years beginning after March 18, 2010. Failure to report foreign financial assets on Form 8938 may result in a penalty of $10,000 (and an additional penalty up to $50,000 for continued failure after IRS notification). Additionally, underpayments of tax attributable to undisclosed foreign financial assets will be subject to an additional substantial understatement penalty of up to 40 percent for certain transactions that should have been reported under the applicable code sections.

In addition to the complying with the FATCA reporting requirements, taxpayers also may be required to file FinCEN Form 114 (FBAR). The FATCA requirements may overlap with and affect the same assets as the FBAR requirements, but they apply separately. The reporting threshold for FBAR is lower than that for FATCA. For FBAR purposes, if at any point during the calendar year, the aggregate value of the accounts exceeds $10,000 an FBAR must be filed. Willfully failing to file an FBAR may result in civil penalties as high as the greater of $100,000 or 50 percent of the total balance of the foreign account per violation. Nonwillful violations that the IRS determines were not due to reasonable cause are subject to a $10,000 penalty per violation. Criminal penalties, including fines and jail time, may also apply.

Moreover, taxpayers that were not previously in compliance must examine the options available to them, such as the 2014 OVDP, and make a determination regarding coming into compliance. Based on recent changes and continual enforcement efforts, it is clear that both the IRS and Congress will continue to maintain their focus on using these new reporting requirements to locate and collect monies owed by U.S. taxpayers.

MODULE 3: EVOLVING ISSUES FOR INDIVIDUALS—Chapter 6: Retirement Plan Rollovers, Conversions, and Distributions

¶ 601 WELCOME

This chapter discusses the tax incentives for retirement savings, and the rules regarding the shifting of savings from one retirement plan or account to another. It also discusses the consequences of dipping into those savings before retirement age.

¶ 602 LEARNING OBJECTIVES

Upon completion of this chapter, you will be able to:

- Identify key features of today's retirement plan accounts and roads to building retirement assets;
- Identify plan assets that may use rollovers and the plans eligible to receive them;
- Recognize the differences between actual distributions and trustee-to-trustee transfers;
- Identify rules for converting traditional IRAs, recharacterizing contributions, and reconverting a recharacterized conversion;
- Identify the merits of keeping retirement assets in a 401(k) account rather than rolling over to an IRA and how distributions for deceased employees are made; and
- Recognize the consequences of early distributions and hardship distributions from retirement accounts.

¶ 603 INTRODUCTION

Retirement planning has become a far bigger challenge for individuals of the generation approaching retirement than it was for the previous generation. Previously, employees could rely on an employer-sponsored defined benefit pension plan that would provide a steady income flow along with generous health plan benefits for life starting at age 65. Social Security benefits would bolster that income. Retirement savings in an IRA or 401(k) account would be a bonus.

Today this model is the exception rather than the rule. Employers have drastically cut back on traditional pension plans, replacing them with 401(k) plans. Employers often contribute a few thousands of dollars per year to these plans for rank-and-file employees, but generally the bulk of the savings has to come from the employee. Going forward, retirement means Social Security payments and a carefully guarded 401(k) balance. Many retirees have to find part-time jobs.

The great post-2008 recession has made retirement planning all but irrelevant to many people in their 50s and 60s, just when they should be topping off their retirement accounts and paying off their mortgages. Many have lost their well-paid career jobs and have had to draw down on their assets just to pay their mortgage. Many who have returned to work have had to take retail jobs that pay a fraction of the baby boomers' old wages.

Maximizing retirement savings is now crucial; fortunately, the tax code reflects the new reality by providing serious incentives for contributing to a 401(k) or individual retirement account (IRA). It is possible to move retirement money among accounts without incurring tax. Choices for people departing jobs enable choices between taking the tax benefits now or in retirement. For account holders in financial need, early distributions are available under certain circumstances.

¶ 604 BUILDING RETIREMENT ASSETS

Traditional defined benefit pension plans for rank-and-file employees are fading into history as employers move to elective deferral plans such as 401(k)s. Under these latter types of plans, the employee elects to defer a part of his or her wages or salary. Within limits, it is up to the employee how much to defer. Usually, the employee has some control over asset selection and allocation over the amounts deferred. The burden is on the employee to save enough, and invest well enough. Employers, which formerly offered to match a percentage of employees' contributions to 401(k) plans, cut back on such perks during the great recession.

Maximizing Elective Deferrals

The first step an individual can and should take to build retirement savings is to contribute the maximum to his or her 'employer-sponsored elective salary deferral plan, particularly to the extent of an employer match. Such plans include 401(k) plans, 403(b) plans (for employees of education organizations), and 457(b) plans (for state and local employers and tax exempt employers). Savings incentive match plan for employees (SIMPLE) IRA plans for small employers also have a deferral feature.

Limits on deferrals. In 2014, the inflation-adjusted deferral limit for 401(k), 403(b), and 457(b) plans is the lesser of $17,500 or 100 percent of compensation. The cap is the lesser of $12,000 or 100 percent of compensation for SIMPLE IRA and SIMPLE 401(k) plans. These amounts are adjusted for inflation in $500 increments annually.

Employer contributions. An employer providing a profit-sharing plan may make discretionary contributions to its employees' 401(k) accounts each year. Some employers make annual matching contributions to encourage participation by lower-paid employees (which helps the employer meet nondiscrimination requirements). For 2014, employer contributions are capped at an inflation-adjusted amount of $52,000 per employee.

> **EXAMPLE:** Sophia Manara elects to defer $1,200 from her $30,000 annual salary to her employer's 401(k) plan. Her employer makes 50 percent matching contributions on its employees' deferrals up to 5 percent of an employee's salary. As a result, Sophia's employer contributes an additional $600 (50 percent × $1,200) to her 401(k) account for the year.

> **EXAMPLE:** Alternatively, Sophia defers $2,000 for her 401(k) account. As a result, her employer adds $750 ($1,500 × 50 percent percent) to the account. Note that the matching contribution is not $1,000 because the plan's match is capped at 50 percent of the deferrals made up to 5 percent of an employee's salary ($30,000 × 5 percent = $1,500, and $1,500 × 50 percent = $750).

> **COMMENT:** An employer plan may limit deferrals and contributions to less than the maximum permitted amounts.

Contributions to more than one plan. In general, the annual deferral limit is applied on a taxpayer-by-taxpayer basis rather than a plan-by-plan basis. Accordingly, the limit applies to all of an individual's contributions for a particular year to the individual's 401(k), 403(b), and SIMPLE 401(k), and IRA plans. The exception is 457(b) plans, for which the limit is applied separately. Taxpayers who file joint returns are nevertheless each considered separately in connection with these limits.

EXAMPLE: In 2014, Jackson Montgomery is 40 years old. During the year, he works for two unrelated employers, each of which offered a 401(k) plan. He defers $10,000 for each plan, which is the maximum amount each plan allows. Jackson exceeds the total annual contribution limit of $17,500 by $2,500.

CAUTION: Typically, if there is an excess deferral in within a plan, the plan administrator discovers the mistake, notifies the participant, and makes a timely corrective distribution. But if there is an excess deferral because the taxpayer makes less than $17,500 in deferrals to more than one unrelated plan, the administrators of the two plans probably will not catch the mistake. In either case, the buck stops with the individual taxpayer for guarding against and correcting excess deferrals.

Correcting excess deferrals. When an individual discovers an excess deferral, he or she should notify the plan administrator to have the excess amount and any income distributed by April 15 (or the next business day if a weekend or holiday) of the following year. If corrected by then, the distribution of the excess deferral is not treated as taxable income (though of course there is no exclusion allowed from income). Distributed amounts attributable to income generated by the excess deferral are taxable in the tax year received.

Failure to meet the deadline. If the April 15 deadline is not met, the excess deferral is taxed twice. First, as is the case where the excess deferral is corrected in time, there is no exclusion for the excess deferral for the year it was made. Second, the amount is taxed when it is distributed. Note that an excess deferral amount is not treated as an after-tax contribution for purposes of basis in the account.

EXAMPLE: Ellen, who is age 30, defers $18,500 in 2013 for her 401(k), which is $1,000 over the limit. She does not correct the deferral by April 15, 2014. She can only exclude $17,500 for 2013, and therefore there is no exclusion for the $1,000 excess deferral for 2013. Unlike after-tax contributions, the $1,000 is not added to her account's basis. When she later takes a distribution, the amount is taxed as ordinary income.

Catch-up contributions for employer plans. For individuals who turn age 50 by the end of the calendar year, deferrals may be increased by an inflation-adjusted annual amount. For 2014, the amount is $5,500 for traditional 401(k) plans, 403(b) plans, and 457(b) plans, and $2,500 for SIMPLE 401(k) and SIMPLE IRA plans. Catch-up contributions are allowed only if the plan provides for them.

Pretax or Designated Roth? Some employers offer their employees the option of deferring part of income to a designated Roth account under their 401(k), 403(b), or 457(b) plan. A designated Roth account is taxed similarly to a Roth IRA, except they the designated account is part of an employer plan and subject to employer plan rules. Deferrals to a designated Roth account are not excluded from income, and they are taxed as compensation in the year of deferral. Like deferrals to traditional plans, the assets grow tax-free-free until distribution. The difference is that when they are distributed, neither the original contribution nor the earnings are taxed.

PLANNING POINTER: Many individuals need the current tax benefit, and for them contributing to a traditional deferral account makes the most sense. But for those who can afford the current tax hit, the Roth contribution might be the better way to go in the long run.

IRA Contributions

If the individual is deferring the maximum into an employer plan, or does not have an employer plan but does have compensation, an IRA contribution can make sense. The maximum contribution is $5,500 for 2014. The maximum is bumped up by $1,000 for individuals ages 50 and up. An individual must have taxable compensation at least in the amount of the contribution.

> **EXAMPLE:** Janice Patterson's income for 2014 consists of $50,000 in dividends and $1,000 in wages. Janice may contribute up to $1,000 (her earned as opposed to unearned income) to an IRA for 2014.

Spousal IRAs. IRAs belong to individual owners and are taxable to the owner's Social Security number. For married taxpayers, each spouse can contribute the respective maximum amounts each year to his or her separate IRA. Taxable compensation, for these purposes, is combined for married joint filers so that a spouse without taxable compensation may still make a contribution.

> **EXAMPLE:** Karen and Irv Glass are married. They are 30 years old. In 2014, Karen earns $11,000 in wages. Irv has no compensation in 2014. Each may contribute the full amount of $5,500 to their IRAs because Karen's compensation may be counted towards Irv's contribution limit.

Deductible contributions. Contributions to a traditional IRA are generally deductible. Contributions grow tax-free until withdrawn. Upon withdrawal, the contributions and all earnings are taxed at ordinary rates.

Nondeductible contributions. Taxpayers may choose to make nondeductible contributions, or they might have to make them because the deduction is limited. In particular, the ability of an active participant in an employer plan to take an IRA deduction is phased out for those whose adjusted gross income (AGI) exceeds $96,000 (for 2014) if a joint filer or $60,000 (for 2014) if a single filer. Nondeductible contributions—whether made by choice or because the taxpayer exceeds the active participant AGI limit—are treated as basis, and those contributions are not taxed when withdrawn. Earnings grow tax-free but are taxed upon distribution.

> **PRACTICE POINTER:** The taxpayer must file Form 8606, *Nondeductible IRAs,* along with Form 1040 or 1040A if he or she makes nondeductible contributions.

Roth IRAs. Contributions to Roth IRAs are not deductible. Earnings grow tax-free, and neither contributions nor earnings are taxed when withdrawn. There is an income phaseout for account holders having Roth IRA contributions beginning at adjusted gross income of $181,000 (for 2014) for joint filers, and $114,000 (for 2014) for single filers.

Nonretirement Account Assets

If an individual has more retirement-earmarked savings than can be absorbed by the individual's retirement plans and accounts, the goal should be to keep the most heavily taxed investments in the retirement accounts. For example, if an investor wants to have bonds that generate ordinary income in the investor's portfolio, it makes sense to have them in a retirement account. If it is a Roth account, there is no tax on what would be taxed as ordinary income. If it's a traditional account, distributions are taxed at ordinary rates no matter what the investment.

Assets held outside of retirement accounts. Assets held outside of qualified retirement plans are generally subject to tax. If a taxpayer wants to avoid tax altogether, tax-free bonds are an option. Annuities allow a deferral of tax until earnings are distributed. Corporate stock that generates qualified dividends and qualified capital gains is taxed at a 20 percent maximum rate (for 2014). If an investor has to hold some investments outside of a retirement account, these sorts of tax-favored investments are prime candidates.

Social Security benefits. Retirement benefits under Social Security increase dramatically for each year that an individual delays the retirement benefit start date between ages 63 and 70. Social Security benefits are an excellent deal compared to private annuities because they are inflation-adjusted (private annuity companies charge dearly for this feature and usually hedge their protection). Individual benefit estimates are readily available by registering on the Social Security Administration website

STUDY QUESTION

1. Which of the following may *not* make nondeductible contributions to a traditional IRA for 2014?

    a. A single taxpayer with earned income of less than $60,000

    b. Joint filers with combined incomes total $95,000

    c. A taxpayer older than age 50 who contributes $6,500 for 2014

    d. Taxpayers (including the taxpayer's spouse) having no taxable compensation for 2014

¶ 605 MANAGING RETIREMENT ASSETS THROUGH ROLLOVERS

Individuals have a great deal of-freedom in transferring their retirement savings tax-free from one type of qualified retirement plan to another by means of a rollover. However, rollovers are limited by certain rules, and they may be further limited by employer plan language or IRA administrator arrangements.

Rollover Basics

The following are the basic considerations and rules that a taxpayer should understand with respect to rollovers.

- Only certain distributions are eligible to be rolled over;
- Not all kinds of plans can accept rollover distributions from every other kind of plan, and the transferor plan and transferee plan must match in that respect;
- Though generally tax-free, rollovers from traditional accounts to Roth accounts generate current tax;
- There are two kinds of rollovers—those involving distributions to the taxpayer and those that do not, and several rules apply to rollovers that involve actual distributions;
- The receiving plan has a duty to ensure that an intended rollover is valid under the rules.

Distributions Eligible for Rollover Treatment

Eligible rollover distributions include those from an eligible plan, other than the following types:

- Required minimum distributions (RMDs);
- Distributions in the form of a substantially equal series of payments;
- Hardship distributions;
- Corrective distributions;

- Loans treated as distributions;
- Cost of life insurance coverage; and
- Dividends on employer securities.

Required minimum distributions. If a taxpayer has begun taking RMDs, the first dollars taken out will be counted toward the taxpayer's RMD for the year. Only after all RMD dollars are distributed can distributed dollars be treated as an eligible rollover distribution.

> **EXAMPLE:** Brewster McKay has an IRA from which he has begun taking RMDs. In 2014, he receives a distribution of $9,801, which is his RMD for the year based on his age and the value of his account as of December 31, 2013. That distribution is not an eligible rollover distribution, and unless Brewster takes a subsequent distribution in 2014, he cannot roll over any amount for 2014.

> **EXAMPLE:** If Brewster takes an additional distribution of $4,000 in 2014, the distribution does not fall under any of the other listed rollover distribution exceptions. Therefore $4,000 may be rolled over during 2014.

Substantially equal payments. Although substantially equal payments from a traditional IRA cannot be rolled over, the traditional (deductible or nondeductible) IRA can be converted to a Roth IRA with the periodic payments continuing as before.

Plans Eligible to Make and Receive Rollovers

Plans eligible for rollovers include:

- IRAs including simplified employee pension (SEP) IRAs and savings incentive match plans for employees (SIMPLE) IRAs;
- Qualified pension plans (which include 401(k), profit-sharing, money purchase, and defined benefit plans);
- Qualified annuity plans;
- Tax sheltered annuity plans (403(b) plans); and
- State or local government deferred compensation plans (457(b) plans).

Eligible plans include traditional plans and accounts, as well as designated Roth 401(k), 403(b), governmental 457(b) accounts, and Roth IRAs. They do not include nongovernmental 457(b) plans sponsored by tax-exempt organizations.

Traditional-to-traditional plan rollovers. Rollovers may be made from any traditional (i.e., non-Roth) account or plan to any other traditional account or plan (assuming the plan accepts such rollovers), except that rollovers cannot be made:

- To a SIMPLE IRA unless it is from another SIMPLE IRA; and
- From a SIMPLE IRA to a non-SIMPLE IRA for at least two years from the initial participation date.

Rollovers to Roth IRAs. Rollovers can be made to a Roth IRA from virtually any kind of plan, including Roth and traditional IRAs, simplified employee pension (SEP) and SIMPLE IRAs, qualified plans (including 401(k) plans), 403(b) plans, and 457(b) governmental plans.

Rollovers from Roth IRAs. Rollovers from a Roth IRA can only be made to another Roth IRA.

Rollovers to designated Roth accounts. Rollovers can be made only from another designated Roth account under a different plan, or by means of an in-plan rollover from a traditional qualified plan, including a 401(k), 403(b), and governmental 457(b) plan.

Rollovers from designated Roth accounts. Rollovers can be made from a designated Roth account to a Roth IRA or other designated Roth account.

> **COMMENT:** Employer plans must generally allow rollovers for eligible distributions to IRAs or other eligible plans, but they are not required to accept them. Plan provisions will control and need to be checked.

Eligible distributions. Distributions eligible for rollover treatment generally include lump-sum distributions rather normal periodic pension payments made after retirement. Eligible distributions do not include RMDs, hardship distributions, or corrective distributions made to keep the plan in compliance. There are number of additional technical exceptions.

STUDY QUESTION

2. Eligible rollover distributions from eligible plans include:

   a. Hardship distributions from a 401(k)

   b. RMDs from an IRA

   c. Distributions from a nongovernmental 457(b) plans

   d. Corrective distributions from a 403(b) account

Tax Treatment of Rollovers

Amounts may be rolled over tax-free from traditional plans to other traditional plans. Amounts from Roth accounts may be rolled over tax-free to other Roth accounts. Amounts from traditional IRA and employer plans may be rolled over to Roth accounts, and are included in income. Amounts from Roth accounts cannot be rolled over into traditional accounts (though recharacterizations of a recently converted traditional-to-Roth account are allowed under certain circumstances).

> **EXAMPLE:** In 2014, Peggy Albrecht is age 30 and has a traditional IRA. She has never made a nondeductible contribution. She withdraws $10,000 on July 1 to pay off consumer debt. She must recognize the $10,000 in gross income for 2014, and because she is younger than age 59½, she owes 10 percent additional tax on the early withdrawal (there are exceptions to the 10 percent tax, but paying off debt is not one of them).

> **EXAMPLE:** If within 60 days Peggy rolls the $10,000 over to a different traditional IRA that belongs to her, Peggy pays no income tax, and she is not subject to any additional tax for an early withdrawal for 2014.

> **EXAMPLE:** If the account to which Peggy rolls over the $10,000 is a Roth IRA, Peggy must recognize $10,000 in income for 2014 but owes no additional early withdrawal tax.

> **EXAMPLE:** If both her original IRA and that to which she rolls over the $10,000 are Roth IRAs, Peggy recognizes no income in 2014, and she owes no additional early withdrawal tax.

> **COMMENT:** Peggy has use of the money for up to 60 days before she has to roll over the amount. She is free to do what she wants with the money during that time, but if she misses the 60-day deadline she will be unable to obtain a waiver from the IRS if she does anything but park the money in an account. Waiver of the deadline is discussed below.

¶605

After-tax contributions to an employer plan. Generally, individuals may roll over the entire amount of any qualified distribution received from a qualified plan into another qualified plan or IRA, including the portion of the distribution representing after-tax contributions. A rollover of after-tax contributions must be made in a trustee-to-trustee transfer. In addition, an employer plan that accepts the rollover of after-tax contributions must separately track these contributions and related earnings. IRAs can take after-tax contributions, but are *not* required to separately track after-tax contributions.

> **COMPLIANCE POINTER:** If only part of a distribution from a 401(k) plan includes both taxable and nontaxable amounts, the amount rolled over is treated as coming first from the taxable part of the distribution. That means if the amount rolled over is less than the taxable amount, the rollover is tax-free. Any rolled over nontaxable portion is treated as basis in a receiving IRA.

> **EXAMPLE:** Jerry Brosnan is age 60, and has a 401(k) plan worth $100,000. He is let go from his job, and is eligible to take a distribution from the plan in the full amount. The after-tax portion in the 401(k) is $40,000. Jerry rolls over the entire $100,000 to a new rollover IRA. He pays no tax, and the IRA has $40,000 in basis.

> **EXAMPLE:** If Jerry rolls over $90,000 instead of the full amount, and takes a distribution of remaining $10,000, the $60,000 taxable amount is protected from tax because in a partial rollover, the taxable portion comes out first. The remaining $30,000 of the rollover represents after-tax contributions, resulting in $30,000 in basis for the IRA. The $10,000 kept by Jerry also represents after-tax contributions, and is not taxable. He does not owe an additional early withdrawal penalty tax because he is older than age 59½.

> **PRACTICE POINTER:** In a partial rollover, the unrolled over amount may be subject to tax, as well as the 10 percent additional early withdrawal tax, if applicable.

Rollovers from IRAs to non-IRA employer plans. Normally, when distributions are made from an IRA that has nontaxable basis, the amount of the basis is a pro-rata portion of all of the basis in all of the taxpayer's IRAs. There is a special rule, however, for rollovers from IRAs to a non-IRA employer plan (such as a 401(k) plan) because no basis may be rolled over into the employer plan. In these cases, the taxable portion comes out first.

> **EXAMPLE:** Laura Rothberg owns two IRA accounts, each worth $100,000. Laura has made $20,000 in nondeductible contributions to the first IRA with Global Equities Fund (hence, it has a basis of $20,000). She has made no such contributions to the second IRA account in the Domestic Bonds Fund. When Laura takes a rollover distribution of $80,000 from the Global Equities IRA and moves it to a different IRA with Latin America Bonds Fund, the amount of basis in the $80,000 distribution is $8,000 (20,000 ÷ 200,000 × $80,000 - $8,000). The same would hold true if she rolled over $80,000 from the Domestic Bonds account to Latin America Bonds.

> **EXAMPLE:** If Laura rolls over the $80,000 from Global Equities to her 401(k), none of the $80,000 is basis. Global Equities still has $20,000, all of which is basis.

> **COMMENT:** 401(k) plans may accept IRA rollovers, but they do not have to. The plans do have to allow rollovers out of the plan for eligible distributions.

> **PRACTICE POINTER:** To recover basis, if any, in an IRA distribution, the taxpayer must file Form 8606, *Nondeductible IRAs,* for the year of the distribution. The rest of the distribution representing earnings and deductible contributions is taxable in the year of distribution.

Eligible rollover distributions involving property. If a distribution from an employer plan includes property other than cash (e.g., stock), the property can be rolled over. It is permissible to sell the property and roll over the proceeds. In that case, no gain or loss is recognized as long as the entire amount is rolled over.

> **EXAMPLE:** Betsy Washington receives nonemployer stock valued at $50,000 in an eligible rollover distribution. She sells the stock for $60,000, and rolls over the $60,000 to a traditional IRA. Betsy recognizes no income, and the amount of the rollover is the full $60,000.

Two Kinds of Rollovers

Rollovers come in two varieties:

- Rollovers that involve a distribution to the taxpayer in the form of a check payable to the taxpayer, and subsequent deposit within 60 days by the taxpayer to the receiving plan; and

- Trustee-to-trustee transfers in which the trustee or administrator of the transferor plan or account issues a check payable to the transferee plan for the benefit of the taxpayer.

A rollover with a distribution to the taxpayer results in the money being under the complete control of the taxpayer for up to 60 days. Trustee-to-trustee rollovers never place the money in the control of the taxpayer (though the taxpayer is typically tasked with forwarding the check to the transferee plan). The rules differ somewhat depending on which form the rollover takes.

> **COMMENT:** The IRS calls rollovers without distributions to the taxpayer "trustee-to-trustee transfers" or "direct rollovers." Trustee-to-trustee transfers are generally permitted for any distribution that would qualify as an eligible rollover distribution if it were actually distributed to the taxpayer. Certain kinds of transfers, however, can only be done as a trustee-to-trustee transfer. To keep the distinction clear, rollovers without an actual distribution to the taxpayer will be called "trustee-to-trustee transfers" in this course.

Rollovers with Distributions

Rollovers that involve actual distributions to the taxpayer are subject to the following rules that do not apply to trustee-to-trustee transfers:

- The rollover must be completed by the 60th day after receipt of the distribution;

- An individual is allowed to make only one rollover from an IRA in a 12-month period that begins on the distribution date; and

- Withholding rules requiring the distributing plan to withhold 20 percent of funds apply.

60-day deadline. If the taxpayer fails to deposit the rollover amount with an eligible retirement plan within 60 days, the distribution is treated as taxable for the year of the distribution (even if the 60-day period extends into the following tax year). The 10 percent additional tax for early distributions may apply. The subsequent deposit with the eligible retirement plan or IRA will be treated as a contribution instead of a rollover and be subject to relevant contribution limits.

Extension due to frozen accounts. The 60-day period is extended if there is a period of time during the 60-day window during which the account is frozen due to bankruptcy or insolvency of the financial institution, or the state where the financial institution is located restricts withdrawals due to possible bankruptcy or insolvency of financial institutions. The period is extended for the period the account was frozen, and cannot end earlier than 10 days after the account was unfrozen.

Waiver of the 60-day rule. Waivers are available under certain conditions. A waiver covers amounts up to the amount received. For example, if the taxpayer takes a distribution of $5,000 and obtains a waiver, the waiver is good for up to $5,000.

Automatic waiver. The 60-day deadline is automatically waived if:

- The financial institution received the funds on time;
- The taxpayer followed the institution's procedures;
- The funds were not deposited on time solely due to an error of the financial institution;
- The funds are deposited correctly within one year from the beginning of the 60-day period; and
- The rollover would have been valid if the financial institution had deposited the funds as instructed.

Hardship waiver. The IRS may waive the 60-day rule if the owner was unable to meet the deadline due to hardship. The types of delays that might qualify include delays caused by:

- Errors committed by a financial institution that do not fall under the automatic waiver requirements; and
- Delays caused by death, disability, hospitalization, incarceration, restrictions imposed by a foreign country, or postal error.

> **PRACTICE POINTER:** To obtain a hardship waiver, the taxpayer must use the IRS letter ruling procedure, along with the appropriate user fee ($500 for a rollover of less than $50,000; $1,500 for $50,000 to $100,000; and $3,000 for amounts of more than $100,000). It is best to apply for a ruling with some urgency after discovering the compliance failure. If the taxpayer does not take the matter seriously enough to act promptly, the IRS might not take it seriously either in entertaining a hardship waiver request.

Nonuse of distributed funds. Normally, the IRS is not interested in what an individual does during the 60-day rollover period with an eligible rollover distribution, unless an extension of the 60-day period is requested. In that case, it is important that during the extension period the taxpayer park the funds and not use them for other purposes. For example, the IRS denied the waiver in the following circumstances:

- The owner used the distribution to pay off an existing mortgage on investment property, and the delay in rolling over the distribution beyond the 60-day period was due to delays in the sale of the property;
- The owner used the distribution for a short-term loan to his elderly mother to buy a new home until she could get a mortgage; and
- The owner used the funds for personal expenses.

> **COMMENT:** The IRS's concern is that the taxpayer is gaming the system by using the tax-sheltered assets to fund other endeavors. This concern also arises with respect to application of the once-per-12-months rule.

Revised 12-months rule for IRAs starting in 2015 . Historically, the IRS has applied the once-per-12-months rule generously by applying it on an IRA-by-IRA basis, rather than on a taxpayer-by-taxpayer basis. Accordingly, a taxpayer with multiple IRAs could roll over amounts from each IRA during the course of a 12-month period, as long as the taxpayer only did it once per IRA. Starting in 2015, the once-per-12-months rule applies on a taxpayer-by-taxpayer basis. Accordingly, if a taxpayer has multiple IRAs, a rollover from one prevents the taxpayer from rolling over again within 12-months from any of the taxpayer's other IRAs as well.

¶605

EXAMPLE: Jackson McGill has two IRA accounts, one for commodities, the other for bonds. On January 1, 2014, he receives a rollover distribution from his Global Commodity account. He completes the rollover by February 28 from that fund to his International Markets Fund account. Jackson may not make another rollover from either account until July 1, 2015. He may, however, roll over amounts from his High Yield Bond Fund account during 2014.

EXAMPLE: If Jackson receives the rollover distribution from Global Commodity on January 1, 2015, he may not make another rollover until January 1, 2016. This ban includes the High Yield Bond account. However, he may make another rollover from the bond account, as long as it is done in 2015.

PRACTICE POINTER: The once-per-12-months rule does not apply to rollovers from employer plans.

COMMENT: Historically, individuals with multiple IRAs could have free access to a portion of their total IRA funds throughout the year by making a series of rollovers and by using the full 60-day window for each. Starting in 2015, individuals can no longer rotate rollovers and are limited to no more than one 60-day period per year.

COMMENT: The opportunity for abuse is absent in the case of trustee-to-trustee transfers because the money never lands in the hands of the individual taxpayer. Accordingly, the once-per-12-months rule does not apply to trustee-trustee transfers.

PRACTICE POINTER: Married spouses are each counted as individual IRA owners or plan participants for retirement account purposes, so a married couple as a unit can roll over twice within a 12-month period as long as they roll over from IRAs that belong to each of them rather than to only one of them. However, when the rollovers are overlapping, it might draw the attention of the IRS if it appears the couple is merely trying to lengthen the 60-day window.

Withholding. Eligible rollover distributions are subject to income tax withholding at a rate of 20 percent even if they are going to be rolled over and thus exempt from tax. This can cause a serious cash flow problem for the taxpayer.

EXAMPLE: Betty Atherton is entitled to a distribution of $100,000 from her employer's plan. If she takes a rollover distribution, she will receive only $80,000 and the remaining $20,000 will be withheld as income tax. If she only rolls over the $80,000, she will owe tax on the $20,000 withheld. Accordingly, if Betty does not have access to $20,000, she will have to borrow the sum to make up the difference for her rollover if she is to avoid tax.

PLANNING POINTER: Withholding is avoided by making a trustee-to-trustee transfer, which is not subject to withholding. If that is not possible, another approach is to adjust wage income tax withholding (because the taxpayer will otherwise be overwithholding by 20 percent of the rollover distribution) to provide temporary cash flow relief.

Withholding exceptions. There are exceptions to withholding for distributions of less than $200 (including all previous eligible rollover distributions for tax year), or for distributions solely of employer securities, plus cash of $200 or less or less in lieu of fractional shares. Rollover withholding does not apply to distributions that are not eligible rollover distributions, though other withholding rules might apply.

PRACTICE POINTER: Rollovers that involve distributions (as opposed to trustee-to-trustee transfers) from one IRA to another are reported on Form 1040, lines 51a and 15b, Form 1014A, lines 11a and 11b, and Form 1040NR, Lines 16a and

16b. If the rollover is made to a qualified plan, the taxpayer must attach an explanation.

Any fees must be paid directly by the taxpayer. If taken from the rollover, a fee is generally considered a taxable distribution.

Trustee-to-Trustee Transfers

A qualified plan must provide that an employee who is eligible to receive a distribution that could be rolled over may elect to have the distribution transferred directly in a trustee-to-trustee transfer to an IRA or other employer plan, thus avoiding withholding. This option is not required for distributions under $200 for the year. If the trustee-to-trustee transfer is partial, withholding applies to the portion that is not transferred in that manner.

> **CAUTION:** Typically, the transfer is to an IRA, but sometimes it is to another employer plan. There is no requirement, however, that a retirement plan eligible to receive the rollover must accept direct transfers. Indeed, a plan can refuse to accept such transfers or limit the circumstances under which it will accept them.

Procedure. A trustee-to-trustee transfer is often done by having the transferring plan or IRA issue a check payable to the receiving plan or IRA trustee for the benefit of the individual, and giving the check to the individual to deliver to the new plan or trustee.

Transfers that can only be done trustee-to-trustee. Although eligible rollover distributions may be accomplished by means of trustee-to-trustee transfers (plans permitting), there are certain transfers that can only be done trustee-to-trustee. These include:

- Recharacterizing traditional IRA contributions as Roth contributions, or vice versa;
- Moving assets from an inherited IRA to another inherited IRA;
- Transfers between different designated Roth accounts;
- Transfers of after-tax contributions from an employer plan to another employer plan; and
- Transfers from employer plans due to the death of the employee to a nonspouse designated beneficiary.

Inherited IRAs. An *inherited IRA* is an IRA an individual acquires upon the death of the owner. Eligible rollover distributions cannot be made from or to an inherited IRA. However, trustee-to-trustee transfers are permitted. There is an exception for surviving spouses who may roll over an inherited IRA or treat it as their own IRA.

Duty of Receiving Plan

Whether the rollover is a trustee-to-trustee transfer or a rollover distribution, a receiving plan's administrator or trustee must make a reasonable effort to determine whether the distributing plan is a plan that qualifies for eligible rollover treatment, and that the amount is in fact intended as a rollover for the benefit of the employee.

Reliance. A receiving plan may reasonably rely on a statement by the administrator or trustee of the distributing plan. Generally, the administrator or trustee for the distributing plan or IRA communicates the source of the funds to the receiving plan, either through a note on the check or check stub, or by other means in the case of an electronic transfer. In the case of a rollover from an IRA, the receiving trustee must verify that the check is not a required minimum distribution (it is sufficient if the individual certifies that he or she will not attain age 70½ by the end of the year).

EFAST2 safe harbor. The IRS has ruled in the context of a plan-to-plan direct rollover that an administrator of the receiving plan may reasonably rely on the distributing plan's

EFAST2 Form 5500 series filings in evaluating whether the distributing plan is a qualified plan for rollover purposes. The EFAST2 database is maintained by the Department of Labor. The receiving plan administrator can search the system for the most recently filed Form 5500 for the distributing plan.

STUDY QUESTION

3. In a trustee-to-trustee transfer:

   a. There is no requirement that a receiving employer plan must accept the transfer

   b. Withholding applies for the whole distribution

   c. Assets from an inherited IRA may be transferred to an employer plan

   d. The taxpayer may not deliver a check from the transferring plan to the receiving plan

¶ 606 ROTH ROLLOVERS AND CONVERSIONS

Traditional IRAs have two key advantages: They defer tax until the assets are withdrawn during retirement, and the taxpayer is usually in a lower tax bracket when retired. The RMD rules apply after the taxpayer hits age 70½, but that is not an issue for taxpayers who need the distributions to pay their living expenses.

> **PLANNING POINTER:** Different considerations apply for wealthier individuals. They may continue to be in a high tax bracket as they age, so there is no tax bracket advantage to being retired. RMDs are a serious problem because they would prefer to pass on the assets to their heirs while the assets are in a tax-protected retirement account. For wealthy taxpayers, a Roth account is generally an excellent means for both protecting investment income from tax and from RMDs during the life of the owner.

Roth Accounts for Higher-Income Taxpayers

Historically, the value of Roth accounts was limited for higher-income taxpayers because of adjusted gross income limits on Roth contributions and conversions. These days, however, the limits only apply for regular contributions, not rollovers. That means traditional IRAs can be converted at will, subject to the taxpayer's tolerance for recognizing current income.

> **COMPLIANCE POINTER:** For 2014, the ability to make regular Roth IRA contributions begins to phase out starting at an AGI of $181,000 for joint filers, and at $114,000 for single filers. Note that active participation in an employer plan does not affect the ability to make a Roth IRA contribution.

Designated Roth Accounts

Many employer plans have designated Roth accounts as part of their 401(k), 403(b), or 457(b) plan. There is no adjusted gross income limit on regular contributions to such plans. Furthermore, employees may initiate in-plan rollovers from their traditional accounts (if the plan permits).

Taxation of Roth Rollovers

A rollover to a Roth account from a non-Roth account means immediate inclusion of the taxable portion of the traditional IRA or 401(k) distribution (the return of basis, if any, is not taxed). Because it is a rollover, there is no early withdrawal penalty.

PLANNING POINTER: Amounts can be moved into a Roth IRA either by a rollover from a qualified plan or by conversion of an existing IRA. Conversions are treated as rollovers.

Converting Traditional IRAs to Roth IRAs

Traditional IRAs (including SEP and SIMPLE IRAs) can be converted to Roth IRAs. Conversions generally follow the rollover rules, but they are not subject to the once-per-12-months rule. Conversions result in current income taxation of the amount that would be recognized had there been no rollover, but the 10 percent additional tax for early withdrawals does not apply. Note that nondeductible IRA contributions, on funds for which tax was paid earlier, would not be taxed upon distribution; therefore, they are not also taxed upon conversion.

CAUTION: The IRS will not abate an individual's penalty for underpayment of estimated taxes arising because of the additional income resulting from a conversion or rollover of traditional IRA assets to a Roth IRA.

Timing. Any amount converted to a Roth IRA is includible in gross income as a distribution for the tax year in which the amount is distributed or transferred from the traditional IRA. When a rollover spans two tax years, the taxable amounts from the traditional IRA are included in gross income in the year in which the amounts are withdrawn from the traditional IRA.

EXAMPLE: On December 20, 2013, Victor Mallory withdraws the $35,000 balance in his traditional IRA, which stems solely from deductible contributions. On February 18, 2014, Victor deposits the $35,000 into a Roth IRA. Although the transaction was not completed until 2014, the Roth conversion is deemed to have occurred in 2013. Consequently, the $35,000 taxable amount is reported on Victor's 2013 tax return.

Methods of conversion . An amount can be converted by any of three methods:

- An amount distributed from a non-Roth IRA can be deposited in a Roth IRA within 60 days after the distribution;
- An amount in a non-Roth IRA can be transferred in a trustee-to-trustee transfer to a different trustee; or
- An amount in a non-Roth IRA can be transferred to a Roth IRA maintained by the same trustee.

COMMENT: Roth IRA contributions are subject to taxpayer income limits, and historically so were conversions. Currently, there is no income limit on conversions.

PRACTICE POINTER: Conversions of SIMPLE IRAs or SEP IRAs to Roth IRAs are reported on Form 8606.

PLANNING POINTER: A postcalendar-year conversion prior to April 15 may be useful in tax years in which the owner is looking to "fill up" a lower tax bracket. For example, if the owner has $5,320 left in the 25 percent tax bracket, the owner can fill up the bracket by making a $5,320 conversion. The owner will owe an extra $1,330 in tax due to the conversion, but the conversion will not push the owner into a higher bracket.

SEP and SIMPLE IRAs . Conversions are allowed from simplified employee pension plans and from savings incentive match plans for employees. However, with regard to SIMPLE IRAs, taxpayers must wait at least two years from the date the individual first participated in any SIMPLE IRA maintained by the employer. Once converted, amounts in these plans are treated as contributions to a Roth IRA. Consequently, no further SEP or SIMPLE contributions can be made to the converted account (though SEP or SIMPLE contributions may continue to be made to a successor traditional IRA).

Recharacterizing IRA Contributions

A taxpayer may use a trustee-to-trustee transfer to recharacterize an IRA contribution or rollover. Recharacterization is used to:

- Change a traditional IRA contribution to a Roth contribution;
- Undo a Roth conversion; or
- Change a Roth IRA rollover from an employee plan to a traditional IRA rollover.

Effect of recharacterizing. The contribution or rollover is treated as having been initially made to the transferee IRA rather than transferor IRA. The amount of the transfer must reflect net income or loss allocable to the contribution.

> **PRACTICE POINTER:** A recharacterization is reported on the taxpayer's return for the year the contribution was made.

> **PLANNING POINTER:** Converting a traditional IRA to a Roth IRA locks in the taxable amount. Ideally, a conversion should be done when the market price of the IRA assets is low. If the market price is trending down, it is better (in theory) to wait until it hits bottom. If it is trending up, then there's no time like the present. There is always the risk, however, of being wrong about the future, such as converting just before a market crash. In such cases, recharacterization may be available to undo the conversion.

> **PRACTICE POINTER:** To recharacterize, the taxpayer must notify the trustees of both the transferor IRA and transferee IRA that he or she elects to treat the contribution as having been made to the transferee IRA rather than transferor IRA. The notice must be given by the date of the transfer. The notice must indicate the type, date, and amount of contribution to the transferor IRA, and year for which it was made. It must direct the trustee of the transferor IRA to transfer directly to the trustee of the transferee IRA the amount of the contribution and any net income or loss allocable to the contribution. The notice must identify the trustees of both IRAs.

> **COMMENT:** The trustee of the transferor IRA generally determines the net income or loss that needs to be reflected in the amount transferred.

> **EXAMPLE:** Hubert Ninsky has a traditional IRA, the value of which has been steadily increasing. In January, Hubert decides to convert it to a new Roth IRA sooner rather than later in order to "lock in" tax on a lower amount. The IRA is worth $50,000 on the conversion date, so Hubert plans to recognize $50,000 in gross income for the tax year. By June, the now safely converted Roth IRA is worth $60,000 and Hubert is congratulating himself on his keen financial sensibilities.

> **EXAMPLE:** In July, the market crashes. Hubert's new Roth IRA is now worth only $30,000. So it turns out that Hubert will have to pay tax on $50,000, even though the IRA is only worth $30,000. Fortunately, Hubert can recharacterize the conversion. He notifies the IRA trustee, and has the trustee set up a new traditional IRA and transfer the assets into it. The conversion is treated for tax purposes as if it never happened.

Timing. The election and transfer must both happen before the due date (including extensions) of the taxpayer's return for the tax year for which the contribution is made. If that deadline is missed, a taxpayer may still recharacterize if:

- The return for the year of the contribution was timely filed; and
- Within six months from the due date of the return (*excluding* extensions) the taxpayer notifies the trustees of his or her intent to recharacterize, provides the trustees with all of the necessary information, and the trustees transfer the contribution.

PRACTICE POINTER: The taxpayer must file an amended return if the deadline is missed.

EXAMPLE: Roberto Mangiare wanted to recharacterize a contribution to a traditional IRA in 2013 as a Roth contribution. The due date for the return is April 15, 2014. He filed for a six-month extension. Roberto has until October 15, 2014, to recharacterize.

EXAMPLE: If Roberto did not file for an extension, he had until October 15, 2014, to recharacterize. He must file an amended return to reflect the recharacterization.

PRACTICE POINTER: If a recharacterization is reported on an amended return, the taxpayer should write "filed pursuant to Section 301.9100-2" on the return. The return should be filed at the same address as the original.

PRACTICE POINTER: Recharacterizations are not subject to the once-per-12-months rule.

Recharacterization for decedents. The administrator or executor of a decedent's estate can elect to recharacterize on the decedent's final tax return.

Reconversion

Typically in recharacterization situations, a Roth contribution or conversion needs to be recharacterized because the market price of the investment assets has gone down. It is at that point that reconverting after a successful recharacterization can make a lot of sense because it locks in a historically low value for taxation.

Delay period. A taxpayer who converts from a traditional IRA to a Roth IRA and then transfers that amount back to a traditional IRA by means of a recharacterization must wait before reconverting that amount from the traditional IRA to a Roth IRA. The taxpayer must wait until the beginning of the tax year following the tax year of the conversion.

Extended delay period. The delay period is pushed back if the recharacterization takes place near the end of the tax year of the conversion or later. The taxpayer must wait until the end of the 30-day period beginning on the day on which he or she transfers the amount from the Roth IRA back to a traditional IRA by means of a recharacterization (regardless of whether the recharacterization occurs during the tax year in which the amount was converted to a Roth IRA or the following tax year).

EXAMPLE: Hubert Ninsky converts his traditional IRA into a Roth IRA in January 2014. He recharacterizes the conversion in July 2014. Hubert must wait until January 1, 2015 (in the new tax year), before he may reconvert the IRA to a Roth IRA.

EXAMPLE: Instead, Hubert recharacterizes on December 20, 2014. He must wait at least 30 days until January 19, 2015 (in the following tax year), before he can reconvert.

EXAMPLE: If Hubert recharacterizes on April 1, 2015, he must wait at least 30 days until May 1 before he may reconvert.

Designated Roth Account Rollovers

Trustee-to-trustee transfer requirement. If all or a portion of an eligible distribution from a designated Roth account is to be rolled over into a designated Roth account under another plan, the funds may not be distributed to the employee, but the distribution must be rolled over in a trustee-to-trustee transfer to the other plan. The other plan must agree to separately account for the amount.

> **EXAMPLE:** Jennie Jones works for Acme Inc., which has a 401(k) plan with a designated Roth feature. Jennie has a balance of $10,000 in a designated Roth account. She changes careers and becomes a teacher, working for the Springfield school district. The district has a 403(b) plan for its teachers, which has a designated Roth feature that accepts rollovers from other designated Roth plans. Jennie can roll over the amount in the 401(k) designated Roth account to a 403(b) designated Roth account in a trustee-to-trustee transfer.

> **PRACTICE POINTER:** Roth accounts are subject to a five-tax-year holding period, which normally begins in the tax year of the first contribution. In the case of a rollover between different Roth plans, the earlier start date between the two plans controls.

Rollover to Roth IRA. If a distribution is made to the taxpayer, the taxpayer can roll over the amount into a Roth IRA within a 60-day period. If only a portion of a distribution is rolled over, the portion that is not rolled over is treated as consisting first of the amount of the distribution that is includible in gross income.

> **PRACTICE POINTER:** Even if the taxpayer's income is too high to allow regular Roth IRA contributions, the taxpayer may set up a Roth IRA for the purposes of receiving a rollover.

STUDY QUESTION

4. Reconversion to a Roth IRA that had been recharacterized as a traditional IRA:

    a. Is delayed until the beginning of the tax year following the conversion

    b. May be implemented only if the traditional IRA's value has increased

    c. Is subject to a 20-day delay after the recharacterization

    d. Is allowed only if to a different receiving Roth account

¶ 607 DISTRIBUTIONS RESULTING FROM TERMINATING EMPLOYMENT

Employees generally have restricted access to their 401(k) plan assets until they retire, but there are exceptions. One of the most common exceptions occurs when the employee leaves the job. At that point, the employee may take a full distribution. This extra money can come in handy for any number of things, but it may come at a significant price if not done in designated ways:

- It is subject to income tax;
- 20 percent is withheld; and
- It may be subject to the 10 percent early withdrawal additional tax if the employee has yet to reach age 59½.

One alternative is to roll the sum over tax-free to an IRA. Another is to keep the money in the 401(k), if permitted, or roll it over to another employer 401(k) that is willing to accept the rollover.

Keeping Assets in 401(k) Plan Versus Rolling Them Over to an IRA

401(k) plan participants typically roll over assets into an IRA when retiring or otherwise leaving an employer. Once any portion of an eligible rollover distribution has been contributed to an IRA, the assets are subject to the IRA rules. Leaving the assets in the 401(k) (or rolling them over into another 401(k)) does offer some advantages, however. The following lists compare the pros and cons.

- Advantages of leaving assets in a 401(k) or transfer to another 401(k) include

  - 401(k) participants generally have stronger protections against creditor liability, which might be especially important for professionals or small business owners;

  - 401(k) participants who would otherwise not have to start taking RMDs at age 70½ because they are still working would have to start making RMDs if they have rolled assets over into an IRA; and

  - 401(k) participants who would otherwise be allowed to borrow against their accounts would lose that right if they roll over assets into an IRA.

- Advantages for rolling assets over into an IRA include

  - IRA owners can take early distributions without incurring the 10 percent additional tax if they use the proceeds for qualified education expenses, qualified first-time home purchases, and, if unemployed, for health insurance premiums;

  - IRA owners can chose a brokerage IRA account for maximum investment flexibility or a mutual fund IRA for low fees;

  - IRA owners have wealth transfer planning advantages because multiple separate IRAs can be created to facilitate estate planning and provide maximum flexibility for postdeath elections, plus IRAs are advantageous for charitable giving;

  - IRA owners have more flexibility regarding the Roth feature because they are not dependent on plan terms to provide for designated Roth accounts and in-plan rollovers, plus recharacterization of rolled over amounts is allowed for Roth IRAs, and additionally, Roth IRAs are-free from RMDs while the owner is living; and

  - IRA owners may take distributions at any time as long as they are willing to pay income tax on the withdrawn amount and (if applicable) the 10 percent additional tax for early withdrawal; employer plans generally cannot allow any distributions until the participant reaches age 59½ (age 70½ for 457(b) plans) unless the employee has severed employment or falls under circumstances such as the hardship exception. Though this difference may be irrelevant if assets remain in an old plan after severance from employment, it is an important consideration that weighs against rolling over old plan assets into a new employer's plan rather than into an IRA.

Distributions for Deceased Employees

Although the employee has the right to the distribution, this right necessarily passes to the named beneficiary when the employee dies. The rules differ a bit depending on whether the beneficiary is a spouse or a nonspouse.

PRACTICE POINTER: If possible, the beneficiary should roll over the distribution to avoid current income tax. The plan may allow the distribution to be spread out over five years, but rolling the distribution over gives the beneficiary much greater control.

Spouse as the beneficiary. An employee's surviving spouse can roll over a distribution attributable to the employee and paid to the spouse on account of the employee's death to the spouse's own IRA rather than as an inherited IRA. The spouse has rollover rights going forward.

> **COMMENT:** Same-sex spouses are treated as married for these and all tax purposes as long as the couple was married in a jurisdiction that recognizes same-sex marriages, even if they currently live in a jurisdiction that does not. Domestic partners, same-sex or otherwise, are not treated as married.

> **EXAMPLE:** Joan Cecchini is a participant in her employer's 401(k). Upon her death, the plan distributes her account balance to Harry Cecchini, her surviving spouse. Harry has the distribution rolled over into an IRA in his own name. He may freely roll over any amount to or from that IRA.

> **EXAMPLE:** Joan Cecchini is married to Helen Cecchini. The marriage took place in a state that recognizes same-sex marriage. The employer distributes Joan's 401(k) balance to a new IRA in Helen's name as Joan's surviving spouse. Helen may freely roll over any amount to or from that IRA.

> **PLANNING POINTER:** A spouse can roll over the distribution into an inherited IRA rather than the spouse's own IRA if the spouse so chooses. That can make sense under certain circumstances, such as when the decedent is older than age 59½, but the spouse is not, and so current withdrawals are not early withdrawals. The spouse may always convert the IRA to the spouse's own account later simply by consistently treating it as his or her own

Nonspouse as the beneficiary. Qualified plans (including 403(b) plans and 457(b) plans), must allow trustee-to-trustee transfers to nonspouse designated beneficiaries upon the death of the participant. A nonspouse beneficiary may establish an IRA for the purpose of receiving such a distribution. The transferee's IRA is treated as an inherited IRA.

> **PRACTICE POINTER:** The nonspouse beneficiary IRA must be established as an inherited IRA, in that it belongs to the deceased owner but is held for the benefit of the beneficiary. For example, wording may read "Maria Doe as beneficiary of Juan Doe," or "Juan Doe, for the benefit of Maria Doe."

> **EXAMPLE:** Louis Fitzgerald is a participant in his employer's 401(k) plan. He dies and is not survived by a spouse. His sole beneficiary is his child, Wilson. Because Wilson is a nonspouse beneficiary, the plan distributes the balance in the account to an IRA in Louis's name for the benefit of Wilson. Wilson may make trustee-to-trustee transfers to other IRAs, which must be set up similarly. He may not make a rollover distribution, and he may not roll over any amount into that IRA.

> **PRACTICE POINTER:** The rollover to a spouse may be made as an inherited IRA with the spouse as beneficiary instead of as the spouse's own IRA. The surviving spouse may convert it to the spouse's own later on. The spouse may want to keep it an inherited IRA if the inherited IRA distribution rules (which key off of the decedent's age) are more favorable. For example, if the spouse needs the money now, and the spouse has not as yet reached age 59½ but the decedent has, it makes sense for the spouse to treat the IRA as an inherited IRA.

STUDY QUESTION

5. A nonspouse beneficiary of a deceased employee:

    a. Must pay income tax on the inheritance in the year the first assets are received

    b. May roll over the distribution in a trustee-to-trustee transfer to an inherited IRA

    c. May not access the distribution before age 59½

    d. Is treated as a surviving spouse if he or she was a domestic partner of the deceased

¶ 608 TAKING RATHER THAN ROLLING OVER A DISTRIBUTION

A taxpayer might not want to roll over a distribution, either in whole or in part, otherwise eligible for rollover treatment. The taxpayer might need quick cash for any number of reasons. If a taxpayer decides to keep some or all of an eligible rollover distribution rather than roll it over the distribution is included in the taxpayer's gross income (minus basis).

10 Percent Early Distribution Additional Tax

The portion of a distribution that is included in gross income is subject to a 10 percent additional tax unless the taxpayer is at least 59½ years old at the time of the distribution, or the distribution falls under an exception. The 10 percent tax applies both to early IRA withdrawals and early distributions from employer plans.

    PRACTICE POINTER: Distributions of basis (including nondeductible IRA contributions and after-tax employer plan contributions) are not included in gross income; hence, they are not subject to the 10 percent additional tax.

    EXAMPLE: Mary Anne Reilly is 45 years old. She withdraws $10,000 from her traditional IRA. She meets none of the exception provisions to the 10 percent additional tax, so the entire withdrawal is an early distribution. Mary Anne never made any nondeductible contributions to her IRA. Mary Anne must include the $10,000 in her gross income for the year of the distribution and pay income tax on it. She must also pay 10 percent additional tax of $1,000 (10 percent × $10,000).

    PRACTICE POINTER: Additional tax for early withdrawals is reported on Form 5329, *Additional Taxes on Qualified Plans (Including IRAs) and Other Tax-Favored Accounts,* which is filed with the taxpayer's Form 1040.

Early Distributions from Roth Accounts

Early distributions from Roth accounts have an added twist because a distribution can be early not only because the taxpayer is younger than age 59½, but also because a five-tax-year holding period must be satisfied. The five-tax-year period begins for designated Roth accounts on the first day of the employee's tax year for which the employee first had designated Roth contributions made to the plan. For Roth IRAs not part of an employer's designated plan, the period begins on the first day of the tax year for which the taxpayer first made a regular Roth IRA contribution or converted an existing traditional IRA to a Roth IRA. For either, the period ends when the five consecutive tax years have been completed.

    EXAMPLE: Maurice Edelstein first made a contribution to his new Roth IRA in March of 2014 for the 2013 tax year. The five-tax-year holding period began January 1, 2013. It terminates at the end of Maurice's 2017 tax year. Starting in

2018, he may take qualified distributions if he otherwise qualifies (e.g., is older than age 59½).

Roth IRAs. Early distributions of regular Roth IRA contributions are treated as a return of basis and not included in gross income. They are not subject to income tax or the 10 percent early withdrawal additional tax. However, early distributions representing earnings are includible in gross income, and are subject to both income tax and the 10 percent additional tax, unless they are part of a qualified Roth distribution. Qualified Roth distributions are not subject to income tax or additional tax.

Designated Roth accounts. Similar rules apply for the taxation of distributions from designated Roth accounts. However, designated Roth accounts are employee plans, and therefore the exceptions to the early withdrawal 10 percent additional tax are different.

Qualified Roth distributions. Qualified distributions can only be made after a five-tax-year holding period. If the holding period is satisfied, a Roth distribution is qualified if one of the following applies: the distribution is made on or after the date the owner turns age 59½, dies, or becomes disabled. In the case of a Roth IRA (but not a designated Roth account), a qualified distribution beyond the five-tax-year period includes a distribution used for a first-time home purchase (up to $10,000 for a lifetime limit).

> **EXAMPLE:** In 2014, John Bellamy is age 60 and has a Roth IRA with a balance of $100,000. He began his regular Roth IRA contributions in 2005. $50,000 of the balance represents regular contributions and $50,000 represents earnings. John withdraws the entire amount in a qualified distribution and does not roll it over. The distribution is qualified because the five-tax-year period requirement is met, and John comes under one of the requirements for a qualified distributions (he is older than age 59½).

Converted amounts. Early distributions representing amounts converted from a traditional IRA are not included in gross income. However, the 10 percent additional tax applies if the conversion took place inside of the five-tax-year period measured from the tax year of the conversion (unless the distribution falls under an exception). For partial withdrawals, the ordering rule is regular contributions first, then conversion amounts, then earnings.

> **EXAMPLE:** In 2014, Fred Templeton is age 60 and has a Roth IRA with a balance of $100,000. The amount represents a conversion in 2002 of $60,000, and $40,000 in earnings. His distribution is qualified, and none of it is subject to income tax or additional 10 percent tax.

> **EXAMPLE:** Fred's conversion to a Roth account took place in 2012, and the five-tax-year period has yet to run. The distribution is nonqualified. The $40,000 in earnings is subject to income tax. The entire amount would be subject to the 10 percent additional tax, except that Fred is older than age 59½.

> **EXAMPLE:** If Fred were age 50, the entire amount would be subject to the early withdrawal tax.

> **COMPLIANCE POINTER:** Note that amounts rolled over from a designated Roth account are treated as regular contributions rather than conversion amounts. Therefore, they are subject to the income limits on contributions.

Early Distributions from Employer Plans

Employer plans that are subject to the 10 percent early withdrawal tax include qualified plans (including 401(k) plans), qualified annuities, and tax-sheltered annuity (403(b)) plans. Distributions from deferred compensation plans of governmental and tax-exempt employers (457(b) plans) are not directly subject to the increased tax. However, an early distribution from the eligible deferred compensation plan of a governmental employer that includes amounts accumulated in a qualified retirement plan and rolled over to the governmental plan are subject to the increased tax.

PRACTICE POINTER: The plan administrator is not required to withhold the amount of the additional income tax on such a distribution.

SIMPLE plans. The tax on early withdrawals is 25 percent in the case of distributions from a SIMPLE plan received during the two-year period beginning on the date the employee first participated in any qualified salary reduction arrangement maintained by the employee's employer under which the employee could elect to have the employer make payments to a SIMPLE account.

Exceptions to the Early Withdrawal Tax

There are a number of exceptions that shield an early distribution or withdrawal from the 10 percent additional tax.

Exceptions for all retirement plans and accounts. These following exceptions apply to distributions from any eligible retirement plan, including IRAs:

- Distributions made to a decedent's beneficiary or estate on or after death;
- Distributions made because the taxpayer is totally and permanently disabled;
- Distributions made as part of a series of substantially equal periodic payments over the taxpayer's life expectancy or combined life expectancies of the taxpayer and the designated beneficiary (if from a qualified plan other than an IRA, the taxpayer must separate from service with the employer before the payments begin);
- Distributions to the extent the taxpayer has deductible medical expenses that exceed 10 percent of adjusted gross income (for 2013-2016 only, 7.5 percent if the taxpayer or taxpayer's spouse is 65 or older) regardless of whether the taxpayer itemizes deductions for the year;
- Distributions made due to an IRS levy; and
- Distributions that are qualified reservist distributions (distributions made to individuals who are called to active duty for at least 180 days after September 11, 2001).

Exceptions for non-IRA employer plans only. The following additional exceptions apply only to distributions from a qualified retirement plan other than an IRA:

- Distributions made after separation from service with the employer if it occurred in or after the year the employee reaches age 55;
- Distributions made from a qualified governmental defined benefit plan if the taxpayer was a qualified public safety employee (state or local government) who separated from service on or after reaching age 50;
- Distributions made to an alternate payee under a qualified domestic relations order; and
- Distributions of dividends from employee stock ownership plans.

Exceptions for IRAs only. The following exceptions apply only to distributions from IRAs (including SIMPLE IRAs and SEP IRAs):

- Qualified first-time homebuyer distributions (up to $10,000);
- Qualified higher education expenses; and
- Medical insurance premiums paid while the taxpayer is unemployed

Qualified longevity annuity contracts. A new option aimed at ensuring retirement assets last long enough allows a taxpayer to buy a deferred income annuity contract called a qualified longevity annuity contract (QLAC). QLACs are bought with IRA, 401(k), or 403(b) assets and held inside the IRA, 401(k), or 403(b) account. They must be annuitized by the time the taxpayer reaches age 85. Until then, they are not subject to RMDs. Taxpayers can pay up to $125,000 in premiums to buy a QLAC. Once annuitized, the QLACs provide a steady stream of income for the rest of the taxpayer's life, with survivor benefits.

> **COMMENT:** Unlike commercially available variable or indexed deferred income annuities tied to stock market performance, QLACs are simple annuities tied to an interest rate. They are very safe and provide predictable benefits for life, but they provide only a modest return in a low-interest rate environment.

¶ 609 HARDSHIP AND UNFORESEEABLE EMERGENCY DISTRIBUTIONS

An employee who has an immediate cash need and no other way to satisfy that need, might qualify for a hardship distribution or unforeseeable emergency distribution from the employee's 401(k), 403(b), or 457(b) account.

Hardship Distributions

Hardship distributions may only be made from accumulated elective deferrals (but not earnings on the deferrals), profit-sharing plan contributions, and regular matching contributions, not from employer contributions or earnings. The distribution is subject to income tax and may be subject to the 10 percent additional tax for early distributions if the taxpayer has yet to reach age 59½. Hardship distributions cannot be rolled over.

> **COMMENT:** Hardship distributions can only be made in conformity with a written 401(k) or 403(b) plan. If not specifically allowed by the plan, the plan is out of compliance if it permits hardship distributions.

Hardship requirements. A plan may permit a hardship distribution if the plan participant:

- Has an immediate and heavy financial need because of certain circumstances; and
- The distribution is necessary to satisfy that need.

Immediate need. A plan participant has an "immediate and heavy financial need" if the distribution would be used to pay for the following items:

- Medical expenses qualifying for the medical expense deduction;
- The purchase of a principal residence for the employee, excluding mortgage payments;
- Tuition, related educational fees, and room and board expenses for the next 12 months of postsecondary education for the employee, or the employee's spouse, children, or dependents;
- Payments necessary to prevent the eviction of the employee from the employee's principal residence or foreclosure on the mortgage on that residence;
- Burial or funeral expenses for the employee's deceased parent, spouses, children, or dependents); or
- Expenses for the repair of damage to the employee's principal residence that would qualify for the casualty deduction.

Needs of beneficiaries. If the plan provides that an event (such as medical expenses) would constitute a hardship if it occurred with respect to the participant's spouse or dependent, the plan must allow a hardship distribution in the event that occurred with respect to the participant's beneficiary under the plan as well. Examples of such beneficiaries might be adult children or domestic partners.

"Necessary" distribution. A distribution is deemed "necessary" to satisfy an immediate and heavy financial need of a participant if:

- The employee has obtained all other currently available distributions and loans that are nontaxable (at the time of the loan) under the plan and all other plans maintained by the employer; and
- The employee is prohibited under the terms of the plan from making elective contributions and employee contributions to the plan and all other plans maintained by the employer for six months.

> **COMPLIANCE POINTER:** Hardship distributions may not be rolled over. They are subject to the early withdrawal additional tax unless the taxpayer is older than age 59½ or the distributions come under an exception to the additional tax.

Unforeseeable emergencies. 457(b) plans may—but are not required to—offer distributions to a participant based on an unforeseeable emergency. Circumstances may include:

- An illness or accident of the participant, the participant's beneficiary, or the participant's or beneficiary's spouse or dependents;
- Loss to the participant's or beneficiary's property caused by casualty (for example, damage from a natural disaster not covered by homeowner's insurance);
- Funeral expenses of the participant's spouse or dependent; and
- Other similar extraordinary and unforeseeable situations resulting from events beyond the control of the participant or beneficiary (for example, imminent foreclosure or eviction from a primary residence, or payments for medical expenses or prescription medications).

Beyond the control of the participant. The emergency must be caused by an event beyond the control of the plan participant. The purchase of a home and payment of college tuition are not unforeseeable emergencies. Neither is accumulated credit card debt. However, residential flood damage qualifies. So does the death of a child (including a nondependent child) that generates funeral expenses.

> **COMPLIANCE POINTER:** The participant seeking the distribution must show that the emergency expenses could not otherwise be covered by insurance, liquidation of the participant's other assets, or cessation of deferrals under the plan.

STUDY QUESTION

---

6. The tax on early withdrawals from a SIMPLE plan is:

    a. 10 percent

    b. 25 percent

    c. 50 percent

    d. No early withdrawals from SIMPLE plans are permitted

¶ 610 CONCLUSION

Through discipline, luck, and the careful use of the various retirement account tax rules, individuals can accumulate significant retirement savings that will allow them to enjoy their retirement years, and maybe pass along something to their children. If hard times come, however, the tax rules allow early access as well.

MODULE 3: EVOLVING ISSUES FOR INDIVIDUALS—Chapter 7: Telecommuting and Traveling for Work

¶701 WELCOME

This chapter describes the issues relevant to individuals who telecommute or travel for work, either full or part time, as well as for the employers of these individuals.

The growth of high-speed internet access has changed the U.S. economy, making the world a more interconnected and smaller place. One repercussion has been the rise of *telecommuting,* also known as *teleworking,* which is considered to take place when an employee works from a location other than an employer's office. Normally, telecommuting employees work from home, although coffee shops and libraries are not uncommon locations. Self-employed individuals, including the rising tide of freelancers, are also finding it easier to work from home or other flexible locations; a trend to keep an eye on is the growth of coworking spaces or *incubators* for entrepreneurs.

The always-connected nature of the internet has also changed the way we travel for work. Whether workers are keeping in contact with their home office or other clients, or are polishing a project while en route to give a presentation to a customer, traveling can be more productive, and more common, than in the past.

As with most business trends, teleworking and traveling for work have tax consequences for the worker and for employers.

¶702 LEARNING OBJECTIVES

Upon completion of this chapter, you will be able to:

- Identify the eligibility requirements for the home office deduction;
- Identify whether the simplified home office deduction should be elected;
- Recognize when a worker may deduct the cost of commuting;
- Identify expenses that may be deductible when traveling for work; and
- Identify the treatment of home office equipment and supplies.

¶703 INTRODUCTION

Both telecommuting and traveling for work raise a variety of tax issues. For those who work from home, a deduction for expenses related to having a home office is available. This deduction may even offset some of the normal costs of running a home, such as utilities and insurance. Individuals may also benefit from deductions for the cost of commuting between their home office and other work locations, or for traveling away from home for business. The cost of purchasing equipment and supplies for a home office is deductible, but not if the individual is reimbursed by his or her employer under an accountable plan.

Telecommuting may also affect whether the worker is classified as an employee or an independent contractor, which has employment tax consequences for both the worker and the service recipient.

Finally, allowing employees to telecommute from another state or country may create a variety of jurisdictional issues for both the employees and employer.

¶ 704 GENERAL IMPLICATIONS FOR EXPENSES

When an expense is incurred in connection with a trade or business, the cost is taken as a deduction in arriving at adjusted gross income (AGI). When an expense is incurred in connection with the performance of services for an employer or investment, hobby, or other income producing use, the deduction is treated as a miscellaneous itemized deduction.

> **COMPLIANCE TIP:** Individuals claim adjustments to gross income related to a trade or business on Schedule C. If the taxpayer is in the business of farming and files Schedule F, business deductions are instead reported on that schedule. Individuals, including employees claiming unreimbursed business expenses, use Schedule A. Employees deducting ordinary and necessary business expenses, including travel expenses, must include Form 2106, *Employee Business Expenses*.

For the home office deduction, whether the individual must also file Form 8829, *Expenses for Business Use of Your Home,* depends on how the deduction is calculated. If the simplified safe harbor method is used (as described later), Form 8829 is not required.

> **PLANNING POINTER:** Each deduction must be adequately substantiated.

¶ 705 HOME OFFICE DEDUCTION

Taxpayers are allowed to claim a deduction for expenses related to a qualifying home office. This deduction is available to individuals as well as trusts, estates, partnerships, and S corporations, but not to C corporations (Code Sec. 280A).

A home office generally must be used exclusively and regularly:

- As a principal place of business for any trade or business of the taxpayer;
- To meet with patients, clients, or customers in the normal course of the taxpayer's trade or business; or
- In connection with the taxpayer's trade or business, if the office is a separate structure (not attached to the rest of the home).

In addition, expenses allocable to the use of a portion of a residence on a regular (but not necessarily exclusive) basis as a storage unit for the taxpayer's inventory or product samples may be deductible.

> **COMMENT:** Daycare providers are also subject to a special rule but are not otherwise discussed here.

For an employee, the home office deduction is allowable only if, in addition to satisfying the exclusive and regular use test in connection with his or her trade or business of being an employee, the home office is for the convenience of the employer.

Taxpayers may deduct either their actual expenses or, for tax years beginning on or after January 1, 2013, a fixed amount determined under what has been dubbed the *simplified safe harbor method.* The deduction is limited, however, if the gross income from the business use of the home is less than the total business expenses.

When a taxpayer sells a residence that contained a home office, the exclusion of gain on the sale may be limited, depending on whether the office was within the main walls of the home and on whether depreciation was claimed for the office.

Exclusive Use

The taxpayer must use the home office exclusively for trade or business purposes to qualify for the deduction (Code Sec. 280A(c)(1)). If the office is used for both business and personal purposes, the exclusive use test is not met.

> **CAUTION:** The exclusive use test can be very troublesome; any personal use of the office area may void the taxpayer's claim for the home office deduction

> **EXAMPLE:** Annie Anopalus uses a den to prepare tax returns and engage in other similar business activities, as well as for personal purposes, such as watching television and allowing her family to use the office space on weekends and holidays. The den is not considered to be used exclusively for a business purpose.

An exception to the exclusive use test is provided in the case of the taxpayer whose trade or business is selling products at retail or wholesale and whose dwelling unit is the sole fixed location of the trade or business. Under this exception, the ordinary and necessary expenses allocable to space within a dwelling unit that is used as a storage unit for inventory or product samples are not disallowed even if the exclusive use test is not met. This space, however, must be used on a regular basis and must be a separately identifiable space suitable for storage (Code Sec. 280A(c)(2)).

Regular Use

A home office must be used on a regular basis for business purposes to qualify for the deduction (Code Sec. 280A(c)(1)). The purpose of this requirement is to prevent a taxpayer from claiming a deduction for a room that is used only sporadically for business purposes. Occasional or incidental business use of a home office does not constitute regular use. Seasonal use may qualify, however.

Trade or Business

The home office must be connected to a trade or business of the taxpayer (Code Sec. 280A(c)(1)). Expenses related to investments or other income-producing activities are not eligible, even if conducted in a business-like manner. Whether an activity is a trade or business is ultimately a question of fact.

Principal Place of Business

The home office must be the taxpayer's principal place of business, unless the office qualifies for the deduction because it is used by patients, clients, or customers or is a separate structure (Code Sec. 280A(c)(1)(A)).

A home office qualifies as the principal place of business if:

- The office is used by the taxpayer to conduct administrative or management activities of a trade or business, and
- There is no other fixed location of the trade or business where the taxpayer conducts substantial administrative or management activities of the trade or business.

If a taxpayer conducts some administrative or management activities at a fixed location of the business outside the home, the taxpayer still is eligible to claim a deduction as long as those activities are not substantial. In addition, a taxpayer's eligibility to claim a home office deduction is not affected by the fact that the taxpayer conducts substantial nonadministrative or nonmanagement business activities at a fixed location of the business outside the home, e.g., meeting with, or providing services to, customers, clients, or patients at a fixed location of the business away from home.

Use by Patients, Clients, or Customers

The home office must be used by patients, clients, or customers in meeting or dealing with the taxpayer in the normal course of his or her trade or business, unless the office qualifies for the deduction because it is the taxpayer's principal place of business or is a separate structure. The use of the office by patients, clients, or customers must be both substantial and integral to the taxpayer's business. Occasional meetings are insufficient to make the exception applicable (Code Sec. 280A(c)(1)(B); Proposed Reg. § 1.280A-2(c)).

Separate Structures

The home office must be a separate structure used in connection with the taxpayer's trade or business, unless the office qualifies for the deduction because it is the taxpayer's principal place of business or is used by patients, clients, or customers (Code Sec. 280A(c)(1)(C)). The separate structure must be appurtenant to, but not attached to, the dwelling unit, such as an artist's studio, a florist's greenhouse, or a carpenter's workshop. The structure cannot share a common wall with the taxpayer's residence.

> **COMMENT:** Because the separate structure exception requires only that the home office be used in connection with the taxpayer's trade or business, it is easier to satisfy than the principal place of business or meeting place tests. Therefore, it is especially useful for artists and self-employed craftspeople with a secondary studio at home, e.g., in their garages.

Storage of Inventory and Product Samples

A taxpayer may be entitled to deduct the expenses attributable to the portion of the residence used to store inventory and product samples, in addition to an area used as a principal place of business, used as a place used by patients, clients, or customers, or that is a separate structure (Code Sec. 280A(c)(2)).

The space within the dwelling unit must be used on a regular basis to store the taxpayer's inventory or product samples. This space is not subject to the exclusive use requirement, however.

The taxpayer must be engaged in the trade or business of selling products at retail or wholesale, and the dwelling must be the sole fixed location for this trade or business. Only the deductions allocable to the space actually used for storage qualify for the deduction. Thus, if a taxpayer stored product samples in a portion of his or her basement, only the expenses allocable to the space so used would be deductible, even if the taxpayer made no use of the rest of the basement. Moreover, the space must be a separately identifiable space suitable for storage.

> **COMMENT:** This exception is mainly designed for door-to-door salespersons for the storage of their merchandise. For example, a salesperson's garage used for that purpose, resulting in there being no room for the car, fits the requirement to perfection.

Convenience of the Employer

A taxpayer who is an employee must establish that the home office is used for the convenience of the employer (Code Sec. 280A(c)(1)). Use that is merely appropriate and helpful to the employer's business does not satisfy this requirement.

> **COMMENT:** It appears that the key to satisfying the convenience of the employer requirement is providing proof that the employer provides either no facilities or inadequate facilities for the employee to otherwise perform activities that are crucial for successful job performance.

Leased Home Offices

A home office deduction is not allowable by reason of business use when the taxpayer leases a portion of his or her home to an employer (Code Sec. 280A(c)(6)). For this purpose, an individual who is an independent contractor is treated as an employee, and the party for whom such individual is performing services is treated as an employer.

CAUTION: The scope of the denial for leased home offices is wide; for example, it bars the deduction where a partner or a shareholder rents a portion of his or her residence to the partnership or the corporation.

This rule, of course, does not affect the deductions of expenses allowable in the absence of any business use, e.g., home mortgage interest expense and real property taxes, if the taxpayer itemizes deductions.

Deducting Actual Expenses

For purposes of the home office deduction, taxpayers may deduct either actual expenses or, for tax years beginning on or after January 1, 2013, calculate the deduction using a simplified safe harbor. Home office expenses for this purpose are those costs attributable to the real estate involved. They do not include equipment, furniture, stationery, or other costs, which may be deducted under other Internal Revenue Code provisions.

When claiming actual expenses, any direct expenses attributable to the home office are deductible in full. These costs may include items such as paint or minor repairs to the office. Indirect expenses, i.e., insurance, utilities, and general repairs to the home, are deductible only to the extent of the percentage of the home used as a home office. Expenses that are not related to the use of the unit for business purposes, such as expenditures for lawn care, may not be taken into account (Code Sec. 280A(c); Proposed Reg. § 1.280A-2(i)(3)). Basic local telephone service charges, including taxes, for the first telephone line into a home are a nondeductible personal expense (Code Sec. 262). If a separate internet line is used exclusively for business, it is fully deductible; if also used for personal purposes, the cost must be allocated based on square footage as would any shared, indirect cost.

COMMENT: Home office expenses can also be divided into those that are deductible (even if the taxpayer does not use any portion of the home for business) and those that are deductible only because the taxpayer has a home office. Expenses that are deductible even if the home is not used for business are expenses that qualify as itemized deductions on Schedule A or as net disaster losses on Schedule L. These deductible expenses include:

- Real estate taxes;
- Qualified mortgage insurance premiums;
- Deductible mortgage interest; and
- Casualty losses.

Because these expenses are deductible as itemized deductions regardless of whether part of the home is used for business, the allocation of part of the expense to business use generally does not affect the amount of the taxpayer's deduction for the expense. However, the allocation is necessary nonetheless because it does affect the limitation on the amount of the taxpayer's home office deduction, discussed below. Taking what would otherwise be itemized deductions as home-office Schedule C deductions also reduces the taxpayer's AGI, which may allow greater entitlement to other AGI-dependent tax benefits, such as deductible individual retirement account (IRA) contributions.

CAUTION: Some repairs might qualify as permanent improvements, in which case they must be depreciated rather than deducted (Code Sec. 263(a)). A permanent improvement increases the value of property, adds to its life, or gives it a new or different use. Examples of improvements are replacing electric wiring or plumbing, adding a new roof or addition, paneling, or remodeling. In addition, normally

¶705

deductible expenses, such as the cost of paint, may need to be treated as a depreciable cost if the expense is included in a larger remodeling project.

Calculating number of rooms versus percentage of total space. A taxpayer may determine the actual expenses allocable to the portion of the home used as an office by any method that is reasonable under the circumstances. For example, if the rooms of the residence are of approximately equal size, the taxpayer may allocate expenses according to the number of rooms used for business purposes. A taxpayer may also allocate expenses according to the percentage of total floor space in the unit that is used for the business purpose. Only the space that could actually be used should be included in the computation for purposes of determining the percentage of space used exclusively for business. For example, an inaccessible attic should not be included in the computation.

> **EXAMPLE:** Dora Delaney's spare bedroom is the principal place of business for her tailoring business. She spends $800 to install special lighting and additional mirrors in the room for her customers to use. This $800 cost is a direct expense that is fully allocable to Dora's home office. Thus, the entire $800 is a home office expense.

> **EXAMPLE:** Dora's home office occupies 20 percent of the total useable area of her home. Generally, her home office expenses include 20 percent of the expenses for operating and maintaining her home, such as utilities, mortgage interest, and insurance. Her annual deduction percentage for these home expenses is claimed in addition to the expenses such as the cost of installing special lighting and mirrors used directly for the tailoring business.

Depreciation of office space. Like most other business property, the portion of a dwelling unit (other than land) that is used as a home office is depreciable. A taxpayer who begins using a home office during the current tax year depreciates the business part of the home as nonresidential real property under the modified accelerated cost recovery system (MACRS) (that is, under the straight-line method over 39 years). A taxpayer who has depreciated the home office in prior years should continue to use the same depreciation method used in those years. The appropriate depreciation rates are applied to the depreciable basis of the home (the part of the cost of the home that can be depreciated) by calculating the percentage of the home used for business and multiplying that percentage by the smaller of the adjusted basis or the fair market value of the home (excluding land) on the date the business use began.

The costs of permanent improvements made before the business use began are added to the basis and depreciated as part of the cost of the home. Indirect costs of permanent improvements made after the business use began are depreciated separately by multiplying the cost of the improvement by the percentage of the home used for business, and then depreciating the result over the recovery period that would apply to the home if the business use began at the same time as the improvement. Thus, for improvements made this year, the recovery period is 39 years.

STUDY QUESTION

1. An employee may deduct expenses for a home office even when his or her employer provides office space at the organization only if:

    a. He or she uses the simplified safe harbor method

    b. The employee uses the home office for business more often than for personal use

    c. The home office use is occasional

    d. The home office is for the convenience of the employer

Simplified Deduction

New for tax years beginning on or after January 1, 2013, an optional simplified safe harbor rule is available to determine the home office deduction. Every tax year, taxpayers are allowed to elect to use either this safe harbor method or to deduct actual expenses. The maximum deductible amount using the safe harbor method is currently limited to $1,500 per tax year, calculated by multiplying the allowable square footage, not to exceed 300 square feet, by the prescribed rate. The prescribed rate is $5, which is not subject to annual inflation adjustment but may be updated by the IRS from time to time as is warranted (Rev. Proc. 2013-13, 2013-6 I.R.B. 478).

> **COMPLIANCE TIP:** The election is made by using the method on a timely filed original return. Once made, the election is irrevocable for that year.

> **COMMENT:** This optional method eliminates the need to substantiate, calculate, and allocate home expenses but still allows taxpayers to deduct expenses on Schedule A that are unrelated to the business but are attributable to the home, such as qualified acquisition mortgage interest, real estate taxes, and casualty losses.

> **EXAMPLE:** John Shackleton uses one bedroom of his two-bedroom Washington, D.C., apartment as a home office. The office is 100 square feet. The total square footage of his four-room apartment is 556 square feet. His monthly rent (which includes utilities) is $1,800/month. Using the regular square foot method, he can deduct 18 percent of his rent (100 ÷ 556). With this method, his deduction is $324 per month or $3,888 per year. Using this method would give John a substantially higher deduction than the $1,500 he could claim using the simplified method.

Multiple offices. Taxpayers sharing a home (for example, roommates or spouses, regardless of filing status), if otherwise eligible, may each use the safe harbor method, but not for a qualified business use of the same portion of the home. For example, a husband and wife, if otherwise eligible and regardless of filing status, may each use the safe harbor method for a qualified business use of the same home for up to 300 square feet of different portions of the home.

An individual with a home office in each of two or more homes may only use the safe harbor for one of the home offices. The actual expense method may be used for all other home offices.

An individual who uses two home offices in the same home may not use the safe harbor for one home office and the actual expense method for the other. If the safe harbor method is elected it applies to both offices but the total square footage taken into account may not exceed 300 square feet. If the total combined square footage of both offices exceeds 300 square feet the taxpayer may allocate the square footage in any reasonable manner.

Minimum use requirements. If a taxpayer only uses a home office for a portion of the tax year (e.g., in a seasonal business or the office is first used after the beginning of the tax year) or the square footage of the office increases or decreases during the tax year, then the square footage of the office for purposes of the safe harbor is based on the average monthly square footage for the tax year. For this purpose no more than 300 square feet may be taken into account in any month and no square footage may be taken into account in any month in which the taxpayer did not have at least 15 days of qualified business use of the office.

EXAMPLE: Alice Sims begins using her 400-square-foot home office on July 20 and continues that use through the end of the year. Her average monthly allowable square footage for the year is 125 square feet (300 square feet for August through December divided by the number of months in the tax year ([300 + 300 + 300 + 300 + 300] ÷ 12)). The deduction is $625 ($125 × $5). July is not considered because the office was not used for more than 15 days in July.

As when a taxpayer deducts actual expenses, the amount deducted using the safe harbor method may not exceed the gross income derived from the qualified business use of the home for the tax year reduced by business deductions unrelated to the qualified use of the home such as advertising, wages, and supplies. However, unlike when the taxpayer deducts actual expenses, any portion of the safe harbor deduction in excess of this amount may not be carried forward.

CAUTION: When the actual expense method is used, a taxpayer may carry forward any portion of the home office deduction that is not allowed because of the gross income limitation. Carryforwards may not be deducted in any year that the safe harbor method is used. Moreover, if the safe harbor method is used, any amount of the otherwise-allowable safe harbor deduction that is disallowed under the gross income limit may *not* be carried forward. Consequently, the actual expense method is usually preferable when a taxpayer has limited gross income, such as a startup business.

Employees with a home office do not qualify for the safe harbor method if advances, allowances, or reimbursements for their home office expenses are received from their employer under a reimbursement or other expense allowance.

If the safe harbor method is chosen for a tax year, then for that tax year, the taxpayer may not deduct any portion of the actual expenses related to the qualified business use of the home and may not deduct any depreciation for the office. The depreciation deduction allowable for that portion of the home for that tax year is deemed to be zero. If, in a later tax year, the taxpayer instead deducts actual expenses, the taxpayer must calculate the depreciation deduction allowable in the subsequent year by using the appropriate optional depreciation table applicable for the property provided in IRS Publication 946, *Depreciation and Amortization.* The table percentages must be used even if the taxpayer was not previously using the table percentages to compute allowable depreciation deductions prior to the first tax year in which the safe harbor method was elected. Thus, generally, taxpayers will use the table percentages for MACRS 39-year real property to compute the depreciation deduction on the home office. These table percentages are applied against the remaining adjusted depreciable basis. In the context of nonresidential real property, remaining adjusted depreciable basis is the original cost or other basis of the entire home that was allocated to the home office without reduction for any depreciation claimed on the home office. The applicable table percentage is the table percentage for the current tax year based on the placed in service year of the home office.

In any year in which the safe harbor is used, the deemed depreciation claimed is $0. Thus, the adjusted basis of the home office used for purposes of determining gain or loss is not reduced by any amount of depreciation in any year that the safe harbor applies.

For purposes of the safe harbor, the home office must be located in a residence that is Section 1250 real property and that is depreciable under MACRS. Thus, in the unlikely situation that a home office is currently being depreciated under ACRS or some other pre-1986 method, the safe harbor does not apply.

Limitation on Amount Deductible

The amount of the home office expense that any taxpayer may deduct is limited if the gross income attributable to the business use of the home is less than the taxpayer's total business expenses. The limitation affects expenses that are deductible solely because they are attributable to the home office, such as insurance, utilities, and depreciation. More specifically, these amounts are limited to the gross income derived from the business use of the home minus the following:

- The business part of expenses that are allowable regardless of whether a home office is claimed, such as mortgage interest, real estate taxes, and casualty and theft losses.
- The business expenses that relate to the business activity in the home but that are not allocable to the use of the home itself, such as expenses for a business phone, supplies, and depreciation on equipment (Code Sec 280A(c)(5)).

> **COMMENT:** Thus, home office deductions are disallowed to the extent that they create or increase a net loss from the business activity to which they relate.

> **PLANNING POINTER:** The no-loss restriction can result in a total disallowance of expenses like depreciation and maintenance attributable to a qualifying home office if:
> - The taxpayer receives no income during the current year from the activities carried on there; or
> - The income received does not exceed the home office's allocable share of such otherwise deductible expenses as real estate taxes and qualified mortgage interest.

When a taxpayer claims actual expenses rather than the safe harbor deduction, any amount not allowable as a deduction by reason of the gross income limitation may be carried forward to subsequent tax years, but the income limitation applies to prevent the use of such deductions to create or increase a net loss in any year from the business activity.

Expenses that are allocable to the business use of the dwelling are deducted in the same order as activities not engaged in for profit. Thus, the deductions must be taken in the following order:

1. The allocable portion of expenses allowable as a deduction with respect to the dwelling unit regardless of business use, e.g., home mortgage interest and real estate taxes;
2. Amounts otherwise allowable as deductions for the tax year by reason of the business use of the dwelling unit, other than those that result in adjustment to the basis of the property, i.e., depreciation; and then
3. Amounts otherwise allowable as deductions for the tax year by reason of the business use of the dwelling use that would result in an adjustment to the basis of the property.

Effect on the Sale of the Home

When a taxpayer sells his or her home, Code Sec. 121 excludes up to $250,000 of the gain ($500,000 for joint filers), subject to certain limitations. If part of the property has been used for another purpose, e.g., a home office, and the portion of the property used for that other purpose is separate from the dwelling portion, only the gain attributable to the portion used as a residence qualifies for the exclusion. Gain must be allocated between the residential and separate, nonresidential, portions of the property and recognized to the extent of the nonresidential portion.

EXAMPLE: Mary Chesterton is a single taxpayer who has lived in her home for 10 years. During that entire time, she used a home office in her unattached garage that took up 10 percent of the space of the home. She sells the home for a gain of $100,000. Ten percent of that gain ($10,000) is attributable to the home office and is taxable. The remainder may be excluded from Mary's income, assuming it qualifies under Code Sec. 121.

No allocation is required if both the residential and nonresidential portions of the property are within the same dwelling unit, but the exclusion nevertheless does not apply to gain to the extent of any depreciation adjustments that may have been made for periods after May 6, 1997 (Reg. § 1.121-1(d)(1)).

EXAMPLE: Mary's office is located within the main walls of the home, rather than being in an unattached garage. She has never claimed depreciation for the home office. She may exclude the entire gain of $100,000 under Code Sec. 121.

STUDY QUESTION

2. Which of the following is *not* a reason a startup business owner may prefer the actual expense method to the simplified safe harbor method for deducting business costs?

   a. The maximum deduction is higher using the actual expense method

   b. The safe harbor method does not allow losses to be carried forward to a subsequent tax year

   c. The actual expense method does not require tax on the gain from sale of property with the home office

   d. The safe harbor method does not allow the taxpayer to claim home office deductions in two or more homes

¶ 706 COMMUTING EXPENSES

Taxpayers generally cannot deduct the cost of travel between their home and their place of business, but exceptions exist for travel:

- Outside the taxpayer's metropolitan area to a temporary work location;
- Within the taxpayer's metropolitan area to a temporary work location; or
- To any regular or temporary work location, for taxpayers whose personal residence is their principal place of business.

   COMMENT: Deductible commuting expenses may include the cost of operating the taxpayer's car, discussed below, or the cost of a bus or subway ride.

Temporary Work Locations Outside the Metropolitan Area

A taxpayer may deduct daily transportation expenses incurred in going between his or her residence and a temporary work location outside the metropolitan area where the taxpayer lives and normally works (Rev. Rul. 99-7, 1999-1 CB 361).

A *temporary work location* is determined using a one-year standard similar to that used for figuring the deductibility of expenses for travel away from home to a temporary work site. Under this standard, if the employment is realistically expected to last a year or less and in fact does last for one year or less, it is temporary. If it is realistically expected to last for more than one year, it is not temporary, regardless of whether it in fact lasts for more than one year.

The Tax Court has repeatedly rejected rigid definitions of a *metropolitan area,* preferring instead to look at the facts and circumstances. For example, the court relied on the ordinary and common meaning of the term as a city and the densely populated and economically and socially integrated area around the city, when the court found that a taxpayer reasonably considered a 35-mile radius from his home town as his metropolitan area (*Wheir v. Commissioner,* TC Summary 2004-117). In another case, the court held that a 45- to 50-mile radius was reasonable under the facts presented (*Marple v. Commissioner,* TC Summary 2007-76).

Temporary Work Locations Within the Metropolitan Area

If a taxpayer has one or more regular work locations away from his or her residence, the taxpayer may deduct daily transportation expenses incurred in going between the residence and a temporary work location within the metropolitan area (Rev. Rul. 99-7, 1999-1 CB 361).

Residence Is Principal Place of Business

If the taxpayer's residence is his or her principal place of business, the taxpayer may deduct daily transportation expenses incurred in going between the residence and another work location in the metropolitan area (Rev. Rul. 99-7, 1999-1 CB 361). For this purpose, whether a residence is a principal place of business is determined under the rules for the home office deduction, although a home office deduction does not necessarily need to be claimed.

> **EXAMPLE:** Jessica Malone is a contractor with a home office that is her principal place of business. She commutes between her home and a house that she is renovating in order to flip it for a profit. The costs of the commute are deductible.

STUDY QUESTION

---

3. Which of the following is *not* a deductible commuting expense?

- **a.** An urban worker's bus fare to and from a temporary suburban work location for two weeks, rather than to his or her regular business location
- **b.** A cement trucker's commute to an expressway's construction site for two years
- **c.** A self-employed editor's commute downtown for a week-long professional meeting
- **d.** An architect's daily commute for six months across San Francisco to oversee a home-building project

---

¶ 707 TRAVEL EXPENSES

A taxpayer engaged in a trade or business is entitled to deduct travel expenses. Travel expenses are deductible from gross income if they are incurred while the taxpayer is away from home in the pursuit of a trade or business and if they are reasonable and necessary to the conduct of the taxpayer's business and directly attributable to such business (Code Sec. 162(a)(2)). The unreimbursed travel expenses of an employee are treated as itemized deductions subject to a limit based on 2 percent of AGI, although an exception allows Armed Forces reservists to claim an adjustment to gross income certain types of travel. Travel expenses incurred for investment are deductible as itemized deductions. Travel expenses for a trip undertaken for personal purposes are nondeductible.

EXAMPLE: Tommy Whittager works in Pittsburgh and takes a business trip to New York City. His business travel totals 750 miles round trip. On his way, Tommy stops in Baltimore to visit family. On the nine days he is away from home, Tommy spends $2,000 on meals, lodging, and other travel expenses. If he had not made the side trip to Baltimore, Tommy would have been gone only six days, and the total cost would have been $1,500. He can deduct only $1,500 for the trip, including the cost of round-trip transportation to and from New York. The deduction for meals is subject to the 50 percent limit on meals discussed below.

Away from Home

For a taxpayer to be considered away from home, the trip must be of sufficient duration to require sleep or rest (Rev. Rul. 54-497, 1954-2 CB 75, 78, superseded in part by Rev. Rul. 75-432, 1975-2 CB 60, modified by Rev. Rul. 63-145, 1963-2 CB 86). The sleep or rest requirement is generally interpreted to mean that the nature of the taxpayer's employment makes it reasonable for the taxpayer to stop for sleep before continuing his or her duties. Merely working overtime, traveling a great distance from the taxpayer's residence, or working a second job is not relevant under this test, and a deduction for travel expenses will be disallowed if the taxpayer returns home without stopping for sleep or rest. Although the away-from-home requirement is often described as the "overnight" rule, it does not necessarily require an overnight stay or for the taxpayer to be away from home for a 24-hour period. For example, a railroad employee who regularly rented a hotel room to sleep during a 6-hour layover in the middle of a 17- to 18-hour workday was allowed a deduction (Rev. Rul. 75-170, 1975-1 CB 60).

Travel away from home means travel away from the taxpayer's tax home, which is not necessarily the taxpayer's family home. A *tax home* is the individual's regular place of business or post of duty, including the entire city or general area in which the business or work is located (Rev. Rul. 56-49, 1956-1 CB 152). If an individual has more than one regular place of business, the tax home is the main place of business, determined by comparing, for each business location, the amount of time spent on business, the type of business activity, and the income generated (***Markey v. Commissioner***, CA-6, 74-1 USTC ¶ 9192, 490 F2d 1249). If an individual has no regular or main place of business, the tax home may be where the individual regularly lives, depending on whether the individual performs work there, whether living expenses are duplicated while the individual is traveling away from that location, and on the individual's personal ties to that location. An itinerant individual with no regular or main place of business and no place where he or she regularly lives cannot claim travel expenses (Rev. Rul. 73-529, 1973-2 CB 37).

Generally, the costs of a taxpayer's local lodging (i.e., staying in a hotel while not away from home) are personal expenses. Under certain circumstances, however, expenses for local lodging may be deductible under as ordinary and necessary expenses of carrying on a trade or business, including the trade or business of being an employee. A safe harbor rule treats local lodging expenses provided or required by an employer as a deductible ordinary and necessary expense of an employee if:

- The lodging is necessary to participate fully in or be available for a bona fide business meeting, conference, training activity, or other business function;
- The lodging is provided for a period not to exceed five calendar days and no more often than once per calendar quarter;
- The lodging is not lavish or extravagant under the circumstances and does not provide any significant element of personal pleasure or benefit; and
- The employee is required by the employer to remain at the activity or function overnight (Proposed Reg. § 1.162-31).

¶707

Primarily for Business

If a taxpayer combines business and pleasure in the same trip, traveling expenses to and from the destination are deductible only if the trip is primarily related to the taxpayer's trade or business. If the trip is primarily personal in nature, the traveling expenses to and from the destination are not deductible even though the taxpayer engages in business activities while at the destination. Expenses incurred while at the destination that are attributable to business activities are, however, deductible (Reg. § 1.162-2(b)(1)).

EXAMPLE: Mark Steiner travels from his home in Washington to Denver for business. He spends $900 on airfare, $300 on his hotel, and $150 on meals in Denver. After his four days of business are concluded, he rents a car for $120 and drives to a mountain camp and spends two days fishing. The camp charges him $200. Mark may deduct his airfare, meals (subject to the 50 percent limitation on business meals under Code Sec. 274(n)), and lodging costs in Denver, but not the cost of the car or the fishing camp. His airfare is deductible in full, even though he took a personal side trip, because the primary purpose of his trip was business.

The determination of whether a trip is related primarily to the taxpayer's trade or business or is primarily personal in nature depends on the facts and circumstances. An important factor is the amount of time spent on personal activities as compared to the amount of time spent on activities directly related to the taxpayer's trade or business (Reg. § 1.162-2(b)(2)).

Traveling with Others (Spouse, Dependent, Employee, or Friend)

A deduction is not allowed for the travel expenses paid or incurred with respect to a spouse, dependent, or other individual accompanying the taxpayer on business travel unless:

- The other individual is an employee of the taxpayer;
- The travel of the other individual is for a bona fide business purpose; and
- Such expenses would otherwise be deductible by the other individual (Code Sec. 274(m)(3); Reg. § 1.274-2(g)).

Traveling Internationally

Restrictions are imposed on the deductibility of travel expenses incurred by an individual for travel outside the United States that involves substantial personal activities not attributable to the taxpayer's trade or business (Code Sec. 274(c)). The United States in such a case includes only the 50 states and the District of Columbia. U.S. possessions and territories, such as the Virgin Islands, Guam, or Puerto Rico, are not considered to be within the United States for this purpose (Reg. § 1.274-4(f)). Nor is travel to Canada or Mexico given any special consideration.

These restrictions apply to an individual who engages in nonbusiness activities during a business trip abroad. A taxpayer who engages in nonbusiness activities must allocate travel expenses between personal nondeductible costs and deductible business expenditures, unless the trip falls within an exception to the allocation rules. The deduction by his or her employer or client who is paying for the trip is unaffected.

COMMENT: These restrictions are in contrast to the travel rules applicable to domestic travel, when no allocation is required for transportation costs to and from the business location if the primary purpose of the trip is the taxpayer's business.

The nondeductible portion is computed on a time basis, usually based on the proportion of the nonbusiness days to all travel days. But the amount on which the allocation is based depends on where the personal portion of the trip takes place. If it takes place beyond the business destination, the amount subject to allocation is the amount that would have been incurred if the taxpayer had traveled directly to the business destination and back, without the personal trip added on.

> **EXAMPLE:** Laurie Masters travels on business from Washington, D.C., to London. While en route to London, she stops in Paris for a vacation. Laurie returns home from London. The amount of travel expense used for the allocation is the expense that would have been incurred in a round trip from Washington to London.

There are several exceptions to the allocation requirement. Expenses for travel outside the United States need not be allocated when:

- The travel is for a period of one week or less;
- Less than 25 percent of the taxpayer's time abroad was spent on nonbusiness activities;
- The taxpayer did not have, as a major consideration in deciding to make the trip, the goal of obtaining a personal vacation or holiday; or
- The taxpayer could not and did not exercise substantial control over arranging the trip abroad (Reg. § 1.274-4(f)(5)).

Armed Forces Reservists

Although employees must take unreimbursed travel expenses as an itemized deduction, a member of the National Guard or military reserve may be able to instead claim travel deduction against gross income. To qualify, the individual must travel more than 100 miles away from home in connection with his or her service. This deduction is limited to the regular federal per diem rate (for lodging, meals, and incidental expenses) and the standard mileage rate (for car expenses) plus any parking fees, ferry fees, and tolls (Code Sec. 62(a)(2)(E)). Expenses in excess of this limit may be treated as an itemized deduction under the normal rules for employees.

Deductible Travel Expenses

Examples of deductible travel expenses include the unreimbursed cost of:

- Travel by car, airplane, train, taxi, commuter bus, or airport limousine;
- Baggage and shipping;
- Lodging;
- Meals;
- Dry cleaning and laundry;
- Internet packages at a hotel or on a plane;
- Business calls; and
- Tips and taxes paid on any of the above.

Expenses that are lavish or extravagant under the circumstances are not allowed, however (Code Sec. 162(a)(2)).

Per diem for lodging, meals, and incidental expenses. Rather than calculating the actual expenses, individuals may claim a deduction based on the per diem allowance as set by the federal government (Rev. Proc. 2011-47, 2011-42 I.R.B. 520). Self-employed individuals cannot claim the per diem rate for lodging, but can use the rate for meals and incidental expenses (M&IE).

The federal per diem rate is equal to the sum of the federal lodging expense rate and the federal M&IE rate for the locality of travel. The IRS generally updates the rules and rates on an annual basis, effective October 1. The rates effective as of October 1, 2013, were listed in Notice 2013-65, 2013-44 I.R.B. 440.

> **COMMENT:** Incidental expenses include items such as fees, and tips given to porters and hotel staff.

Employers may use the per diem rates to reimburse employees for travel costs. The arrangement must satisfy the accountable plan requirements. Amounts paid under the arrangement must be ordinary and necessary business expenses incurred, or which the employer reasonably anticipates will be incurred, by an employee for lodging, meals, and incidental expenses for travel away from home in connection with the performance of services as an employee and must be reasonably calculated not to exceed the amount of the expenses or the anticipated expenses.

Meals. The costs of meals consumed while a taxpayer is away from home on business are deductible. If the actual cost is used rather than the M&IE rate, only 50 percent of the unreimbursed cost is deductible. A higher 80 percent limit applies for meals consumed while away from home by individuals subject to the Department of Transportation hours of service limitations, e.g., interstate truck and bus drivers, and certain railroad employees (Code Sec. 274(n)).

Automobiles. There are two methods that may be used to compute the deductible automobile expenses:

- The standard mileage rate; and
- The actual cost.

> **COMMENT:** A taxpayer is free to use the method producing the larger deduction; however, whichever method is used, the deduction must be properly substantiated.

Standard mileage rate. The simplest method of computing automobile expenses is the standard mileage rate method. It is figured in lieu of using the actual costs of operating the vehicle. Only self-employed individuals and employees may use this method (Rev. Proc. 2010-51, 2010-51 I.R.B. 883). In 2014, the rate is 56 cents per mile (Notice 2013-80, 2013-52 I.R.B. 821).

> **COMMENT:** An individual with high business mileage generally benefits more using the standard mileage method than the actual cost method, especially if the taxpayer drives a fuel-efficient vehicle.

A taxpayer may use the business standard mileage rate with respect to a vehicle, including a van, pickup, or panel truck, that he or she either owns or leases. A deduction computed using the standard mileage rate for business miles is in lieu of all operating and fixed costs, e.g., depreciation, maintenance, fuel, and repairs, of the automobile allocable to business purposes. However, parking fees, tolls, car loan interest, and state and local property taxes attributable to business use of an automobile may be deducted as separate items.

> **EXAMPLE:** In 2014, Sally Tipps used the standard mileage rate to determine her automobile expense deduction. Sally drove the car a total of 16,000 business miles. She claimed a deduction of $8,960 (16,000 × 56 cents per mile).

If the standard mileage rate is used, the automobile is considered, for purposes of basis adjustment, to have been depreciated at a standard rate per mile. In 2014, the rate is 22 cents per mile. If actual costs were used for any year, these rates do not apply, however. Depreciation reduces the basis of the automobile, but not below zero, in determining adjusted basis.

The standard mileage rate method may not be used if:

- The automobile was previously depreciated under the actual cost method using a depreciation schedule other than straight line;
- A Code Sec. 179 deduction was claimed for the vehicle; or
- The taxpayer had used the accelerated cost recovery system (ACRS) or the modified accelerated cost recovery system (MACRS).

By using the standard mileage rate, the taxpayer has elected to exclude the automobile, if owned, from MACRS. If, after using the standard mileage rate, the taxpayer uses actual costs, the taxpayer must use straight-line depreciation for the automobile's remaining estimated useful life subject to the applicable depreciation deductions under Code Sec. 280F for any passenger automobile.

In addition, the business standard mileage rate may not be used to compute the deductible business expenses of an automobile leased by a taxpayer unless the taxpayer uses either the business standard mileage rate or a fixed and variable rate (FAVR) allowance to compute the deductible business expenses of the automobile for the entire lease period including renewals.

Actual costs. All operating and fixed costs connected with maintaining a business automobile are deductible under the actual cost method. Deductible costs include depreciation, maintenance and repairs, tires, gasoline, gasoline taxes, oil, insurance, lease payments, and license and registration fees (Rev. Proc. 2010-51, 2010-51 I.R.B. 883).

Parking fees and tolls attributable to using an automobile in business may also be deducted. The cost of the car itself is generally not currently deductible as a business expense, nor is the cost of any replacements that prolong the useful life of the car or increase its value. These costs must be taken into account through depreciation.

The actual cost method must be used by all taxpayers other than self-employed individuals and employees. It also must be used by businesses operating five or more automobiles simultaneously (such as in fleet operations). Taxpayers eligible to use the standard mileage rate method may elect to use the actual cost method.

STUDY QUESTION

4. In addition to the 56 cents per business mile standard rate for a business vehicle in 2014, the owner may separately claim deductions for the vehicle's:

- **a.** Car loan interest
- **b.** Fuel
- **c.** Repairs costing more than $250
- **d.** Depreciation

¶ 708 EQUIPMENT AND SUPPLIES
Full and Partial Deductions Versus Depreciation

Equipment and supplies that enable a worker to perform services at home and that are an ordinary and necessary business expense may be fully deducted or depreciated; they are not subject to the requirements of the home office deduction. Items that have a useful life of less than one year, such as pens and printer paper, may be fully deducted in the current tax year. Items with a longer useful life, such as computers, may instead be depreciated over several years (Code Secs. 162 and 167). A 100 percent deduction may be available for depreciable property, however, under Code Sec. 179, subject to annual limitations.

> **COMMENT:** Items that are used for both business and personal uses, such as cell phones or internet services, may be only partially deducted.

> **COMMENT:** If extended by Congress, first-year bonus depreciation may also be available. In 2013, it allowed a depreciation deduction of up to 50 percent of the cost of qualifying new property.

Listed Property

"Listed property" used in a home office is subject to special rules. *Listed property* includes computers and related equipment and any property of a type generally used for entertainment, recreation, and amusement (including photographic, phonographic, and video recording equipment) (Code Sec. 280F). Computers and related equipment used exclusively in a home office, with no personal use, are not listed property, however.

For listed property to be deductible under Code Sec. 179 or depreciable using MACRS, more than 50 percent of its use must be for business purposes. Listed property used 50 percent of the time or less must be depreciated using the alternative depreciation system (ADS) (straight-line method) (Reg. § 1.280F-6(d)).

Listed property used by an employee is deductible only if its use is:

- For the employer's convenience; and
- Required as a condition of the worker's employment (Code Sec. 280F(d)(3)(A)).

> **EXAMPLE:** Alex Howell occasionally takes work home at night rather than work late in the office. To complete this work, Alex owns and uses a personal computer that is similar to the computer in his office. The use of the computer is not for the convenience of the employer and is not required as a condition of his employment; therefore, Alex cannot claim a depreciation deduction for it.

¶ 709 REIMBURSED EXPENSES

An employee's expenses that are reimbursed by an employer under an accountable plan cannot be deducted by the employee, although the reimbursement is excluded from the employee's income. Conversely, if the reimbursement is not made under an accountable plan, the expense can be deducted, and the reimbursement is included in the employee's wages (Reg. § 1.62-2).

> **COMMENT:** To simplify matters, employers may make reimbursements for lodging, meals, and incidental expenses by using the federal per diem rates, and for miles driven by using the standard mileage rate.

To be an accountable plan, the employer's reimbursement or allowance arrangement must require that:

- Employees properly and timely substantiate expenses;
- Any amounts in excess of substantiated expenses be returned to the employer; and
- A business connection must exist between the amounts advanced and the expenses incurred.

If the worker is reimbursed for travel or transportation under an accountable plan, but at a per diem or mileage rate that exceeds the federal rate, the excess refunded is included in wages. If the worker's actual expenses exceed the federal rate, the individual may be able to claim the excess cost as a miscellaneous itemized deduction.

STUDY QUESTION

5. Listed property that an employee uses 50 percent of the time or less for business purposes is:

    a. Nondeductible

    b. Depreciated using the straight-line method

    c. Up to 50 percent deductible in the year of purchase

    d. Fully deductible if an employer requires its purchase

¶710 MANAGERS AND EXECUTIVES

It is becoming increasingly unnecessary for managers and executives to be in the office every day. Just as regular employees are telecommuting more and more, many managers and executives are also finding advantages in working from home. Indeed, employers frequently require managers and executives to keep an office at home, and may even provide all the supplies and equipment needed to furnish the office. As with other employees, managers and executives may claim the home office deduction only if the office is used regularly and exclusively, and for the convenience of the employer.

> **COMMENT:** It may be difficult for a telecommuting manager or executive to deduct the cost of telecommuting between his or her home and the office provided by the employer. In most cases, the individual would need to prove that his or her home was the principal place of business, and that the executive therefore performed only an insubstantial amount of administrative or management activities at the office provided by the employer. Such a burden would be difficult for a manager or executive to prove in most cases but nonetheless depends on the facts and circumstances.

¶711 EMPLOYMENT TAX ISSUES

Whether a business is liable for employment taxes with respect to a worker turns on whether the worker is classified as an employee or an independent contractor. For most workers, this determination depends on the common law rules: the level of behavioral and financial controls that the service recipient has over the worker, and on the relationship between the parties (IRS Training Manual 3320-102 (October 1996), Independent Contractor or Employee).

> **COMMENT:** Independent contractors generally must pay self-employment tax.

Telecommuting by itself does not make a worker an independent contractor, but the facts of the situation contribute to the determination. For example, if the worker makes significant investments in office equipment for his or her home, that factor may indicate that the service recipient lacks financial control, and that the worker may be an independent contractor. On the other hand, if the service recipient may, at any time, revoke the telecommuting arrangement, that indicates that the service recipient has behavioral control, and the worker is an employee. All relevant factors are considered in making the determination, however, and no one factor is decisive.

¶ 712 MULTIJURISDICTIONAL ISSUES

The Telecommuter Tax for Employees

Telecommuting may create state income tax consequences for employees. The employee may be liable for a "telecommuter tax," which is an increase in overall state income taxes, not a separate and distinct tax. Some states tax the entire income of nonresident telecommuting employees who occasionally physically work in the state, meaning that the state taxes employees who occasionally work within the state but who live and telecommute from another state. The employee's home state may offer a tax credit to offset the tax, but the overall rate of taxation may still be higher than if the individual were taxed by his or her home state alone.

> **COMMENT:** The telecommuter tax may also apply on a more local level with respect to cities and counties that levy their own income taxes.

Employer Considerations

Depending on the states involved, an employer that allows an employee to telecommute from another state may end up owing corporate and employment taxes in the telecommuter's state, even if the telecommuter is the only connection between the employer and the state.

> **COMMENT:** Along with the chance of higher taxes, the employer may be responsible for following laws related to compensation and benefits in the telecommuter's home state. This is an evolving area of the law.

¶ 713 INTERNATIONAL TELECOMMUTING

Employees who telecommute from a foreign country may find themselves subject to tax in that country as well as in the United States, which taxes the worldwide income of U.S. citizens and residents. However, the foreign earned income exclusion, foreign housing exclusion, and the foreign tax credit or deduction may limit the employee's tax exposure, as may any tax treaties between the two countries.

Employers that mandate or allow employees to work in a foreign country may open themselves up to a range of complications, such data security and liability for employee benefits. Foreign tax liability is also an issue, and therefore an employer should be mindful of taking into account any tax and payroll obligations that may arise.

STUDY QUESTION

6. Which of the following does **not** mitigate the tax burden on employees who telecommute internationally?

- **a.** The U.S. does not tax wages earned while abroad
- **b.** The foreign tax credit
- **c.** The foreign earned income exclusion
- **d.** Tax treaty terms between the United States and the government where the telecommuter resides

¶ 714 CONCLUSION

It is inevitable that telecommuting/teleworking will become more widespread and that traveling for work will become both easier and more productive. These workers and their employers are already subject to a variety of tax provisions, as discussed here, but the application of these provisions will likely be adapted in response to the needs and demands of an ever-changing workforce. The recent availability of the simplified home office deduction is one such example.

MODULE 3: EVOLVING ISSUES FOR INDIVIDUALS—Chapter 8: Trusts: Income Tax Strategies

¶ 801 WELCOME

This chapter examines some of the strategies that are available to achieve income tax savings in the administration of trusts. The recent increase in the top tax rate to 39.6 percent and the imposition of a new 3.8 percent surtax on net investment income (NII) have increased the importance of income tax planning. This is particularly the case for trusts, which are subject to a highly compressed tax rate schedule.

¶ 802 LEARNING OBJECTIVES

Upon completion of this chapter, you will be able to:

- Identify the rules used to make allocations of receipts and disbursements between principal and income;
- Recognize the mechanism by which trust distributions are taxed to the beneficiaries;
- Identify the methods for shifting the tax on capital gains from the trust to beneficiaries; and
- Identify the classes of income subject to the NII tax and opportunities to minimize its impact.

¶ 803 INTRODUCTION

Administering a trust has never been easy. A trustee must be a prudent investor who is able to balance the often competing interests of the beneficiaries. The trustee is also expected to have a proficient understanding of the complex rules of trust accounting and to maintain meticulous records of the trust's receipts and disbursements. It is no wonder, then, that many trustees seek the professional advice of accountants, lawyers, and investment managers in helping them to discharge their duties. A significant portion of this advice invariably focuses on tax matters.

¶ 804 TRUST BASICS

A *trust* is a legal arrangement by which a fiduciary holds property on behalf of designated individuals. The fiduciary is referred to as the *trustee*, the property held by the trustee is the *corpus* of the trust, and the individuals with an interest in the corpus are the *beneficiaries*. Often, there are two classes of beneficiaries:

- Income beneficiaries, who have an interest in the income generated by the corpus; and
- Remainder beneficiaries, who are entitled to receive the trust's corpus when the income interest ends.

Typically, a trust is created when an individual, the *grantor*, executes a trust agreement and transfers property to the trustee, who manages the corpus for the beneficiaries according to the terms of the trust agreement. In addition to following the instructions contained in the trust agreement, the trustee is required to comply with state laws that govern trust administration and adhere to the duties placed upon a fiduciary.

> **COMMENT:** The trustee has a duty to deal impartially with all beneficiaries, always putting their interests first, and is prohibited from taking any action for his or her own personal benefit. Article 8 of the *Uniform Trust Code* explains the many duties of a trustee.

The Trust as a Separate Taxpayer

Once the grantor signs the trust agreement and transfers the property to the trust, the trust has independent legal status and is recognized as a separate legal entity. The income generated by the corpus, along with any gain from the sale of assets that compose the corpus, are treated as trust income. The trust is subject to federal tax on this income, with exceptions as noted later in this chapter.

> **COMMENT:** Form 1041, *U.S. Income Tax Return for Estates and Trusts,* is used to report trust income and compute the amount of tax due. Form 1041 is due by the 15th day of the fourth month following the close of the trust's tax year. Accordingly, a calendar year trust must file Form 1041 by April 15th. A trust can apply for an automatic five-month filing extension.

Simple Versus Complex Trust

For federal tax purposes, a trust may be classified as either *simple* or *complex.* A simple trust is one that is required to distribute all income currently, is not permitted to pay any amounts for charitable purposes, and does not distribute trust corpus. A complex trust (sometimes referred to as a "discretionary" trust) is any trust that does not qualify as a simple trust.

> **COMMENT:** In computing taxable income, a simple trust is allowed a $300 personal exemption and a complex trust is allowed a $100 personal exemption.

Principal and Income Allocations

In administering the trust, the trustee must make decisions as to the allocation of receipts and disbursements between *principal* (another term commonly used for the corpus) and income. These allocation decisions directly impact the interests of the beneficiaries and the taxation of the trust. The terms of the trust agreement may specifically instruct the trustee on how these allocations should be made or give the trustee discretion to make those decisions as he or she deems appropriate.

Many states have adopted some version of the *Uniform Principal and Income Act* (UPIA). The UPIA is designed to be a comprehensive set of rules governing the allocation of receipts and disbursements between principal and income. A trustee is required to administer the trust in accordance with the UPIA if the terms of the trust agreement do not contain a different provision or give the trustee a discretionary power of administration.

Under the UPIA, capital gains are allocated to principal. Amounts received as rent from real property or as interest on promissory notes, to cite two other examples, are allocated to income.

Section 104 of the UPIA permits a trustee to make adjustments between principal and income if the trustee finds it necessary to administer the trust impartially. For example, a trustee may transfer cash from principal to income to the extent the trustee deems it necessary to increase the amount distributed to the income beneficiary. The purpose of this "power to adjust" provision, according to a comment to the UPIA text, "is to enable a trustee to select investments using the standards of a prudent investor without having to realize a particular portion of the portfolio's total return in the form of traditional trust accounting income such as interest, dividends, and rents."

> **COMMENT:** A Prefatory Note to the UPIA states that the power to adjust "helps the trustee who has made a prudent, modern portfolio-based investment decision that has the initial effect of skewing return from all the assets under management, viewed as a portfolio, as between income and principal beneficiaries."

The UPIA approach is broadly consistent with IRS regulations under Code Sec. 643, which define *"income"* as the amount of trust income for the tax year determined under the terms of the trust agreement and applicable local law. "[I]tems such as dividends, interest, and rents are generally allocated to income," the regulations state, "and proceeds from the sale or exchange of trust assets are generally allocated to principal." The regulations also allow the trustee, if state law permits, to make adjustments between income and principal to fulfill the trustee's duty of impartiality between the income and remainder beneficiaries.

¶ 805 TRUST INCOME TAX RATES

Trusts have a separate federal income tax rate schedule. For the 2012 tax year, there were five brackets, with the rates ranging from 15 to 35 percent. The top 35 percent marginal rate applied to taxable income of trusts in excess of $11,650. In contrast, the 35 percent rate did not kick in for single individuals' income until reaching a threshold amount of $388,350.

The *American Taxpayer Relief Act of 2012*, which applies to tax years beginning after December 31, 2012, raised the top tax rate from 35 to 39.6 percent. As a result, a trust was subject to a 39.6 percent tax on amounts of taxable income exceeding $11,950 for 2013. In 2014, the 39.6 percent bracket applies to a trust's taxable income in excess of $12,150. The *American Taxpayer Relief Act of 2012* did not reduce the wide disparity in the income levels required to trigger application of the maximum 39.6 percent rate when comparing income of trusts and individual taxpayers. In 2014, the 39.6 percent rate does not come into play until taxable income exceeds $406,750 for a single individual and $457,600 for married individuals filing jointly.

Also, for tax years beginning after December 31, 2012, trusts (and individuals) are subject to a 3.8 percent net investment income (NII) tax (Code Sec. 1411). The NII tax is discussed later in this chapter.

Preferential Rates for Capital Gains and Qualified Dividends

In the calculation of the tax due on the trust's taxable income, not all types of income are created equal. Like individual taxpayers, trusts may be eligible for lower tax rates on their net long-term gain from the sale of a capital asset. Whether a capital gain is long term depends on the length of time that the trust held the capital asset before it was sold (generally keyed to a holding period of more than 12 months).

> **COMMENT:** Generally, the trust's holding period for a capital asset includes both the time that the grantor held the property before transferring it to the trust and the time that the property was held by the trust.

Dividends are generally taxed as ordinary income. However, qualified dividend income is taxed at capital gains rates. *Qualified dividend income* includes the dividends received during the tax year from a domestic corporation or a qualified foreign corporation.

For 2013 and thereafter, the capital gains rate on net capital gains and qualified dividend income for trusts is:

- 20 percent if the trust is in the 39.6 percent income tax bracket;
- 15 percent if in the 25, 28, or 33 percent bracket; and
- 0 percent if in the 15 percent bracket.

The Tax Interplay Between Trust and Beneficiary

Income received by a trust is taxed either to the trust or to the beneficiary who receives the income as the result of a distribution by the trustee. To ensure that trust income is not taxed twice—once at the trust level and again at the beneficiary level—the trust receives an income distribution deduction for the amounts that were distributed or paid to beneficiaries during the tax year. The trust claims the income distribution deduction on its tax return (Form 1041), and the beneficiary reports the distribution on his or her individual return.

To the extent that a beneficiary is in a lower tax bracket than the trust, which often is the case, income tax savings can be realized by having the trust's income taxed to the beneficiary rather than the trust. The ability to achieve these tax savings depends on the terms of the trust agreement, the state law governing administration of the trust, and the tax code and regulations.

> **EXAMPLE:** The Bleeker Family Trust received $25,000 of interest income during the 2014 tax year. The trustee has discretion to distribute income to Trevor Bleeker to provide for his wellbeing. Trevor is the only beneficiary of the trust during his lifetime. Trevor, who is single, has taxable income (not counting any trust distributions) of $50,000 a year. If the trustee does not distribute any of the income to Trevor, it is taxed to the trust, and the trust incurs an income tax of approximately $8,230. On the other hand, if the income is distributed to Trevor, it is added to his $50,000 income, giving him $75,000 in taxable income for the year. The $25,000 is taxed at a 25 percent rate, generating a tax of $6,250. Distributing the income to Trevor results in net tax savings of almost $2,000.

Distributable Net Income

In calculating the amount of the income distribution deduction, it is first necessary to determine the trust's *distributable net income* (DNI). DNI plays a key role in establishing both the maximum income distribution deduction that can be taken by the trust and the character of the distribution taxable to the beneficiaries.

> **COMMENT:** Because it is one of the cornerstones of trust taxation, it is essential that the trustee understands the fundamentals of DNI.

The trust's DNI generally consists of the same income and deductions that make up the trust's taxable income. However, as specified in Code Sec. 643(a), several important modifications are made to taxable income to arrive at the trust's DNI. Chief among them:

- No deduction is allowed for distributions to beneficiaries;
- No deduction is allowed for the personal exemption (typically $100, or $300 in the case of a trust that is required to distribute all of its income currently);
- Adjusted tax-exempt interest is included;
- In the case of trusts that distribute current income only, extraordinary dividends or taxable stock dividends are excluded to the extent that they are allocated to corpus; and
- Capital gains are excluded to the extent that the gains are allocated to corpus and are not
  - Paid, credited, or required to be distributed to any beneficiary during the tax year, or
  - Paid, permanently set aside, or to be used for a charitable purpose.

STUDY QUESTION

---

1. A trustee may prefer to have trust income distributed to beneficiaries when:

    a. The beneficiary is in a lower tax bracket than the trust

    b. The trust can claim the distribution as a deduction in determining DNI

    c. The beneficiary allocates capital gains of the trust to income.

    d. The distribution enables the personal exemption to be deducted in calculating DNI

¶ 806 INCLUDING CAPITAL GAINS IN DNI

The last item mentioned, capital gains, deserves special attention. As previously discussed, capital gains are allocated to principal under the UPIA. This treatment reflects traditional trust accounting principles. In addition, capital gains will generally be excluded from the computation of DNI. This means that, in most instances, capital gains will be taxed at the trust level.

Because of the highly compressed nature of the tax brackets that apply to trusts when compared to those that apply to individuals, to achieve tax savings a trustee may explore opportunities for shifting the tax on capital gains from the trust to the beneficiaries, who will usually reside in a lower tax bracket. Although capital gains are usually excluded from DNI, IRS regulations do allow for exceptions to the rule in certain cases under Reg. § 1.643(a)-3(b).

The inclusion of capital gains in DNI requires that the trustee act either:

- Pursuant to the terms of the governing instrument (i.e., the trust agreement) and applicable local law; or

- Pursuant to a "reasonable and impartial exercise" of discretion, in accordance with a power granted to the trustee by applicable local law or by the governing instrument (if not prohibited by local law).

Assuming that one of these two conditions is met, capital gains are includible in DNI to the extent that they are:

- Allocated to income;

- Allocated to corpus, but treated consistently by the trustee on the trust's books, records, and tax returns as part of a distribution to a beneficiary; or

- Allocated to corpus, but actually distributed to the beneficiary or used by the trustee in determining the amount that is distributed to a beneficiary.

A closer look at each of these three avenues for including capital gains in DNI follows.

Allocation of Capital Gains to Income

The allocation of capital gains to income would appear, at first glance, to be the most straightforward method available to include capital gains in DNI. However, given that allocating capital gains to income departs from traditional trust accounting principles, its actual use may be limited. Many trust agreements expressly state that capital gains are to be allocated to corpus. If the trust agreement is silent on the matter, the trustee may be obliged to follow local (state) law. In that case, if state law is based on the UPIA, capital gains would be allocable to principal.

Assuming that state law does not expressly give the trustee the ability to allocate capital gains to income, the trust agreement would need to grant the trustee that discretion. If the trust agreement gives the trustee the discretion to allocate capital gains to income and that discretion is exercised in a manner that is fair and reasonable to all the beneficiaries, the allocation should be respected by the IRS.

Depending on the specifics of state law, the trustee may have the "power to adjust" provision at his or her disposal, providing a basis for allocating capital gains to income. However, relying on the power to adjust would not provide the same level of comfort that would come from language in the trust agreement authorizing the trustee to allocate capital gains to income in his or her discretion.

> **CAUTION:** A remainder beneficiary may be more likely to object if the trustee's action is not directly traceable to language in the trust agreement.

Allocation of Capital Gains to Corpus, Treated Consistently as Distribution

Capital gains are included in DNI to the extent they are allocated to corpus, "but treated consistently by the [trustee] on the trust's books, records, and tax returns as part of a distribution to a beneficiary." The onus is on the trustee to document that capital gains are included in the distribution and to perform the necessary recordkeeping evidencing such treatment.

The key question in using this method to include capital gains in DNI is what is meant by "treated consistently." Does it require that the trust adopt this practice from the beginning of its existence? If so, the availability of this method would be limited to those trusts in which, beginning with the trust's first tax year, discretionary distributions of principal were treated as being paid from capital gains realized during the year. Or is it possible for a trust that is already in existence to demonstrate consistent treatment by adopting the practice at some point in time (after the first tax year) and continuing to follow the practice for some period of time thereafter?

Unfortunately for a trustee looking for clarity on this point, the examples that accompany the IRS regulations offer little guidance on how to meet the "treated consistently" requirement. All of the examples discuss a trust that is in its first tax year, during which the trustee decides to follow a "regular practice" in future years.

> **CAUTION:** The ambiguity in the regulations may cause a trustee concern in going this route to shift the tax on the trust's capital gains to the beneficiaries.

Allocation of Capital Gain to Corpus, Actually Distributed to Beneficiary

Lastly, capital gains are includible in DNI to the extent they are allocated to corpus but actually distributed to the beneficiary or used by the trustee in determining the amount that is distributed to a beneficiary. The examples in the IRS regulations illustrating this concept refer to a trust in which the trustee is required to distribute one-half of the principal when the beneficiary reaches a certain age. The trust assets consist entirely of corporate stock. In order to make the required distribution, the trustee sells half of the stock and distributes the proceeds to the beneficiary. In that case, all the capital gain attributable to the sale is actually distributed to the beneficiary and therefore included in DNI (Reg. § 1.643(a)-3(e), *Example 9*).

In another example, a trust has capital gain from the sale of securities. The trustee decides that discretionary distributions will be made only to the extent that the trust has realized capital gains during the year. The trustee then makes a distribution in the amount of the capital gain to the beneficiary. Because the trustee uses the amount of the capital gain to determine the amount of the discretionary distribution, the capital gain is included in the trust's DNI for the tax year (Reg. § 1.643(a)-3(e), *Example 5*).

COMMENT: The IRS regulations do not indicate the degree of discretion the trustee has to use this method when it is not being done on a consistent basis. For that reason, the governing instrument should expressly provide that the trustee has discretion to deem distributions of principal as being paid from capital gains realized during the year, particularly when such discretion is not a feature of applicable local law.

¶ 807 DISTRIBUTIONS OF PROPERTY RATHER THAN SALES PROCEEDS

In seeking tax savings by shifting income from the trust to the beneficiaries, the trustee may also want to consider making in-kind distributions to the beneficiary (Code Sec. 643(e)). In an in-kind distribution, the trustee distributes appreciated trust property rather than the proceeds from the trust's sale of that property. The beneficiary, not the trust, will then pay the capital gains tax on the property when it is sold. The trust does not recognize gain on the in-kind distribution (unless the trustee elects to do so under Code Sec. 643(e)(3)),

EXAMPLE: Among other assets, the Lundberg Family Trust holds appreciated stock with a fair market value of $30,000 and a basis of $15,000. During the 2014 tax year, the trust received $15,000 in interest income. The trustee has the discretion to make distributions to a beneficiary in kind, in cash, or through a combination of both. The trustee decides to make a $30,000 distribution to the beneficiary, Bill Lundberg, in 2014. Bill has taxable income (not counting any trust distributions) of $45,000 in 2014. If the trustee sells the stock and uses the proceeds to effect the distribution, the trust will incur the capital gains tax. Because the trust is in the 39.6 percent bracket, it is subject to a 20 percent rate on the capital gains. However, were the trustee to distribute the stock in kind, Bill would pay the capital gains tax when he sold the stock. Because Bill is in the 25 percent bracket, he would be subject to only a 15 percent rate on the gain.

CAUTION: However, a trustee should be aware that this provision regarding in-kind distributions does not apply in the case of specific bequests (see Code Sec. 663(a)).

The trustee should consult the trust agreement to see whether he or she has the power to make in-kind distributions of principal in lieu of making cash distributions. The trust agreement may also allow the trustee to make distributions partially in kind and partially in cash. If the trust agreement does not address the issue of in-kind distributions, the trustee should examine local law to determine what is permissible.

Remaining Mindful of Fiduciary Duties

In pursuing income tax savings for the trust, the trustee must remember that he or she has an overriding obligation to balance the sometimes conflicting interests and needs of the beneficiaries. For example, allocating capital gains to income instead of principal will enhance the rights of the income beneficiary to the possible detriment of the remainder beneficiary. It is possible that certain strategies for shifting income from the trust to the beneficiaries to take advantage of tax rate differentials will conflict with the trustee's duty to administer the trust impartially.

COMMENT: Even when the trust agreement and/or applicable local law affords the trustee considerable discretion in administering the trust, that discretion must be exercised in a fair and reasonable manner. The pursuit of tax savings cannot be undertaken in a vacuum. The trustee would be well advised to carefully document the thought process that led to his or her particular action.

¶ 808 THE NET INVESTMENT INCOME TAX

The *Health Care and Education Reconciliation Act of 2010* created a new tax—the net investment income (NII) tax—to help fund health care reform. For tax years beginning after December 31, 2012, a 3.8 percent surtax is imposed on the NII of individuals and trusts. Specifically as applied to trusts, the tax applies to the lesser of:

- Adjusted gross income (AGI) in excess of the highest income tax bracket threshold for trusts; or
- Undistributed net investment income.

As previously noted, the highest income tax bracket threshold applicable to trusts is $11,950 for 2013 and $12,150 for 2014. These amounts, which are adjusted for inflation each year, are significantly less than the thresholds that apply to individuals (which are not adjusted for inflation). For example, the thresholds for single and joint filers are $200,000 and $250,000, respectively.

> **COMMENT:** Final regulations clarifying the application and operation of the NII tax were published in December 2013 (T.D. 9644).

Computing AGI

For trusts, AGI is generally computed by subtracting the following amounts from total income:

- The income distribution deduction;
- The personal exemption; and
- Administration costs that would not commonly or customarily be incurred by an individual.

> **EXAMPLE:** The Langer Family Trust receives interest and dividends totaling $50,000 in 2014. Setting aside the effects of the personal exemption and administration costs, if none of this income is distributed, the 3.8 percent tax applies to the lesser of: (a) $50,000 - $12,150 ($37,850), or (b) $50,000. This creates a NII tax liability of $1,438. If $25,000 income is distributed, the NII tax applies to the lesser of: (a) [$50,000 - $25,000] - $12,150 ($12,850), or (b) $50,000 - $25,000 ($25,000). In that case, the trust is subject to a NII tax of $488.

Costs Not Subject to the 2 Percent Floor

The above-mentioned third item, administration costs, merits special attention. Many of the costs incurred in administering the trust will be subject to the 2 percent floor on miscellaneous itemized deductions. That is, the costs are deductible only to the extent that they exceed 2 percent of the trust's AGI. However, under Code Sec. 67(e), costs that are paid in connection with the administration of a trust and that would not have been incurred if the property were not held in trust are not subject to the 2 percent floor.

The IRS recently published regulations that provide guidance on the classification of a trust's administrative costs (T.D. 9664). A cost is subject to the 2 percent floor if it "commonly or customarily" would be incurred by a hypothetical individual holding the same property. The regulations address four specific categories of costs with respect to the "commonly or customarily" test: ownership costs; tax preparation fees; investment advisory fees; and appraisal fees. The trustee should refer to the regulations in deciding whether a particular administrative expense is subject to the 2 percent floor on miscellaneous itemized deductions.

> **COMMENT:** The regulations require that, for purposes of computing AGI, a single fee or commission (a "bundled fee") paid by a trust must be allocated

between the costs that are subject to the 2 percent floor and those that are not. However, if a bundled fee is not computed on an hourly basis, only the portion of the fee that is attributable to investment advice is subject to the 2 percent floor, with the remaining portion not subject to the 2 percent floor.

Costs subject to the 2 percent floor on miscellaneous deductions are not subtracted from the trust's income in computing AGI, unlike costs that would not commonly or customarily be incurred by an individual. Therefore, in lessening the potential exposure to the NII tax, the trustee will want to maximize the amount of "above-the-line" deductions not subject to the 2 percent floor.

The regulations apply to tax years beginning after December 31, 2014.

¶ 809 DETERMINING NET INVESTMENT INCOME

Three classes of income are subject to the NII tax under Code Sec. 1411:

- Gross income from interest, dividends, annuities, royalties, and rents, other than such income that is derived in the ordinary course of a trade or business;
- Gross income from a passive activity or income by a financial trader (i.e., trading in financial instruments or commodities); and
- Net gain attributable to the disposition of property, other than property held in a trade or business.

NII is the sum of these three classes of income, less "properly allocable" expenses.

> **COMMENT:** Several types of income are not subject to the NII tax, including salary, wages, bonuses, and distributions from individual retirement accounts (IRAs) or qualified plans.

Calculating Undistributed Net Investment Income

A trust's undistributed NII is its NII, reduced by:

- The NII included in the distribution to beneficiaries which is deductible by the trust (i.e., eligible for the income distribution deduction); and
- The NII for which the trust was entitled to a deduction under Code Sec. 642(c) (which relates to amounts paid to charity).

Amounts of NII distributed by the trust to a beneficiary are included in the beneficiary's income and the beneficiary is required to include the distribution in his or her income to determine whether the 3.8 percent NII tax applies.

Types of Trusts Not Subject to the NII Tax

Not all trusts are subject to the NII tax. Some of the trusts excluded from the reach of the NII tax include business trusts, common trust funds, designated settlement funds, cemetery trusts, Alaska Native settlement trusts, and trusts exempt from tax imposed under Subtitle A of the tax code (e.g., charitable remainder trusts). However, although a charitable remainder trust is not itself subject to the NII tax, annuity and unitrust distributions may constitute NII to a noncharitable beneficiary. The regulations detail the special rules relating to the classification of charitable remainder trust income and distributions from a charitable remainder trust (Reg. § 1.1411-3(d)). In addition, specific computational rules apply to electing small business trusts (ESBTs).

> **COMMENT:** A detailed discussion of the trusts excluded from the NII tax and the special rules that apply to particular kinds of trusts is beyond the scope of this chapter. Trustees should familiarize themselves with the NII tax rules that apply to the particular type of trust they are administering to ensure they are acting appropriately in their compliance and planning activities.

The Murky Issue of Material Participation

The enactment of the NII tax increased the need to be able to determine how a trust "materially participates" in an activity. This is because a trust's income from a trade or business activity in which it materially participates does not constitute income from a passive activity for purposes of the NII tax. The definition of passive activity is found in Code Sec. 469.

Currently, there is uncertainty in this area of the law, because guidance supplied by the IRS appears to conflict with some of the case law. Some argue that the legislative history indicates that only the trustee's involvement, solely in his or her capacity as trustee, should matter in deciding whether the trust materially participates in a trade or business activity. However, in certain instances, courts have concluded that the participation of beneficiaries and employees should also be considered in making the determination. A recent Tax Court case (*F. Aragona Trust,* 142 TC -, No. 9, CCH Dec. 59,859) held that a trust materially participated in its real estate operations. The Tax Court ruled that the activities of the trustees as employees of a limited liability company that was wholly owned by the trust and managed much of the trust's real estate should be considered in determining whether there had been material participation by the trust.

COMMENT: The issue of material participation by trusts is currently under study by the IRS and may be addressed in guidance issued under Code Sec. 469 at a later date. Until such time, trustees will have to navigate through the ambiguities as best they can. Trustees may want to take a conservative approach in dealing with the issue until greater clarity is provided.

STUDY QUESTION

2. Which amounts received by a beneficiary from a trust will be included in determining the beneficiary's NII tax liability?

    a. Dividends

    b. IRA distributions

    c. Income derived from a business operated by the trust

    d. No amounts may be included because individuals are not subject to the NII tax

¶ 810 MINIMIZING THE IMPACT OF THE NII TAX

As previously discussed, trusts face a tax rate schedule with brackets that are significantly more compressed than those that apply to individuals. The same kind of phenomenon is on display with respect to the NII tax. In 2014, the threshold for a trust begins at $12,150 for purposes of the NII tax, compared to $200,000 for a single individual and $250,000 for married couples filing jointly.

In light of this disparity, a trustee will be able to generate tax savings by distributing income to the beneficiaries, where it will be taxed at a lower marginal rate, instead of letting the income remain inside the trust, where it will be subject to the compressed rate schedule. The NII tax will be avoided altogether if the beneficiary's modified AGI (MAGI) is less than the applicable threshold amount.

Making Discretionary Distributions

If the trust provides that income is to be distributed at the discretion of the trustee, the trustee may consider exercising that discretion to "carry out" DNI to the beneficiaries, rather than retaining the income in the trust. This would be especially advantageous were the beneficiaries to have a MAGI below the threshold amount applicable to their particular filing status. For purposes of the NII tax calculation, the trust's AGI is reduced by the amounts distributed to the beneficiaries. If the trust has multiple beneficiaries, even greater potential tax savings can be achieved by spreading the trust's income among the beneficiaries.

The trustee should examine the trust agreement to determine the breadth of his or her discretion to make distributions. If distributions are permitted in order to meet particular needs or objectives of the beneficiaries, the trustee must exercise his or her discretion within the boundaries set forth by the grantor. Failing to do so will raise the possibility that other beneficiaries will object to the trustee's administration of the trust.

Although making discretionary distributions seems like a simple, straightforward, and obvious way to save tax, the trustee must consider whether there are other considerations that would counsel against making a distribution. For example, there may be legitimate concerns that the beneficiary will not use the money wisely or it will end up in the hands of the beneficiary's creditors.

> **COMMENT:** In such cases, a trustee may conclude that it is better, on balance, to have the trust retain the income and pay any resulting NII tax.

Making the 65-Day Election

The trustee has the ability to treat any amount, or portion thereof, distributed to a beneficiary within the first 65 days of the tax year as if it was paid on the last day of the preceding tax year (Code Sec. 663(b)). In order to receive this treatment, the trustee must make an election on the trust's income tax return (Form 1041).

> **CAUTION:** The election, which is made on a year-by-year basis, cannot be revoked once it is made.

The amount to which the 65-day election applies is limited to the greater of:

- The trust's DNI for the tax year for which the election is made (reduced by any other amounts distributed in such year); or
- The trust's accounting income for such year.

The 65-day rule allows the trustee to take a second look at the trust following the close of the tax year and determine whether there would be a benefit to increasing the amount of the distributions considered to have been made during that tax year. For example, the trustee may decide, upon further reflection, that it would be advantageous to distribute additional amounts to the beneficiaries in order to reduce the trust's liability for the NII tax. This might be the case when the trustee was not fully aware of the beneficiary's level of income at the close of the trust's tax year (which typically corresponds to the December 31 end of the calendar year), which led the trustee to be more conservative than necessary in making distribution decisions.

Including Capital Gains in DNI and In-Kind Distributions

Capital gains are subject to the NII tax. Because capital gains are typically taxed at the trust level, the NII tax will exacerbate the trust's income tax liability unless the capital gains can be included in DNI and carried out to a beneficiary in a lower tax bracket. The same strategies discussed earlier in this chapter in the context of reducing the trust's tax exposure generally will have similar applicability in minimizing the impact of the NII tax.

In addition, the trustee's ability to make in-kind distributions of trust property will have equal application in devising strategies to curtail the effects of the NII tax (as discussed earlier for distributions of property). In an in-kind distribution, the beneficiary inherits the trust's basis in the property ("carryover basis") for income tax purposes.

¶810

The beneficiary will not recognize gain until the property is sold. This enables the beneficiary to time the sale of the property so that it occurs in a tax year when he or she is in a lower tax bracket and has a MAGI beneath the NII tax threshold.

> **COMMENT:** It should also be noted that if the beneficiary holds the property until death, the basis will be "stepped up" to fair market value, which eliminates the tax on any appreciation that occurred during the beneficiary's life.

STUDY QUESTION

3. In-kind distributions of trust property help to mitigate the NII tax because:
   a. The trust pays NII tax on gain attributable to the in-kind distribution
   b. The NII tax is calculated on the current fair market value of the property
   c. Any gain from selling the property will be taxed to the beneficiary
   d. The beneficiary receives a stepped-up basis in the property

¶ 811 CONCLUSION

A trustee can achieve income tax savings by making distributions to beneficiaries who are in a lower tax bracket than the trust. This will often be the case because of the highly compressed rate schedule that applies to trusts, for which any income in excess of $12,150 (in 2014) is subject to the top marginal rate of 39.6 percent, as well as the additional 3.8 percent NII tax.

In order to successfully shift the tax burden to the beneficiaries, the trustee must be cognizant of the rules governing principal and income allocations and understand key tax code concepts like DNI and AGI. In pursuing this tax planning, the trustee must adhere to the language in the trust agreement and the dictates of applicable local law, while acting in an impartial manner that is fair and reasonable to all beneficiaries. The trustee must also recognize that there may be times when pursuing an optimal tax savings strategy can be counterproductive, such as in the case of a beneficiary who is a spendthrift. In such cases, the trustee may refrain from making tax-motivated distributions in order to achieve a greater good.

MODULE 3: EVOLVING ISSUES FOR INDIVIDUALS—Chapter 9: Conservation Easements

¶ 901 WELCOME

Recognizing the need to preserve our heritage, Congress allows an income tax deduction for owners of property who give up certain rights of ownership to preserve their land or buildings for future generations. The IRS has seen abuses of this tax provision that compromise the policy Congress intended to promote. This chapter provides an update on charitable contributions easements to tax-exempt organizations, an area where the IRS and the courts have been especially active, with particular focus on fulfilling the requirements for claiming a conservation easement deduction.

¶ 902 LEARNING OBJECTIVES

Upon completion of this chapter, you will be able to:

- Identify the requirements for a qualified conservation easement;
- Recognize the elements of a qualified appraisal;
- Recognize the president's conservation easement proposals; and
- Identify the contiguous parcel and enhancement rules as they relate to conservation easements.

¶ 903 INTRODUCTION

The IRS has seen taxpayers, often encouraged by promoters and armed with questionable appraisals, take inappropriately large deductions for charitable contribution of easements. In some cases, taxpayers claim deductions they are not entitled to (for example, when taxpayers fail to comply with the law and regulations). Also, taxpayers have sometimes used or developed these properties in a manner inconsistent with the Code Sec. 501(c)(3) requirements. In other cases, recipient charities have allowed donor property owners to modify the easement or develop the land in a manner inconsistent with the easement's restrictions.

Another problem arises in connection with historic easements, particularly façade easements. Here again, some taxpayers are taking improperly large deductions. They agree not to modify the façade of their historic house and they give an easement to this effect to a charity. However, if the façade is already subject to restrictions under local zoning ordinances, the taxpayers may be giving up little or nothing. Taxpayers cannot give up a right that they do not have.

As of June 2014, the courts were facing more than 150 pending cases relating to the charitable conservation easement deduction, which was established to offset certain costs and losses associated with preserving property of historical, educational, or other public value. The increasing use (or often abuse) of the deduction by some taxpayers, however, has caused the IRS and Tax Court to heighten their scrutiny of charitable tax deductions for contributions of conservation easements. In other areas, however, the Tax Court has controversially upheld deductions claimed for contributions of property that arguably benefit mostly high-income taxpayers.

In light of these developments, this course highlights some of the important requirements relating to the deduction. This review includes background on conservation easements, current government treatment, and a discussion of interesting cases and a ruling in this area.

¶ 904 CRACKDOWN ON CHARITABLE CONSERVATION EASEMENT DEDUCTIONS

A deduction is generally available for charitable contributions of cash and property. This deduction is limited, or disallowed entirely, for certain types of hard-to-value property. To be eligible for an income tax charitable deduction, an individual must donate his or her entire interest in property. However, there is an exception for partial interests in property that are "qualified conservation contributions" (Code Sec. 170(f)(3)(B)(iii)). A *qualified conservation contribution* is a contribution of a "qualified real property interest" to a qualified organization exclusively for conservation purposes. A *qualified real property interest* is:

- The entire interest of the donor other than a qualified mineral interest;
- A remainder interest; and
- A restriction granted in perpetuity on the use that may be made of the real property.

A qualified conservation contribution must fulfill one of four conservation purposes:

- The preservation of land areas for outdoor recreation by, or for the education of, the general public;
- The protection of a relatively natural habitat of fish, wildlife, plants, or similar ecosystem;
- The preservation of open space when the preservation will yield a significant public benefit and is either for the scenic enjoyment of the general public or under a clearly described federal, state, or local governmental conservation policy; and
- The preservation of a historically important land area or certified historic structure. To qualify as a certified historic structure, a building must be either located in a registered historic district or be listed in the National Register of Historic Places.

Advantages of a qualified conservation easement to a donor include:

- A current income tax deduction for the value of the easement;
- No requirement that the property on which the easement is granted ever be transferred to the charity; and
- Preservation of the donor's intent for the property use after death.

The conservation deduction is limited to 30 percent of a donor's adjusted gross income because it is a contribution of property. From 2006 through 2013, this limit was temporarily increased to a 50-percent AGI deduction (Code Sec. 170(b)(1)(E)). Proposed legislation (H.R. 2087, The Conservation Easement Incentive Act of 2012)) would reinstate and make permanent the temporary provision. As of the time of publication, the legislation has not been enacted.

President's Proposal Includes Limiting Easements

In recent years, the Tax Court has been perceived as showing leniency for conservation easements on land that is or is intended to be used as a golf course as the result of the outcome of several cases. Among the more prominent cases is the court's 2009 decision in *Kiva Dunes Conservation, LLC v. Commissioner* (97 TCM 1818, T.C. Memo. 2009-145 (2009)). There, the Tax Court upheld most of a deduction for a contribution of an easement on golf course land that the IRS valued at roughly one third of the value claimed by the taxpayer. The court rejected the IRS expert appraiser's method of valuing the easement after the contribution due to his failure to take into account significant expenses in computing the net income from the course.

Meanwhile, the supposedly favorable Tax Court treatment of conservation easements for golf courses has become a point of contention among politicians. Although on the one hand conservation easements may preserve large tracts of land, they can also be used to reap unfair tax benefits for high-income taxpayers, particularly where golf courses are surrounded by luxury housing developments. In February 2012 President Obama announced in his fiscal year 2013 budget that he would pursue an amendment to the charitable contribution deduction provision that would prohibit a deduction for any contribution of property that is, or is intended to be, used as a golf course. This proposal was also contained in the fiscal year 2014 budget (*General Explanation of the Administration's Fiscal Year 2014 Revenue Proposals* (April 2013)).

> **COMMENT:** The president's budget reports:
>
> These contributions have raised concerns both that the deduction amounts claimed for such easements (often by the developers of the private home sites) are excessive, and also that the conservation easement deduction is not narrowly tailored to promote only bona fide conservation activities, as opposed to the private interests of donors . . . .Easements on golf courses are particularly susceptible to overvaluation, as private interests often profit from the contribution of an easement. Because of the difficulty determining both the value of the easement and the value of the return benefits provided to the donor—including indirect benefits, such as the increase in the value of home sites surrounding the golf course—it is difficult and costly for the Internal Revenue Service to challenge inflated golf course easement deductions. Thus, to promote the kinds of public benefits intended by the charitable deduction provision and to prevent abuses, no charitable deduction should be allowed for contributions of easements on golf courses.

> **COMMENT:** House Ways and Means Committee Chairman Dave Camp (R-Mich.) released a discussion draft of comprehensive tax reform on February 26, 2014. His *Tax Reform Act of 2014* also includes a prohibition of a conservation easement for golf courses.

> **COMMENT:** There is a concern that the conservation easement deduction is too broad, structured inappropriately, and should be reined in, according to Ruth Madrigal, attorney advisor at the Office of Tax Policy at the U.S. Treasury, speaking at the 2013 AICPA Not-for-Profit Industry Conference in Washington, D.C. The Office of Tax Policy not only provides guidance for rules already on the books but also looks at where those rules possibly can be changed. The office, she said, participates in the president's budget.

Another budget proposal would limit the Code Sec. 170 charitable deduction for historic preservation easements. Specifically, the proposal would disallow a deduction for any value of a historic preservation easement associated with forgone upward development above a historic building. It would also require contributions of conservation easements on buildings listed in the National Register to comply with the same special rules currently applicable to buildings in a registered historic district.

The reason for the change, according to the budget proposal, is that concerns have been raised that the deduction amounts claimed for historic preservation easements are excessive and may not appropriately take into account existing limitations on the property. Some taxpayers have taken large deductions for contributions of easements restricting the upward development of historic urban buildings even though such development was already restricted by local authorities.

In both of these proposals, Madrigal said the restriction on deductibility is "driven by a concern that values for these things are unbelievably high." These are very difficult cases for the IRS to pursue in any cost effective way, she said. To prove valuation is a costly and time-consuming process.

Madrigal added that especially in the case of historic preservation easements, there is a concern existing zoning laws or the rules of developing in a historic district already prevent much development of the property.

Therefore, an additional restriction might not restrict the value any further. "And certainly the prospect of building up 50 stories on top of a brownstone would likely not be allowed under current restrictions."

A 2013 TIGTA report (*Treasury Inspector General for Tax Administration (TIGTA) Report: Many Taxpayers Are Still Not Complying with Noncash Charitable Contributions Reporting Requirements* (Reference Number: 2013-40-009, January 16, 2013)) was very surprising to Madrigal. She noted the report indicated that roughly 20 million individuals claimed noncharitable contributions annually over a period that included 2011 and 2012. The report found a 60 percent error rate in the sample data, which projects to almost $200 million in unsubstantiated contributions. "And it's not just the little guys. They found a 41 percent error rate in contributions over $500,000."

Finally, the report estimated that 273,000 taxpayers claimed $3.8 billion in unsubstantiated noncash contributions, leading to a $1 billion tax loss. Madrigal commented that the figure was "really startling."

STUDY QUESTION

---

1. Which of the following is **not** one of the four conservation purposes of a qualified conservation contribution?

    a. Preserving land for outdoor recreation

    b. Offering a public benefit for scenic enjoyment of open space

    c. Lowering population density of older neighborhoods

    d. Preserving a historically important land area

Substantiation Requirements

Substantiation issues are common means for which courts will disallow deductions. They are simpler to rule on than valuations of fair market value (FMV) and benefits. And because the charitable contributions of conservation easements are so often subject to abuse, courts are more apt to be suspicious and to disallow deductions based on faulty Forms 8283, *Noncash Charitable Contributions*; lack of or insufficient contemporaneous written acknowledgments of contributions; and nonqualifying appraisals. Thus, when drafting their documents, it is important for potential donors to hire good attorneys, specialists, and accountants experienced in the area of conservation easements.

    PLANNING POINTER: Using such experts can result in a considerable expense for taxpayers. However, such costs may be itemized as a miscellaneous deduction.

In an area governed by nearly 100 pages of regulations and in which many IRS agents who review the deduction may not have extensive experience with conservation easements, it is clearly important to provide as much information on the contributed property as possible and in an upfront manner. Form 8283 should be properly completed and accompanied by a detailed baseline report. A copy of the conservation easement deed describing the property should be attached, as should the contemporaneous written acknowledgment letter from the donee.

> **COMMENT:** Because the deduction for charitable contributions conservation easements is, in essence, another layer of the deduction for noncash charitable contributions, conservation easement donors are required to provide a contemporaneous written acknowledgment of their contribution.

The letters, as with all noncash donations of more than $250, should state whether the donee provides any goods or services in consideration for the contribution, and if so, the value of those goods or services.

Valuation

Finding good, qualified appraisers is important for donors who do not want their contribution deductions challenged. In most of the court cases, overvaluation is an issue, with the IRS view being that appraisals of the FMV of donated property are improper or inflated.

There are so many requirements for an appraisal to be qualified that a regular appraiser is not experienced enough to represent the donor (Code Sec. 170(f)(11)(E)(i); Reg. § 1.170A-17).

A qualified appraisal must include all of the elements shown in Figure 1.

Figure 1. Code Sec. 170 Requirements for Qualified Appraisals

(A) The following information about the contributed property:

    (i) A description in sufficient detail under the circumstances (taking into account the value of the property) for a person who is not generally familiar with the type of property to ascertain that the appraised property is the contributed property.

    (ii) In the case of real or personal tangible property, the condition of the property.

    (iii) The valuation effective date.

    (iv) The fair market value of the contributed property on the valuation effective date;

(B) The terms of any agreement or understanding by or on behalf of the donor and donee that relates to the use, sale, or other disposition of the contributed property, including, for example, the terms of any agreement or understanding that—

    (i) Restricts temporarily or permanently a donee's right to use or dispose of the contributed property;

    (ii) Reserves to, or confers upon, anyone (other than a donee or an organization participating with a donee in cooperative fundraising) any right to the income from the contributed property or to the possession of the property, including the right to vote contributed securities, to acquire the property by purchase or otherwise, or to designate the person having income, possession, or right to acquire; or

    (iii) Earmarks contributed property for a particular use;

(C) The date (or expected date) of the contribution to the donee;

(D) The following information about the appraiser:

   (i) Name, address, and taxpayer identification number.

   (ii) Qualifications to value the type of property being valued, including the appraiser's education and experience.

   (iii) If the appraiser is acting in his or her capacity as a partner in a partnership, an employee of any person (whether an individual, corporation, or partnership), or an independent contractor engaged by a person other than the donor, the name, address, and taxpayer identification number of the partnership or the person who employs or engages the qualified appraiser;

(E) The signature of the appraiser and the date signed by the appraiser;

(F) The following declaration by the appraiser: "I understand that my appraisal will be used in connection with a return or claim for refund. I also understand that, if a substantial or gross valuation misstatement of the value of the property claimed on the return or claim for refund results from my appraisal, I may be subject to a penalty under section 6695A of the Internal Revenue Code, as well as other applicable penalties. I affirm that I have not been barred from presenting evidence or testimony before the Department of the Treasury or the Internal Revenue Service pursuant to 31 U.S.C. section 330(c);"

(G) A statement that the appraisal was prepared for income tax purposes;

(H) The method of valuation used to determine the fair market value, such as the income approach, the market-data approach, or the replacement-cost-less depreciation approach; and

(I) The specific basis for the valuation, such as specific comparable sales transactions or statistical sampling, including a justification for using sampling and an explanation of the sampling procedure employed.

Moreover, the appraiser must be qualified (Code Sec. 170(f)(11)(E)(ii)). Qualified appraisers with local expertise are particularly recommended. Even if an appraiser arrives at the correct amount and fulfills every requirement, if he or she is not qualified, the deduction would not be allowed.

STUDY QUESTION

2. The IRS considers donation of charitable conservation easements to be a type of:

   a. Remainder interest
   b. Noncash charitable contribution
   c. In-kind exchange
   d. Cash donation

¶ 905 *BUTLER:* DEDUCTIONS ALLOWED FOR EASEMENTS

As discussed above, the increasing use, and often abuse, of the conservation deduction by some taxpayers has caused the IRS and Tax Court to heighten their scrutiny of charitable tax deductions for contributions of conservation easements. This does not mean, however, that all challenges to a taxpayer's conservation deduction will be upheld. For example, in one case a charitable contribution was allowed for conservation easements on their property although the conservation deeds reserved some rights for a married couple (*James E. Butler, Jr. v. Commissioner*, 103 TCM 1359, T.C. Memo. 2012-72 (2012)). The couple included language to ensure the intended conservation purposes would be protected.

> **COMMENT:** Generally, the amount of a charitable contribution is the FMV of the contributed property at the time it is contributed. The taxpayers had retained conservation advisors who helped them to select several appraisers, but the court found that the taxpayers overstated the value of their charitable contribution. However, the taxpayers had reasonable cause and acted in good faith with respect to their underpayment, and the court declined to impose accuracy-related penalties.

Background

The taxpayers contributed conservation easements to a limited liability company (LLC). The LLC subsequently contributed the easements to a separate entity. The LLC passed through to the taxpayers the charitable contribution deductions with respect to its donations during 2003 and 2004, and the taxpayers claimed those deductions on their joint return for each year.

The IRS determined that the taxpayers did not show that their contributions of conservation easements were qualified conservation contributions under Code Sec. 170(h). Alternatively, the IRS determined that the taxpayers' appraisal reports did not establish the proper value of the conservation easements.

Court's Analysis

Generally, taxpayers may deduct the value of a contribution of a partial interest in property that constitutes a qualified conservation contribution. For a contribution to constitute a qualified conservation contribution, the taxpayer must show that the contribution is of a qualified real property interest, to a qualified organization, and exclusively for conservation purposes. The taxpayers and the IRS agreed that the contributions were qualified real property interests and that the contributions were made to qualified organizations.

Reg. § 1.170A-14(e)(2) disallows any deduction for which the conservation easement would preserve one of the conservation purposes but would permit destruction of other significant conservation interests. The area around the properties was becoming attractive to developers because of population growth. The taxpayers had received offers to purchase all or portions of the properties. The taxpayers declined these offers, the court found, because they wanted to preserve the land.

The conservation deeds placed significant restrictions on the properties. The deeds limited water usage and commercial timber harvesting. Mineral exploitation and commercial/industrial facilities were expressly not allowed. The properties also were not open to the general public. The taxpayers, however, did reserve certain rights, such as the right to engage in small-scale farming and grazing. They could also use certain fertilizers and pesticides. Additionally, a portion of the property could be subdivided into tracts of at least 200 acres.

In some cases, conservation easements permit no development at all, guaranteeing that the land will continue to exist in its current state. Here, the taxpayers reserve certain rights. If the properties were developed to the full extent permitted by the conservation deeds, the conservation purpose would still be preserved, the court found. The court in *Butler* concluded that the conservation deeds satisfied the statute and regulations.

¶ 906 *GRAEV:* CONDITIONAL DONATIONS DISALLOWED

In *Graev,* a couple's charitable contributions of cash and a façade conservation easement that they donated to a charitable organization were not deductible because the donations were conditional gifts (*Lawrence G. Graev v. Commissioner,* 140 TC - No. 17 (2013)).

A gift is considered conditional if:

- The charitable contribution is not considered made because the possibility that the receiving organization's interest in the contribution would be defeated by a subsequent event is "not so remote as to be negligible;"
- The charitable contribution constitutes less than the donor's entire interest in a property and there is a likelihood that the receiving organization's interest in the contribution would be defeated by a subsequent event is "not so remote as to be negligible;" or
- The conservation easement is not considered a qualified conservation contribution because the possibility that the receiving organization may be divested of its interest in the easement by a subsequent event is "not so remote as to be negligible."

A tax treatment contingency could be considered a subsequent event.

In *Graev,* the likelihood that a charitable organization would be divested of its interest in the couple's donations of cash and the façade conservation easement was "not so remote as to be negligible."

COMMENT: Valuing a conditional gift is difficult because of the refund feature. Therefore, the value of conditional gifts are often heavily discounted.

Background

Before the couple made the donations to the National Architectural Trust, the charitable organization, at the couple's request, issued them a side letter in which it promised to refund the entire cash contribution and immediately remove the façade easement from the property's title if the IRS were to disallow the couple's deductions for the donations. Asking for this letter was evidence that the couple was aware that there was a risk that their deductions would be disallowed. In addition, the fact that it was standard policy for the organization to return a donation to the extent that a deduction was not allowed by the IRS was evidence that it believed that there was risk that the IRS might disallow a deduction. The tax treatment contingency in the letter was considered a subsequent event because there were no prior decisions that held otherwise.

The couple claimed that the organization could not be divested of its interest in the façade easement because the letter was not enforceable under New York State's environmental conservation statutes. However, the organization had the ability to honor its promises in the letter because the subscribed and recorded deed, which clearly was the instrument creating the easement, reserved for the organization the power to do so.

COMMENT: There has been a string of cases challenging deductions for the donation of façade easements to the NAT (e.g., *J. Maurice Herman v. Commissioner,* 98 TCM 197, T.C. Memo. 2009-205 (2009); *1982 East, LLC, v. Commissioner,* 101 TCM 1380, T.C. Memo. 2011-84 (2011); *George Gorra v. Commissioner,* 106 TCM 523, T.C. Memo. 2013-254, (2013)).

Court's Analysis

The common law doctrine of merger, even if it were to apply, also did not extinguish the letter. Although the doctrine of merger generally extinguishes terms of preliminary contracts or negotiations upon the recording of a deed, so that only the terms in the recorded deed remain, the letter fell within one of the exceptions to this general rule. Specifically, a contract for real estate is merged in the deed only when the deed is intended to be accepted in full performance of the contract and the promises made in the letter to return the donations showed the parties' clear intent that the letter would survive the deed.

Also, the letter was not a nullity, which would extinguish the letter, even though it provided the couple with a potential recovery of the donations in the event of unwanted tax consequences, because:

- The letter did not discourage the collection of tax;
- The possibility of the subsequent return of the contributions did not render this case moot; and
- The return of the donations to the couple would have no effect on their tax liabilities.

There was a negligible possibility that the charitable organization would voluntarily extinguish the easement and return the cash contributions because there was no evidence that the organization might renege on it promises made in the letter to return the donations to the couple. However, even if this could be assumed, there was still a nonnegligible possibility that it would do as it promised.

¶ 907 *TROUT RANCH:* COMPARABLE-SALES METHOD

The value of a conservation easement is the FMV of the perpetual conservation restriction at the time of the contribution. Determining value is a factual inquiry. One method used is to ascertain the difference between the FMV of the property the easement encumbers *before* the granting of the restriction and the FMV of the encumbered property *after* the granting of the restriction. Another method is the comparable-sales method, which looks at data from the sales of similar properties to estimate the market value.

One appellate court found that the Tax Court's valuation of a conservation easement was not clearly in error (*Trout Ranch, LLC, v. Commissioner,* CA-10, 2012-2 USTC ¶ 50,524). The Tax Court was free to construct its own model, which did not use the comparable-sales method, and its use of postvaluation data was not an abuse of discretion.

Background

The taxpayer purchased 450 acres intending to develop a residential community. The locality had no zoning laws and under state law developers could subdivide the property into 35-acre parcels as a matter of right. However, the locality had a conservation program that rewarded developers that preserve 75 percent of their property, which effectively allowed for subdivision of the property into 22 three-acre lots. Ultimately, the taxpayer preserved 85 percent of the property under a conservation easement.

The taxpayer claimed a charitable deduction of $2.2 million. The IRS initially valued the deduction at $485,000 but subsequently adjusted the deduction to zero.

The taxpayer filed for relief in the Tax Court. Experts for the taxpayer and the IRS testified before the court. The taxpayer's expert was the only expert to perform a valuation based on the comparable-sales method, which estimated the value of the conservation easement between $1.59 million and $2.3 million. The IRS's experts performed before-and-after appraisals using discounted cash-flow models to determine the most profitable use of the property before and after the easement. The IRS's experts determined that the value of the conservation easement was zero. The Tax Court declined to accept any of the expert appraisals in their entirety. Instead, it constructed its own model, concluding that the value of the conservation easement was $500,000.

Tenth Circuit's Analysis

The taxpayer argued that the Tax Court improperly admitted the testimony of the IRS's experts because they did not use the comparable-sales method. The Tenth Circuit disagreed. As professional appraisers, the IRS's experts determined the value of the conservation easement by calculating and comparing the best use of the property before and after the taxpayer donated the easement. The experts acknowledged the comparable-sales method in their appraisal and chose not to follow it. The experts were not required by the regulations to explain why they did not use the comparable-sales method, the court found.

> **COMMENT:** The Tenth Circuit found that the IRS experts were correct to overlook comparable sales because the easement was less restrictive than comparable ones.

The Tenth Circuit further found that the Tax Court's valuation of the conservation easement was not clearly in error. Contrary to the taxpayer's claims, the Tax Court could take into account data released after the date of valuation.

The Tenth Circuit found that a reasonable buyer is a conceptual device intended to illustrate the objective nature of the inquiry and not a limitation on the evidence that can inform it. Data from events after the donation can be just as informative, and just as distorting, as data from events before the donation, the court found. The use of postvaluation data was not an abuse of discretion.

STUDY QUESTION

---

3. Why did the Tenth Circuit Court uphold the IRS valuation position in *Trout Ranch?*
- **a.** The donor used the fair market value of the donated property
- **b.** The IRS experts were correct in overlooking comparable sales
- **c.** The Tax Court's valuation was higher than the taxpayers
- **d.** The Tax Court and IRS experts agreed that the easement's value was zero

---

¶ 908 *BELK:* "FLOATING EASEMENT"

A taxpayer did not donate an interest in real property subject to a use restriction granted in perpetuity because a conservation agreement permitted substitution of the donated property. Therefore, the taxpayer could not claim a charitable deduction for a conservation easement of real property containing a golf course (*B.V. Belk, Jr. v. Commissioner,* 105 TCM 1878, T.C. Memo. 2013-154 (2013)).

> **COMMENT:** The conservation easement in this case was characterized by the IRS as a "floating easement." Before the Tax Court, the IRS successfully argued that a conservation easement that does not relate to a specific piece of property cannot be a qualified conservation contribution.

Background

Belk owned 410 acres in North Carolina. An LLC controlled by the taxpayer intended to build more than 400 homes and a golf course on the property. The LLC executed a conservation easement agreement with a nonprofit land conservancy. The conservation easement reflected that the golf course possessed recreational, natural, scenic, open space, historic, and educational values and prohibited the golf course from being used for residential, commercial, institutional, industrial, or agricultural purposes. The agreement also permitted the parties to substitute what property would be subject to the conservation easement.

The LLC's charitable contribution passed through to the taxpayer. The taxpayer claimed a $10.5 million charitable contribution deduction for the contribution of the conservation easement, which the IRS disallowed.

The Tax Court found that under the conservation easement agreement both the LLC and the nonprofit could change what property was subject to the conservation easement. Therefore, the use restriction was not granted in perpetuity under Code Sec. 170(h)(2)(C). The parties could remove portions of the golf course and replace them with property currently not subject to the conservation easement, the court concluded.

Reconsideration

The taxpayer asked the Tax Court to reconsider its decision. However, the court rejected the taxpayer's argument that it had misinterpreted the tax code. The Tax Court had found that Code Sec. 170(h)(2) defines *qualified real property interest* as any of the following interests in real property:

- The entire interest of the donor other than a qualified mineral interest;
- A remainder interest; and
- A restriction (granted in perpetuity) on the use that may be made of the real property.

The court reiterated that Code Sec. 170(h)(2)(C) requires taxpayers to donate an interest in an identifiable, specific piece of real property.

The court also rejected the taxpayer's argument that it had erred in deciding that the conservation easement agreement allowed substitutions. The LLC and the nonprofit had included a provision in the agreement permitting substitutions, the court found. Although the substitution provision stated that a substitution was not binding or final on the nonprofit until the agreement would be amended to reflect the substitution, the court had found that the substitution and amendment provisions were in conflict.

Additionally, the court rejected the taxpayer's claim that its decision imposed an impossible and impractical requirement on taxpayers and qualified organizations.

¶ 909 *MITCHELL:* LACK OF SUBORDINATION AGREEMENT AT TIME OF GIFTS

A contribution is not treated as exclusively for conservation purposes unless the conservation purpose is protected in perpetuity. No deduction will be permitted for an interest in property that is subject to a mortgage unless the mortgagee subordinates its rights in the property to the right of the donee organization to enforce the conservation purposes of the gift in perpetuity (Reg. § 1.170A-14(g)(2)).

The Tax Court has held that the requirements of the subordination regulation, with respect to a qualified conservation contribution deduction, cannot be avoided by use of the "so remote as to be negligible" standard (***Ramona L. Mitchell v. Commissioner,*** 138 TC 324 (2012)). The court upheld the IRS's disallowance of a deduction related to seller-financed property. The taxpayer and the seller failed to have a subordination agreement in place on the date of the gift.

Background

In 1998 Chris and Ramona Mitchell, a married couple, purchased unimproved property. The couple installed a water line and electricity on the property, and built a home. Sometime later, the couple approached the same seller to purchase some adjoining property. The couple and the seller agreed to an installment sale ($600,000 to be paid in installments of $60,000 per year plus interest).

The couple formed a family limited partnership (FLP) in 2002 and transferred the property to the partnership. The FLP granted a conservation easement on a portion of the unimproved land to Conservancy. The seller subsequently agreed to subordinate his deed of trust to the conservation easement but received no consideration for the subordination. The partnership claimed a $500,000 charitable contribution deduction, which flowed through to the couple, who claimed a charitable contribution deduction on their 2003 tax return. The IRS disallowed the charitable deduction.

Court's Analysis

The IRS and the taxpayer agreed that the contribution was a qualified real property interest and Conservancy was a qualified organization. They disagreed whether the contribution had been made exclusively for conservation purposes.

A subordination agreement must be in place at the time of the gift. Here, the subordination agreement was signed nearly two years after the grant of the conservation easement. Consequently, the conservation easement was not protected in perpetuity at the time of the gift.

The taxpayer also argued that the conservation easement was still protected in perpetuity because the probability of default on the promissory note was so remote as to be negligible. The court noted this presented a case of whether the court must consider the "so remote as to be negligible" standard in determining whether petitioner satisfied the subordination regulation.

The court concluded that the subordination regulation should not be read in tandem with the "so remote as to be negligible" standard. A taxpayer cannot avoid meeting the strict requirement of the subordination regulation by showing that the possibility of foreclosure on that deed of trust is so remote as to be negligible.

Easement Disallowed

In **Minnick,** another subordination case, married taxpayers were not allowed charitable contribution deductions for the grant of a conservation easement because a bank mortgage on the donor's land was not subordinated to the conservation easement when it was granted (**Walter C. Minnick v. Commissioner,** 104 TCM, T.C. Memo. 2012-345 (2012)).

The taxpayers owned a parcel of real property that they subdivided into residential lots. They donated a conservation easement on the remainder of the land in the parcel, claimed a deduction for the year of the grant, and carried the unused portion of the deduction over for two subsequent years.

The grant contained a warranty that the property was not encumbered by any mortgages. However, the land was subject to a mortgage at the time of the grant of the easement, and the bank holding the mortgage did not subordinate the mortgage to the easement until several years after the grant.

Again, a subordination agreement must be in place at the time of the grant of an easement for there to be a charitable contribution deduction. The alleged intent of the taxpayers that the mortgage be subordinated and the alleged willingness of the bank to subordinate its mortgage at the time of the grant did not avoid the explicit requirement that a subordination agreement be in effect at the time of the grant. Further, state law imposing the doctrine of *cy pres* did not cause the mortgage to be subordinated because the bank was not a party to the agreement granting the easement.

Accuracy Penalties

In addition, the taxpayers were subject to accuracy-related penalties under Code Sec. 6662 for the years for which they claimed the deductions. They were negligent and did not exercise reasonable care, in that they should have known the deduction would not be allowed because of the lack of a subordination agreement for the donated easement. The fact that they hired an appraiser was irrelevant, because the appraiser was hired only to value the easement, not to give an opinion about the subordination agreement.

The taxpayers failed to solicit advice from their certified public accountant about the deductibility of the easement, and the CPA only gave advice on easements generally, not on the particular grant at issue. Therefore, the taxpayers could not have reasonably relied on such advice.

An IRS appraiser's opinion as to the value of the conservation easement was not relied on as a basis for the court's decision. It was an expert opinion and had not been brought before the court in the form of an expert report or provided to the taxpayers 14 days before trial.

¶ 910 CONTIGUOUS PARCEL AND ENHANCEMENT RULES

The amount of the deduction in the case of a charitable contribution of a perpetual conservation restriction covering a portion of the contiguous property owned by a donor and the donor's family (as defined in Code Sec. 267(c)(4)) is the difference between the FMV of the entire contiguous parcel of property before and after the granting of the restriction (the Contiguous Parcel Rule; Reg. § 1.170A-14(h)(3)(i)).

If the granting of a perpetual conservation restriction after January 14, 1986, has the effect of increasing the value of any other property owned by the donor or a related person, the amount of the deduction for the conservation contribution must be reduced by the amount of the increase in the value of the other property, whether or not the property is contiguous (the Enhancement Rule; Reg. § 1.170A-14(h)(3)(i)).

The IRS has provided scenarios illustrating the application of the contiguous parcel and enhancement rules for valuing perpetual conservation easements for charitable contribution deduction purposes (CCA 201334039).

According to the chief counsel's advice:

- The deduction allowed for a qualified conservation contribution when the donor owns a parcel and a contiguous parcel is either owned by the donor or the donor's family is equal to the difference between the FMV of the entire contiguous parcel owned by the donor or the donor's family before and after granting the easement;

- The deduction when contiguous and noncontiguous parcels are owned by the donor is first determined by valuing the entire contiguous parcel before and after the granting of the easement. Then the deduction is reduced by the value of the noncontiguous parcel owned by the donor;

- When the contiguous parcels are owned by the donor and a disregarded single-member limited liability company (SMLLC), the deduction is equal to the difference between the FMV of the entire contiguous parcel before and after granting the easement. Similarly, the same deduction rule applied when the donor's daughter was the single member of the disregarded entity that owned the contiguous parcel; and

- When contiguous parcels are owned by a donor and the donor's SMLLC, the deduction is first determined by valuing the parcel before and after granting the easement. The deduction is reduced by the value of the enhancement of the second parcel because a related party that is not a family member (the LLC) owns the contiguous parcel. However, the contiguous parcel rule does not apply when an entity classified as a partnership owns the contiguous property.

The deduction for the conservation contribution is reduced by the amount of the increase in the value of the other property, whether or not the property is contiguous under the enhancement rule.

Further, the contiguous parcel rule does not apply when a partnership owns contiguous property, the donor owns a parcel, and an LLC owns a contiguous parcel when the donor and an unrelated person each own 50 percent of the LLC. In this case, the LLC is classified as a partnership because it has not elected otherwise, and the donor does not own more than 50 percent of the partnership.

¶ 911 *WHITEHOUSE HOTEL:* FAÇADE EASEMENT DONATION OVERVALUED

A limited partnership overstated its charitable contribution deduction for donation of a façade easement on a historic building the Tax Court, on remand from the Fifth Circuit Court of Appeals, held (***Whitehouse Hotel Limited Partnership v. Commissioner,*** 139 TC 304 (2012)).

> **COMMENT:** According to the Fifth Circuit Court, the Tax Court had erred in declining to consider the highest and best use of the historic building and adjoining buildings in the light of probable combination of the buildings into a single functional unit. The Fifth Circuit also instructed the Tax Court to reconsider the experts' reports and valuation methods and their conclusions regarding highest and best use as a hotel. Although the assumption from the Fifth Circuit's directions may have been that a significantly higher value from the Tax Court's initial valuation was in order, the Tax Court raised its value of the façade easement only slightly, from $1.7 million to $1.8 million, far below the taxpayer's $7.4 million amount. The court's value was just not enough higher to automatically exempt the taxpayer from the 40 percent overvaluation penalty under Code Sec. 6662(h). There is a substantial valuation misstatement if the value of any property claimed on the return is 200 percent or more of the amount determined to be correct.

Background

In 1995, the Whitehouse Hotel partnership acquired a historic building housing a department store in New Orleans' French Quarter. Several years later, the partnership began extensive and costly renovations on the building and to adjoining buildings, with the ultimate goal of operating a hotel. The partnership also donated a façade easement to a local nonprofit organization. The partnership claimed a $7.4 million charitable deduction for the façade easement, which the IRS reduced to $1.15 million.

The Tax Court valued the easement at nearly $1.8 million. The court found that the comparable-sales approach was applicable and that the FMV of the easement on the valuation date was $1.792 million. The court further found that the taxpayer had made a gross valuation misstatement of more than 400 percent of the value of the conservation contribution, thus justifying IRS's assessment of the Code Sec. 6662(a) overvaluation penalty of 40 percent.

Remand

On remand, the Tax Court looked to the "highest and best use" of the property. The court agreed with the Fifth Circuit that finding a property's highest and best use is critical for determining its FMV. The term *highest and best use* is the reasonably probable and legal use of vacant land or an improved property that is physically possible, appropriately supported, and financially feasible and that results in the highest value. However, the highest and best use of property does not itself identify the FMV of the property: It forms the foundation for the opinion of value, according to the Tax Court.

The Tax Court found that the highest and best use of the property may have been the luxury hotel development. Its second best use, the court assumed, would be as a nonluxury hotel. After reviewing all of the evidence and revisiting the experts' valuations, the court concluded that the value of the easement was $1.85 million.

¶ 912 *ESGAR CORPORATION:* TAXPAYER'S OVERSTATED VALUE

The battle line has shifted recently in most litigation from determining the right to a conservation easement charitable deduction to determining the size of the deduction based on valuation. In one example, the Court of Appeals for the Tenth Circuit has upheld a Tax Court decision relating to the valuation of charitable conservation easements (*Esgar Corporation v. Commissioner,* CA-10, 2014-1 USTC ¶ 50,207). The Tax Court chose the correct methodology for valuing conservation easements of agricultural land donated by taxpayers but at overstated values during the 2004 tax year, the appellate court found.

> **COMMENT:** The Tax Court in *Esgar* agreed with the IRS that the taxpayers had not correctly determined the conservation easements' values, finding that the easements' highest and best use for purposes of determining the land's before and after value under Reg. § 1.170A-14 would have been as agricultural land, not a gravel mine.

Background

Two corporations and two married couples held land in partnership and leased a large portion of it to a gravel mining operation. In December 2004, the partnership transferred 163 acres from the unleased portion of land, split equally three ways, to the one corporation and to each of the married couples. In mid-December 2004, the taxpayers donated their acres subject to a conservation easement, which an appraiser valued at $570,500, $867,500, and $836,500, based on the properties' relinquished value as a gravel mining operation.

The taxpayers all claimed charitable deductions for the donations on their respective 2004 tax returns, with carryforwards into 2005 and 2006. At trial over the methodology used to determine the values of the conservation easements, the Tax Court agreed with the IRS that the "highest and best" use of the properties was as agricultural land, which resulted lower values than the original appraisal.

Court's Analysis

The Tenth Circuit in *Esgar* ruled that the Tax Court's decision that agriculture was the properties' highest and best use would stand "if it is supported by substantial evidence and is not clearly erroneous." The Tenth Circuit found that the Tax Court had correctly applied the highest and best use standard by looking for the use of the land that was most reasonably probable in the reasonably near future.

The Tax Court had not clearly erred by concluding that use was agriculture rather than gravel mining, the Tenth Circuit found. In 2004 there was no unfulfilled demand for gravel in the county, demand for gravel was unlikely to increase in the reasonably near future, and current gravel supply was sufficient to satisfy any demand increase. Therefore, developing the donated land into a gravel mining operation was not a reasonably foreseeable possibility in 2004, the court concluded.

STUDY QUESTION

4. The focus of much litigation concerning qualified conservation contributions of land is currently:

   a. The size of the deduction

   b. The correctness of methodology for valuing easements

   c. The stipulation by donors to use land for agriculture

   d. The common use of the comparable-sales method versus before-and-after valuations

¶ 913 *ROTHMAN:* LACK OF QUALIFIED APPRAISAL

A charitable deduction for a conservation easement can be denied if the deduction was not based on a qualified appraisal, as required by Reg. § 1.170A-13(c) (***Steven Rothman v. Commissioner,*** 104 TCM 126, T.C. Memo. 2012-218 (2012). The court in ***Rothman*** found that the appraisal failed to satisfy a majority of the regulation's requirements for a qualified appraisal.

> **COMMENT:** The IRS has successfully challenged many easements by arguing that the appraisal was not qualified. This generally is easier than a challenge to the value of the easement. The court's opinion will encourage the IRS to maintain its challenges of appraisals for not being qualified.

Case History

The Tax Court first rejected the easement in a June 2012 decision (***Steven Rothman v. Commissioner,*** 103 TCM 1864, T.C. Memo 2012-163 (2012)). Relying on ***Huda T. Scheidelman v. Commissioner*** (100 TCM 24, T.C. Memo. 2010-151 (2010)), the Tax Court concluded in the first ***Rothman*** decision that the appraisal of the conservation easement was not "qualified" under the regulations, because it lacked a method and a specific basis for the valuation. As a result, the appraisal did not provide sufficient information for the IRS to evaluate it.

Subsequently, in ***Scheidelman*** (2012-1 USTC ¶ 50,402), the Second Circuit Court of Appeals overturned the Tax Court's decision. The ***Scheidelman*** appeals court said that the appraisal was "qualified," even if its accuracy was uncertain.

On a motion for reconsideration, the taxpayers in ***Rothman*** argued that their appraisal was qualified under the appeals court's reasoning in ***Scheidelman.***

Reconsideration

The Tax Court disagreed. There are many distinct requirements for a qualified appraisal under the regulations, the court noted. The appeals court's decision only addressed two of them and did not discuss any of the other regulatory requirements. Although the Tax Court vacated the part of its decision on the two requirements, it concluded that it was not obligated to vacate the rest of its decision and approve the appraisal. Instead, the court concluded that the appraisal submitted by the Rothmans failed to satisfy eight of the regulatory requirements and still was not a qualified appraisal.

COMMENT: The Tax Court stated that it was not necessarily denying a charitable deduction to the Rothmans, because they could claim reasonable cause for failing to obtain a qualified appraisal. The existence of reasonable cause is factual and would not be decided in the motion for summary judgment before the court.

¶ 914 *FRIEDBERG:* APPRAISALS WERE QUALIFIED

In *Friedberg,* based on an intervening change in the law, the Tax Court determined that an easement appraisal and a separate appraisal of development rights were both qualified appraisals under Code Sec. 170 despite being of questionable reliability (*Barry S. Friedberg v. Commissioner,* 106 TCM 360, T.C. Memo. 2013-224 (2013) (Friedberg II)). Consequently, the court reversed its prior decision that the taxpayers were not entitled to a charitable deduction. Instead, the issue of valuation of the easement and the rights must be decided at trial.

Background

Friedberg purchased a townhouse in New York City. He agreed to donate a façade easement and the development rights for the property. The taxpayer obtained an appraisal from an independent third party for both the easement and the rights. Friedberg claimed a charitable deduction of $3.7 million and attached a copy of the appraisals to his tax return.

In *Barry S. Friedberg v. Commissioner* (102 TCM 356, T.C. Memo 2011-238 (2011) (Friedberg I)), the Tax Court granted partial summary judgment to the IRS, concluding that the taxpayer had not obtained a qualified appraisal for the easement, but that there were factual issues to determine whether the appraisal of the development rights was qualified.

Requirements for a Qualified Appraisal

In *Friedberg I,* the Tax Court found that the appraisals did not satisfy the requirements for a qualified appraisal. The court found that the appraisals were inadequate and unreliable; therefore, they did not provide a method of valuation or the specific basis for the valuation.

The Appeals Court in *Scheidelman II* (2012-1 USTC ¶ 50,402) applied a different analysis. It found that the regulations provided reporting requirements for a qualified appraisal. It was not necessary that the appraisal be reliable, only that it identify the appraiser's valuation method and basis for valuation. The purpose of the regulations on qualified appraisals is to provide the IRS with sufficient information to evaluate the claimed deduction and to deal more effectively with potential overvaluations. This requirement is met if the appraiser's analysis was present, even if the IRS deemed it unconvincing.

Reconsideration

Based on *Scheidelman II,* the Tax Court concluded that the appraisals provided for both the easement and the development rights were qualified. The Tax Court, in its prior opinion, had concluded that the appraisal explained both the method and specific basis of valuation.

The taxpayer argued successfully that the reliability of the appraisal was not a factor for determining whether it was a qualified appraisal. The court rejected the IRS's arguments that the appraisal lacked a method of valuation or a specific basis for the valuation.

Qualified Appraiser Issue

The IRS also argued that the appraiser was not a qualified appraiser of the development rights because he had never appraised other development rights. The Tax Court found that this was irrelevant. A qualified appraiser is one who makes the declarations, as required by the regulations, that he or she holds him- or herself out to the public as an appraiser or performs appraisals regularly, and that he or she is qualified to make appraisals of the type of property being valued. Here, the appraiser made the required declarations.

¶ 915 IRS BARS APPRAISERS FOR FIVE YEARS

The IRS has imposed a five-year suspension on appraisers who overvalued building façade easements for charitable contribution deductions (Internal Revenue News Release IR-2014-31, March 7, 2014). The appraisers prompting the suspension acknowledged violating Treasury Department Circular 230's due diligence requirements in agreeing to the suspension. In addition, the appraisers agreed to disclosure of the settlement terms.

> **COMMENT:** The IRS has discovered valuation problems with façade easements. In some cases, the façade was already subject to restrictions under local zoning ordinances. As a result, the taxpayer would be giving up nothing, or very little. In elevating the suspensions to a news release from its National Office, the IRS is clearly sending a warning to other appraisers that it will be aggressive in contesting valuations.

Background

As discussed above, taxpayers may claim a charitable deduction for the value of a qualified conservation contribution. Façade easements may qualify as a qualified conservation contribution. Generally, taxpayers agree not to modify the façade of their historic building and they give an easement to this effect to a charitable organization. The easement must be granted exclusively for conservation purposes.

Settlement

In the news release, the IRS reported that the appraisers prepared reports valuing façade easements donated over several tax years. On behalf of each donating taxpayer, an appraiser completed Form 8283, *Noncash Charitable Contributions,* Part III, Declaration of Appraiser, certifying that the appraiser did not fraudulently or falsely overstate the value of the façade easement. In valuing the façade easements, the appraisers applied a flat percentage diminution, generally 15 percent, to the FMVs of the underlying properties prior to the easement's donation.

The appraisers acknowledged violating Section 10.22(a)(1) of Circular 230, for failing to exercise due diligence in the preparation of documents relating to IRS matters. The appraisers also acknowledged violating Section 10.22(a)(2) of Circular 230 for failing to determine the correctness of written representations made to Treasury.

> **COMMENT:** In the IRS news release, Karen Hawkins, director, IRS Office of Professional Responsibility, said:
>
> Appraisers need to understand that they are subject to Circular 230, and must exercise due diligence . . . .Taxpayers expect advice rendered with competence and diligence that goes beyond the mere mechanical application of a rule of thumb based on conjecture and unsupported conclusions.

The appraisers agreed to a five-year suspension of valuing façade easements and undertaking any appraisal services that could subject them to penalties under the tax code. The appraisers also agreed to abide by all applicable provisions of Circular 230, the IRS reported.

> **COMMENT:** If the claimed value is based on an appraisal and results in a substantial valuation misstatement, a substantial estate or gift tax valuation understatement, or a gross valuation misstatement, the appraiser may be liable for the Code Sec. 6662 penalty.

STUDY QUESTION

5. The Tax Court in *Friedberg II* rejected the IRS position that the appraiser was not qualified because:

   a. He was a member of the state's board of accountancy

   b. He held himself out to the public as an appraiser and was qualified to make appraisals

   c. He had substantial experience appraising development rights to make appraisals

   d. The appraisal was reliable

¶ 916 *WACHTER:* STATE LAW LIMITATION

State law may also limit the availability of an easement deduction. For example, the Tax Court denied a claimed charitable contribution deduction after finding that a purported easement granted in perpetuity was subject to a 99-year term under state law (*Patrick J. Wachter v. Commissioner,* 142 TC - , No. 7 (2014)). However, the taxpayers were allowed to proceed to trial on the merits relating to whether contemporaneous written acknowledgments of cash contributions substantiated their deductions.

> **COMMENT:** Code Sec. 170(h)(2)(C) requires that a qualified conservation contribution of qualified real property can be subject to a restriction only if that restriction is granted in perpetuity. However, the law of the state in which the real property existed in *Wachter* provided a maximum duration of 99 years for an easement on real property. The Tax Court noted that the case was unique in that this was the first time it had encountered a state law limiting the duration of an easement that could not be overcome by agreement.

Background

The taxpayers were four individuals (two married couples) who held interests in a partnership and also in an LLC taxed as a partnership. The LLC operated under two different, but similar, names. For 2004, the LLC made cash contributions to a charity, which the donee acknowledged in a letter along with a statement that the LLC had not received any goods or services in exchange for the donation. The letter used the name of the partnership in the acknowledgment. In response to a donation to the same donee in 2005, the donee addressed an unsigned acknowledgment letter to the LLC, using its second name. In 2006, this happened again. The taxpayers claimed their shares of the contribution deductions on their joint returns for these three years.

For these same three tax years, the partnership had sold conservation easements. The taxpayers claimed charitable deductions for their shares of the contributions on their returns.

The IRS determined that the cash contributions lacked contemporaneous written acknowledgments because the donee addressed the letters to the wrong entities. The IRS also determined that because state law restricted easements to 99 years, the donated land was not a qualified real property interest that could be donated in a qualified conservation contribution. Therefore, the taxpayers could not claim deductions for the value of the conservation easements.

Court's Analysis

The Tax Court found that the easements were not restrictions granted in perpetuity and were therefore not qualified conservation contributions. The 99-year period specified under state law was not a remote possibility, but an inevitable event.

However, the Tax Court found that there remained a genuine issue of material fact regarding whether the taxpayers could produce additional documents to meet the requirements of a contemporaneous written acknowledgment of their cash contributions. The government had not proved that the taxpayers expected to receive a benefit in exchange for their donations. Therefore, the issue was allowed to proceed to trial.

¶ 917 ESTATE TAX EXCLUSION

The executor of the estate of a decedent dying after 1997 may elect to exclude from the gross estate up to 40 percent of the value of land that is subject to a qualified conservation easement. The amount that may be excluded from the gross estate is limited to $500,000 in 2002 or thereafter. In addition, the exclusion applicable in any year is reduced by the amount of any charitable deduction that was taken with respect to the land under Code Sec. 2055(f).

Rule Changes Effective Beginning in 2013

The repeal of a distance requirement for the exclusion of a qualified conservation easement has been made permanent for the estates of decedents dying after December 31, 2012 (Code Sec. 2031(c)(8)(A); P.L. 112-240). Accordingly, for the estates of decedents dying after December 31, 2012, the exclusion for a qualified conservation easement will be available to any otherwise qualified real property that is located in the United States or any possession of the United States, that was owned by the decedent or a member of the decedent's family during the three-year period ending on the date of the decedent's death, and is subject to a qualified conservation easement granted by the decedent or a member of the decedent's family.

Previously, the exclusion for a qualified conservation easement was otherwise qualifying real property that was restricted to property located within 25 miles of a metropolitan area, national park, or wilderness area, or 10 miles of an Urban National Forest.

Date Used to Determine Values Extended

The clarification of the date used for determining the amount of the exclusion has also been made permanent for the estates of decedents dying after December 31, 2012. As a result, the values used in calculating the applicable percentage, including the value of the property subject to the easement and the value of the easement, for estates of decedents dying after December 31, 2012, will be determined as of the date of contribution.

> **COMPLIANCE NOTE:** The qualified conservation exclusion election is made by filing Form 706, *United States Estate (and Generation-Skipping Transfer) Tax Return,* Schedule U, Qualified Conservation Easement Exclusion, and claiming the exclusion on Page 3, Part 5, line 12. Once made, the election is irrevocable.

STUDY QUESTION

6. The exclusion rules effective starting in 2013 provide for all of the following *except:*
   a. Reducing the exclusion by any deduction amount claimed previously
   b. Application as of the date of the decedent's death
   c. A limit of 40 percent of the value of land, up to $500,000
   d. The exclusion election for estates is irrevocable

¶ 918 CONCLUSION

The IRS is responsible for ensuring that organizations and individuals do not abuse their tax deductions to charitable organizations. At the same time, it is also responsible for providing taxpayers with clear guidance and details regarding the specific compliance requirements donors and exempt organizations must follow. Legislative changes to the tax code provisions keep the IRS busy on one hand, whereas ever-inventive individuals and organizations challenge the IRS oversight abilities on the other hand. Constant attention to the rules and any changes is essential for any practitioner in the exempt organizations area.

MODULE 4: TAX REFORM/DEVELOPING LEGISLATIVE ACTION—Chapter 10: Tax Reform: Policy and Proposals

¶ 1001 WELCOME

Since enactment of the *Tax Reform Act of 1986* (P.L. 99-514), the U.S. tax code has steadily acquired new layers of complexity as Congress has inserted provisions designed to benefit myriad special interests, social goals, or certain economic behavior. Although interest in tax reform has never abated, the rash of corporate inversions has increased lawmakers' awareness of the mounting need for corporate tax reform. Numerous proposals have emerged for addressing these issues through fundamental tax reform, and in many cases they involve a complete overhaul of the existing tax code. The enormity of the task, however, means that final tax reform legislation is unlikely to happen quickly, according to Roger C. Altman, former deputy Treasury secretary. As an additional challenge, corporate tax reform and individual tax reform enacted in isolation would be difficult to achieve because the systems are highly interconnected. For example, many of the corporate tax preferences also benefit unincorporated businesses, like partnerships and Subchapter S corporations, which are subject to the individual income tax.

This chapter presents some of the important issues relating to tax reform that are currently under consideration.

¶ 1002 LEARNING OBJECTIVES

Upon completion of this chapter, you will be able to:

- Identify many possible reforms for corporate, small business, and individual taxation;
- Recognize the obstacles and concerns facing policymakers and lawmakers in addressing tax reform;
- Identify the proposals currently under debate in Congressional committee as a possible framework for tax reform in 2015 and beyond; and
- Identify who will be "winners and losers" depending upon which reforms eventually are approved.

¶ 1003 INTRODUCTION

Since the 1986 reform more than 15,000 changes have been made to the U.S. tax code. The resulting tax law has so many tax deductions, credits, exemptions, and exclusions that compliance is very burdensome: As of November 2013, the IRS estimated that it took the average Form 1040 filer 15 hours to do his or her own tax return—24 hours if a Schedule C, E, or F was involved. Reformers claim that the broken U.S. tax system stifles businesses and job growth, and these reformers have pushed for an overhaul of the current business tax system. Many reformers warn that high corporate tax rates and the tax on American businesses' foreign income deter profitable multinational corporations from setting up shop within our borders, and existing U.S. corporations that pay higher taxes are left with less capital to reinvest, innovate, and create jobs. However, there seems to be little public support for reducing high-end or corporate tax rates as part of tax reform unless the promise of jobs and economic prosperity are considered as equal partners in any "grand bargain."

Moreover, although most lawmakers believe that the patchwork tax code is broken, they have not been able to agree on how to fix it. On the Republican side, the proposed Tax Reform Act of 2014 would flatten the individual and corporate rate structures, with a top rate of 25 percent, and would collapse the current income brackets, adopt a larger standard deduction, enhance the child tax credit, and repeal more than 220 sections of the tax code, cutting its size by 25 percent. The Republican bill also claims to modernize the international tax code for the first time in more than 50 years. The Democrats want to close wasteful tax loopholes and special-interest subsidies that have benefitted the wealthiest Americans and biggest corporations. There are also proposals to simplify the tax-filing process, remove dead wood from the tax code, and leverage the technological advances that have been made since Congress last reformed the tax code in 1986. Both the Senate Finance Committee (SFC), controlled by Democrats, and the House Ways and Means Committee, controlled by Republicans, have held hearings on corporate, international, small business, and individual tax reform that have generated volumes of information about what should be done, how it should be done, and what might happen without tax reform. The road to tax reform will not be a straight one, but the gathering consensus among experts is that reform is coming.

¶ 1004 FUNDAMENTAL TAX REFORM: AN OVERVIEW

According to the Congressional Research Service Report, *Tax Reform in the 113th Congress: An Overview of Proposals* (March 24, 2014), comprehensive tax reform may be achieved either by modifying the existing income tax system ("base-broadening") or by adding a new source of tax revenue. Either approach could raise enough tax revenue to reduce marginal tax rates or to reduce the deficit. It is generally understood that effective and responsible tax reform should be structured so that the government will receive no fewer tax dollars than before reform (revenue neutrality). To be revenue neutral, any decrease achieved through lower rates must be offset either by increasing the number of taxpayers or finding new sources of revenue.

Base-Broadening

In the tax reform context, *base-broadening* means eliminating or restricting many of the exclusions, deductions, and credits currently available so that the tax rates can be applied to a larger portion of income. It also means increasing the number of taxpayers by including those who otherwise might not pay income taxes. Some individual deductions that could be targeted by base-broadening tax reform include the home mortgage interest deduction for owner-occupied residences and the deduction for property taxes on residences. Although these and other incentives are popular with taxpayers, reformers argue that Congress should consider whether the costs exceed the benefits and whether the exclusion, deduction, or credit is supporting the policy goal of the expenditure.

New Taxes

Some experts have argued that an alternative revenue source or tax, such as a consumption tax, is an option for improving economic efficiency. As an add-on tax, it could also allow for more tax expenditures to be retained or continued with fewer restrictions. The alternatives or add-ons to income taxes are a value-added tax, federal sales taxes, and other new tax varieties.

Value-added tax. A *value-added tax* (VAT) is a consumption tax on the value added to a product at each stage of production. The value added is the difference between the company's sales and its purchases from other companies. The VAT is collected by each company at every stage of production.

COMMENT: Similar to the VAT is the so-called flat tax, which is essentially a modified VAT, with wages and pensions subtracted from the VAT base and taxed at the individual level and a cash-flow tax for businesses.

EXAMPLE: Matthew Brady, a farmer, grows cotton and sells it to Spinex, a textile manufacturer for $110 ($100 + $10 VAT). Matthew then remits the $10 to the government. Spinex produces cloth and sells it to Forwear, a shirt manufacturer, for $550 ($500 + $50 in VAT). Spinex then remits $40 to the government ($50 - $10 paid to Matthew). Forwear makes 100 shirts and sells them to Buynow, a retailer, for $11 a piece or $1,100 ($1,000 + $100 in VAT). Forwear then remits $50 to the government ($100 - $50 paid to Spinex). Buynow sells the 100 shirts to consumers for $2,200 ($2,000 + $200 VAT) and remits $100 to the government ($200 - $100 paid to Forwear). The consumers end up paying $22 a piece for the shirts, which includes the entire 10 percent VAT.

COMMENT: Like state sales taxes, value-added taxes are regressive: They impose a heavier burden on low-income taxpayers as the ultimate consumer pays the entire tax. Unlike many state sales taxes, a federal VAT would most likely include sales of services. However, a VAT would be a great source of new revenue; many European countries already have one as an add-on to an income tax.

Sales tax. A *retail sales tax* is a consumption tax levied only at the retail stage. A federal retail tax would operate in much the same way as a state sales tax. The retailer would collect and remit a specific percentage of the retail price of a good or service. Because sales tax is collected only at one point in the production process, customers and sellers can work together more easily to evade it as the only way to ensure collection is an audit by the revenue authority.

Other taxes. Other potential new revenue sources include environmental taxes and financial services taxes. *Environmental taxes* may provide the dual benefit by simultaneously discouraging pollution and raising revenue. The most frequently discussed energy tax is a carbon tax that would be levied on the volume of carbon companies emit. Another energy tax option would be to raise gasoline taxes. In addition, taxes on the financial sector, including a securities transaction tax or taxes on systemically important financial institutions, have been discussed.

Tax Committees and Proposals

Several tax reform proposals have been introduced in the 113th Congress and lawmakers continue to consider various tax reform options. One goal of tax reform is to enhance economic efficiency by removing provisions that adversely affect decision making and economic output. Because the current tax code is widely seen as being overly complex, tax reform provides an opportunity to simplify the U.S. tax system while enhancing its equity and efficiency. Some of the current proposals are discussed below.

House Ways and Means Committee. In February 2014 Ways and Means Committee Chairman Dave Camp (R-Mich.) released a discussion draft bill: the Tax Reform Act of 2014. This proposal:

- Broadens the tax base;
- Restructures the statutory tax rates for both individual and corporate taxpayers;
- Changes the tax treatment of foreign-source income for U.S. multinational corporations; and
- Makes dozens of other changes to the federal tax system.

¶1004

Camp's bill also proposes a number of changes to existing passthrough and partnership tax rules, including rules related to partnership audits and adjustments and rules to restrict the use of publicly traded partnerships.

Senate Finance Committee. Former Finance Committee Chairman Max Baucus (D-Mon., now U.S. Ambassador to China) also released several discussion drafts related to international tax reform, tax administration, cost recovery and accounting, and energy tax policy. Under the international tax reform proposal, passive and highly mobile forms of foreign source earned income would be taxed at the U.S. rate, as would income earned from goods ultimately consumed in the United States. One option would subject all foreign earned income to a minimum tax; another would tax 60 percent foreign active business income at the U.S. rate. Reforms to cost recovery and accounting rules include eliminating the modified accelerated cost recovery system (MACRS) and replacing it with a system that uses asset pools and longer useful lives that more closely approximate economic depreciation. Certain intangibles, including research and experimentation as well as advertising expenses, would be capitalized and amortized. Last-in, first-out (LIFO) inventory rules would be repealed and small-business expense allowances would be increased so that more businesses would be allowed to use cash accounting.

The president's FY 2015 budget proposals. The tax proposals in the president's fiscal year (FY) 2015 budget comprise two groups. The first group contains business tax reforms that would pay for a reduction in the corporate tax rate by restricting or eliminating favorable depreciation and inventory methods. The business tax proposals include incentives for research, manufacturing, clean energy, and small business. This group also includes proposed changes to the U.S. international tax system, changes in the tax treatment of derivatives and insurance products, repeal of certain tax incentives for fossil fuels, and other changes.

Other proposals. Some tax reform efforts appear to be focused on reforming, rather than replacing, the current tax code. The Family Fairness and Opportunity Tax Reform Act (S. 1616) proposes substantive changes to the current income tax, including:

- Consolidating the tax brackets;
- Repealing the alternative minimum tax (AMT);
- Providing additional dependent and personal credits; and
- Eliminating the standard deduction and most itemized deductions but retaining, with modifications, the deductions for mortgage interest and charitable contributions, in addition to other changes.

However, several proposals would replace the current income tax system with an alternative federal tax:

- The Fair Tax Act of 2013 (H.R.25/S. 122) would repeal the current federal income tax system and replace it with a system that taxes consumption;
- The Flat Tax Act (H.R. 1040) and The Simplified, Manageable, and Responsible Tax (SMART) Act (S. 173) would impose a flat tax as an alternative to the current tax system; and
- The American Growth & Tax Reform Act of 2013 (H.R. 2393) would require the Treasury Secretary to submit a legislative proposal for a progressive consumption tax that would eliminate the public debt under three scenarios—
  - A consumption tax in addition to other taxes,
  - The consumption tax replacing the individual income tax, and
  - The consumption tax replacing the corporate income tax.

STUDY QUESTION

---

1. House Ways and Means Committee Chairman Dave Camp released the _____ bill in 2014.

    a. Tax Reform Act of 2014

    b. Family Fairness and Opportunity Tax Reform Act

    c. Fair Tax Act of 2013

    d. Flat Tax Act

¶ 1005 CORPORATE TAX REFORMS

The general consensus is that corporate tax reform is necessary because the United States has the highest corporate tax rate among the world's developed economies. All the member nations of the Organisation for Economic Cooperation and Development (OECD) have corporate tax rates that are lower than the combined U.S. rate. Thus, when companies are looking for a home from which to do business, they are less likely to select the United States. Reducing the corporate tax rate, it is thought, would increase after-tax corporate profits, raising stock values, inducing greater capital investment, and creating job growth.

> **COMMENT:** When reformers discuss the U.S. corporate tax rate, they include not only the statutory federal corporate rate of 35 percent but also state and local corporate taxes, which totals a rate of 39.10 percent on average. However, it is important to note that reformers also point out that many, if not most, U.S. corporations actually pay the 35 percent statutory rate as their effective tax rate when deductions, credits, and other tax benefits are computed.

Corporate Tax Reform Proposals

Lower corporate tax rate. There is a wide consensus in Congress that the U.S. corporate tax rate, especially the top rate of 35 percent applicable to most corporations with international business, must be decreased. The United States now has the highest corporate tax rate in the developed world, as shown in Table 1.

> **COMMENT:** The tax rate for corporations is:
>
> - 15 percent on the first $50,000 of taxable income;
>
> - 25 percent on the next $25,000;
>
> - 34 percent on taxable income exceeding $75,000 and not exceeding $10 million; and
>
> - 35 percent on taxable income of more than $10 million.

The U.S. corporate tax rate structure discourages businesses from investing in the United States, limits domestic growth, and increasingly pushes domestic corporations to increase their footholds in foreign jurisdictions where they can shield overseas earnings from U.S. taxes. A lower corporate tax rate would place the United States on an equal (or better) footing with other OECD members throughout Europe and Asia. According to the OECD, the current average combined corporate tax rate for the 33 developed countries listed in the table below is 26.03 percent.

Table 1. Comparative Corporate Tax Rates of Developed Countries

Country	Combined Corporate Income Tax Rate (%)
Australia	30.0
Austria	25.0
Belgium	34.0
Canada	26.3
Chile	20.0
Czech Republic	19.0
Denmark	24.5
Estonia	21.0
Finland	20.0
France	34.4
Germany	30.2
Greece	26.0
Hungary	19.0
Iceland	20.0
Ireland	12.5
Israel	26.5
Italy	27.5
Japan	37.0
Korea	24.2
Luxembourg	29.2
Mexico	30.0
Netherlands	25.0
New Zealand	28.0
Norway	27.0
Poland	19.0
Portugal	31.5
Slovak Republic	22.0
Slovenia	17.0
Spain	30.0
Sweden	22.0
Switzerland	21.1
Turkey	20.0
United Kingdom	21.0
United States	39.1

The proposed Tax Reform Act of 2014 provides for lowering the statutory corporate tax rate over five years from 35 to 25 percent. The proposal would also modify or eliminate a number of business tax expenditures. For example, the proposal would eliminate MACRS depreciation, modify the NOL deduction, phase out the domestic production credit, and repeal the LIFO inventory accounting method.

President Obama, within his annual budget, has proposed a lower corporate tax rate—28 percent. During the 2012 election year he proposed to do this by repealing LIFO for inventories, taxing carried interest income of hedge fund managers as ordinary income, and slashing oil and gas tax preferences. Obama's opponents remain unconvinced, and two years later all serious negotiations about comprehensive international tax reform—including how to lower the corporate tax rate—have broken down.

COMMENT: Because of the number of tax benefits available to corporate taxpayers, there is a great deal of variation in the current effective corporate tax rate among industries. Table 2 shows what S&P 500 companies in certain industries paid in combined corporate income taxes—federal, state, local, and foreign—from 2007 through 2012, according to the S&P Capital IQ.

Table 2. U.S. Effective Corporate Tax Rate by Sector*

Industry	Effective Tax Rate (%)
Energy	37
Financial	33
Health Care	28
Industrials (Manufacturing)	24
Information Technology	21
Pharma	26
Retail	34
Utilities	12

* **Source:** http://www.nytimes.com/interactive/2013/05/25/sunday-review/corporate-taxes.html.

Corporate inversions. Many U.S.-owned multinational corporations have decided that foreign incorporation is preferable to waiting for Congress to reform the tax code or enact a repatriation holiday like it did in 2004. The latest news of 2014 is that more and more U.S. domestic corporations are planning to "invert," meaning they will reorganize as a subsidiary of a foreign parent company incorporated in a lower-tax jurisdiction. Under current 2004 law, a U.S. corporation may take advantage of the lower corporate tax rates in a foreign jurisdiction through an inversion as long as at least 20 percent of its shares are held by the foreign company's shareholders after the merger. New anti-inversion proposals call for the foreign ownership requirement to be raised from 20 percent to as high as 50 percent.

One of the primary tax-related objectives of a corporate inversion is to lower taxes paid on foreign earnings. The U.S. government looks on inversions unfavorably because these foreign reorganizations will lower its corporate tax revenue potentially forever. Some lawmakers, including President Obama, Sen. Carl Levin (D-Mich.), and Rep. Sander Levin (D-Mich.) have pressed for antiinversion legislation as a temporary solution pending comprehensive tax reform. On the other hand, many policymakers and lawmakers hope that the fear of corporate inversions could pressure Congress to enact much-needed tax reform. The Obama Administration has also considered putting

¶1005

certain restrictions on inverted corporations, for instance by restricting the use of intercompany loans to U.S. subsidiaries and accompanying interest deductions.

Currently, most companies are not intimidated by the political discussions surrounding corporate inversions. Those that were planning mergers in May 2014 are for the most part still planning them. Some experts have noted the current political climate lacks the same momentum toward antiinversion legislation that existed in 2003 when current limitations were first developed. Yet as the nation moves closer to the presidential election year, corporate inversions will inevitably continue to be an important talking point.

Corporate Alternative Minimum Tax

The Tax Reform Act of 2014 would also repeal the corporate AMT and the rules that apply to personal service corporations.

> **COMMENT:** The Joint Committee on Taxation (JCT) analysis of the Tax Act of 2014 found that even though the statutory tax rates would be reduced, base-broadening provisions—including repeal of accelerated depreciation—would lead to higher effective tax rates on some capital investments. Overall, the JCT estimates that the increased cost of capital for domestic firms would lead to reduced investment in domestic capital stock. The net result of the JCT estimate suggests that the provisions would increase economic output.

STUDY QUESTION

2. The current rules allow U.S. corporations to invert and use foreign tax rates if _____ of shares are held by foreign company shareholders after the merger.

   a. 10 percent

   b. 20 percent

   c. 40 percent

   d. 51 percent

Business Tax Expenditures

Because of the relatively smaller corporate tax base, corporate tax expenditures are small relative to those for individuals. It is estimated that eliminating all corporate tax expenditures would only allow a reduction in the statutory tax rate from 35 percent to 28 or 29 percent. Therefore, in return for a 25 percent statutory tax rate, businesses would have to give up many, if not all, tax preferences. Moreover, for every tax preference retained, revenue would need to be raised elsewhere to keep the change revenue neutral. The tax preferences affecting corporations and other businesses most likely to face repeal include: MACRS, research and experimentation (R&E), advertising, domestic production activities, and LIFO.

MACRS. Tangible depreciable property placed in service after enactment of the *Tax Reform Act of 1986* must generally be depreciated over time in accordance with the modified accelerated cost recovery system (MACRS). The Tax Reform Act of 2014 would eliminate the recovery period and methods of MACRS and replace it with a system that uses asset pools and longer lives to more closely approximate actual economic depreciation. A system similar to the alternative depreciation system (ADS) rules would apply to depreciable property. The proposal would also lengthen the depreciable lives for depreciation of property placed in service after December 31, 2016.

The Senate Finance Committee draft from 2013 would have also overhauled the complex MACRs system and replaced it with one that would better approximate economic depreciation based on estimates from the Congressional Budget Office. The SFC draft bill would have reduced the number of major depreciable categories from 40 to 5. In addition, businesses would not have needed to calculate depreciation separately for each of their assets (other than real property).

COMMENT: Public companies already must use the straight-line method for purposes of depreciation on financial statements, so switching to a slower depreciation method does not affect the earnings statements they provide to investors and the Securities and Exchange Commission (SEC). Thus, most public companies generally support trading accelerated depreciation for a lower tax rate.

Research expenses. The Tax Reform Act of 2014 would change current treatment of research expense deductions. Under the proposed reform, all R&E expenditures would be amortized over a five-year period beginning with the midpoint of the tax year (mid-year convention) in which the expenditure is paid or incurred. The taxpayer would continue to amortize any property over the five-year period even if the property were abandoned or retired. Software development expenditures would be treated as R&E. Generally, the provision recognizes that R&E has a useful life beyond the tax year in which the expenses are incurred.

Research credits. The Tax Reform Act of 2014 features a modified research credit equal to:

- 15 percent of the qualified research expenses that exceed 50 percent of the average qualified research expenses for the preceding three tax years; plus
- 15 percent of the basic research that exceed 50 percent of the average basic research payments for the preceding three tax years.

Lawmakers and policy makers generally agree that the credit is essential to encouraging technological innovation, which in turn stimulates long-term economic growth. The credit has been renewed 15 times since its enactment. However, it has never been permanent. Most tax reform proposals would make the research credit permanent, although various modifications have been proposed.

Under Camp's proposal, a taxpayer would be able to claim a reduced research credit if the taxpayer had no qualified research expenses in any one of the preceding three tax years. The general 20 percent credit would be repealed, as well as the 20 percent credit for amounts paid for basic research and the 20 percent credit for amounts paid to an energy research consortium. In addition, amounts paid for supplies or with respect to computer software would no longer qualify as qualified research expenses. In addition, the special rule allowing 75 percent of amounts paid to a qualified research consortium and 100 percent of amounts paid to eligible small businesses, universities, and federal laboratories to qualify as contract research expenses would be repealed (though such amounts still would qualify as contract research expenses subject to the 65 percent inclusion rule). The election to claim a reduced research credit in lieu of reducing deductions otherwise allowed would also be repealed.

COMMENT: Making the alternative simplified research credit (ASC) the only method for calculating the credit would ease administrative burdens for taxpayers and the IRS by eliminating substantial amounts of recordkeeping, documentation issues, and controversy connected with the historical base-period credit. For example, using only the ASC would eliminate the need to document gross receipts, a key component of the historic base-period credit and a source of controversy with the IRS. Other changes, such as removing the cost of supplies from the credit calculation, would also reduce controversy with the IRS.

COMMENT: A number of bills introduced in Congress would permanently extend the research tax credit. In May 2014 the House passed the American Research and Competitiveness Act of 2014 (H.R. 4438), which would permanently extend a research tax credit for 20 percent of the qualified or basic research expenses that exceed 50 percent of the average qualified or basic research expenses for the 3 preceding taxable years, at an estimated 10-year cost of approximately $155.5 billion according to the Joint Committee on Taxation. The bill would also allow a 20 percent credit for amounts paid to an energy research consortium for energy research. On the Senate side, a tax extenders bill (S. 2260) that includes extension of the research tax credit through 2015 is under consideration. No further action has been taken on either bill since May.

Advertising expenses. The Camp proposal would allow only 50 percent of advertising expenses to be currently deducted and 50 percent would be amortized over a 10-year period. Advertising expenses would include any amount paid or incurred for development, production, or placement of any communication to the general public to promote the taxpayer's trade or business. Advertising expenses would also include wages paid to employees primarily engaged in activities related to advertising and the direct supervision of employees engaged in such activities. No deduction of unamortized expenses would be allowed if any property for which advertising expenses were paid or incurred were retired or abandoned during the 10-year amortization period.

Net operating losses. Under the proposed reform, C corporations could deduct an NOL carryover or carryback only to the extent of 90 percent of the corporation's taxable income (determined without regard to the NOL deduction). The special carryback rules for specified liability losses, bad debt losses of commercial banks, excess interest losses relating to corporate equity reduction transactions, and certain farming losses would be repealed. In addition, the proposal would repeal the expired special rules for losses incurred in 2008 and 2009, losses of certain electric utility companies, and losses related to the Hurricane Katrina and the Gulf Opportunity Zone. The provision would be effective for tax years beginning after 2014 and losses incurred after 2014 and carried back to prior years.

Domestic production activities. Under Code Sec. 199, taxpayers currently may claim a 6 or 9 percent deduction for qualified production activities. The deduction is limited to 50 percent of the W-2 wages paid by the taxpayer during the calendar year. The Code Sec. 199 deduction is one of the largest business tax breaks and cost the federal government approximately $14 billion in tax revenue for the 2013 tax year, according to the Joint Committee on Taxation. The deduction allows U.S. manufacturers to deduct a certain percentage of their gross receipts that are derived from qualified domestic production activities. Lawmakers and other stakeholders looking for ways to raise revenue by cutting tax breaks have argued that the definition of "qualified domestic production activities" is far too broad and complicates tax compliance.

Qualified production activities income is domestic production gross receipts less the cost of goods sold and expenses allocable to such receipts. Qualifying receipts are derived from:

- Property manufactured, produced, grown, or extracted within the United States;
- Qualified film productions;
- Electricity, natural gas, and potable water production;
- Construction activities within the United States; and
- Certain engineering or architectural services.

Under the reform Camp has proposed, the deduction for domestic production activities would be phased out, with the deduction reduced to 6 percent for tax years beginning in 2015, 3 percent for tax years beginning in 2016, and zero for tax years beginning after 2016.

> **COMMENT:** President Obama's Framework for Business Tax Reform, released in February 2012, vaguely hinted at a proposal to "focus the deduction more on manufacturing activity," proposed an increase in the deduction to 10.7 percent, and suggested pairing this favorable treatment of domestic manufacturing with a special 25 percent corporate tax rate for manufacturers. Neither plan has been much discussed since its release.

LIFO. Camp's Tax Reform Act of 2014 is the latest of a slew of proposals calling for the repeal of the LIFO accounting method. Its repeal would bring the United States in line with international financial reporting standards (IFRS). President Obama's proposed FY 2015 budget also would repeal LIFO and provide any Code Sec. 481(a) adjustment would be taken over 10 years.

Under the LIFO method of accounting, it is assumed that the last goods purchased or produced (i.e., the most recently purchased goods) are the first goods sold. The LIFO method of accounting is meant to match the most current sales against the most current inventory. However, the LIFO method can also be used to manipulate the cost of goods sold to inaccurately reflect profit margins and tax liability. In 2013, the Joint Committee on Taxation issued a report in conjunction with the president's FY 2014 budget proposal stating that if Congress were to repeal LIFO, the measure would generate more than $78 billion in federal tax revenue during the 10-year period between 2013 and 2023.

> **COMMENT:** Support for repeal is far from unanimous. Manufacturers holding inventory would be especially hurt by repealing LIFO because it pairs the newest income with the newest cost. In conjunction with the repeal of LIFO, the reform proposal would repeal the "lower of cost or market" method of inventory valuation.

In early June 2014, more than 110 bipartisan lawmakers led by Reps. Mike Thompson (D-Calif.) and James Lankford (R-Okla.) wrote to Rep. Camp, urging him to drop proposals to repeal. Thompson wrote that a repeal of LIFO would "have a devastating impact on businesses across our districts and country . . . .It will put people in the communities I represent out of work, punish businesses who have depended on this type of accounting for 70 years, increase their tax burden, and cause further economic uncertainty."

STUDY QUESTION

3. Which of the following is *not* a reason to repeal the LIFO accounting method?
   a. Repeal would align U.S. standards with IFRS
   b. Rep. Camp's and President Obama's proposals cite revenue increases possible with repeal
   c. Repeal would lower tax burdens for businesses using the LIFO system
   d. Repeal would curb manipulations of the cost of goods sold

¶ 1006 OTHER PROVISIONS

Accounting Method Changes

Cash method. Current law includes an array of rules for determining whether a taxpayer may use the cash method of accounting, with different kinds of businesses subject to different sets of rules. For example, a business that has inventory generally must use an accrual method of accounting, whereas personal service corporations may use the cash method. Under Camp's proposed reform, businesses with average annual gross receipts of $10 million or less could use the cash method, and businesses with more than $10 million would be required to use accrual accounting. The provision would not apply to farming businesses, which would continue to be subject to current law accounting rules, and sole proprietors could use the cash method regardless of the amount of gross receipts. Generally, taxpayers would be allowed to include any positive adjustments to income resulting from the provision over a four-year period beginning after 2018 or the taxpayer could elect to include the adjustments before 2019.

> **COMMENT:** Current law contains an array of complicated tax accounting rules and disjointed thresholds that make it difficult for small businesses to determine which method of accounting—cash or accrual—they may use for tax purposes. The provision simplifies and harmonizes this area of law for many businesses. Generally, the cash method is simpler and follows more closely the cash flows of their income and expenses. On the other hand, the accrual method provides a more accurate reflection of income. The provision strikes a balance between these two objectives that respects small businesses' need for simplicity.

Long-term contracts. Currently, a taxpayer that produces property under a long-term contract must use the percentage-of-completion method (PCM) to determine taxable income. However, small taxpayers that are building homes or that have contracts that should be completed within two years may use the completed-contract method, under which income is included when the contract is completed. Under the reform proposed, the completed-contract method would be limited to contracts estimated to be completed within two years for taxpayers having average gross receipts of $10 million or less over a three-year period. The special exception to the PCM rules for multiunit housing and shipbuilding contracts would be repealed.

International Tax System

There is much talk of changing the current U.S. system, which theoretically taxes worldwide income but defers tax on foreign earned income until it is repatriated to the United States, into a territorial system. A territorial system would tax U.S. source profits of multinational corporations but would exempt profits earned abroad. Changing from a worldwide to a territorial tax system would also create "winners and losers," even if a transition period accompanied the change. Concern over use of current foreign tax credit carryovers, for example, has been raised as a major issue if the international system changes too abruptly.

The Tax Reform Act of 2014 would make significant changes to the tax treatment of foreign source income earned by U.S. multinational corporations by adopting a 95 percent exemption for dividends received by U.S. corporations from foreign subsidiaries. In addition, there would be a one-time tax on previously untaxed foreign subsidiaries' earnings and profits (E&P), and E&P retained as cash would be taxed at 8.75 percent, whereas any remaining E&P would be taxed at 3.5 percent. Subpart F rules would be modified, providing broad taxation for intangible income of foreign subsidiaries when earned, with foreign intangible income subject to a phased-in 15 percent rate.

> **COMMENT:** According to the Treasury Department, a purely territorial system would aggravate many of the problems of the current tax code. If foreign earnings of U.S.-owned multinational companies are not taxed at all, for instance,

these firms would have greater incentive to locate operations overseas or use accounting mechanisms to shift profits out of the United States. Shifting profits abroad would also erode the U.S. tax base, requiring that more taxes be collected from U.S. taxpayers.

Dividends received deduction. Under the current U.S. tax system, foreign income earned by a foreign subsidiary of a U.S. corporation generally is not subject to U.S. tax until the income is distributed as a dividend to the U.S. corporation. To mitigate the double taxation on foreign earnings, the U.S. corporation is allowed a credit for foreign income taxes paid. A U.S. taxpayer may also elect to deduct foreign income taxes paid rather than claim the credit. Under the Tax Reform Act of 2014, the current system of taxing U.S. corporations on the foreign earnings of their foreign subsidiaries when the earnings are repatriated would be replaced with a dividend-exemption system. Under the exemption system, 95 percent of dividends paid by a foreign corporation to a 10 percent or more U.S. corporate shareholder would be exempt from U.S. taxation. No foreign tax credit or deduction would be allowed for any foreign taxes (including withholding taxes) paid or accrued with respect to any exempt dividend. The provision would be effective for tax years of foreign corporations beginning after 2014, and for tax years of U.S. shareholders in which or with which such tax years of foreign subsidiaries end.

> **COMMENT:** The dividend exemption would also apply to capital gains from sales of shares in foreign companies by 10 percent U.S. corporate shareholders. Thus, the effective U.S. tax rate on most foreign dividends would be 1.25 percent. Also, the provision would eliminate the "lockout" effect that discourages U.S. companies from bringing their foreign earnings back to the United States.

Deferred foreign E&P tax. The 10 percent U.S. shareholders of a foreign subsidiary would include in income their pro-rata share of the post-1986 historical E&P of the foreign subsidiary to the extent it had not been previously subject to U.S. tax. The E&P would be bifurcated into E&P retained in the form of cash, cash equivalents, or certain other short-term assets, versus E&P that had been reinvested in the foreign subsidiary's business (property, plant, and equipment). The portion of the E&P that consisted of cash or cash equivalents would be taxed at a special rate of 8.75 percent, whereas any remaining E&P would be taxed at a special rate of 3.5 percent. Foreign tax credits would be partially available to offset the U.S. tax.

If the U.S. shareholder were an S corporation, the provision would not apply until the S corporation ceased to be an S corporation, substantially all of the assets of the S corporation were sold or liquidated, the S corporation ceased to exist or conduct business, or stock in the S corporation were transferred.

Base erosion prevention. Currently, a U.S. parent is taxable on its pro-rata share of a foreign subsidiary's subpart F income, regardless of whether the income is distributed. Additionally, the U.S. parent's royalty income is subject to U.S. tax upon receipt of the income. However, under the transfer pricing rules, if a foreign subsidiary owns intangible property outside the United States, the U.S. parent may allocate profits to the foreign subsidiary without violating the subpart F rules, deferring U.S. tax on that income until it is distributed. The Tax Reform Act of 2014 would create a new category of subpart F income—*foreign base company intangible income* (FBCII)—consisting of the excess of the foreign subsidiary's gross income over 10 percent of the foreign subsidiary's adjusted basis in depreciable tangible property (except commodities). The U.S. parent would get a deduction for a percentage of the FBCII that relates to property used, consumed, or disposed of outside the United States.

> **COMMENT:** This provision would remove tax incentives to locate intangible property in low-tax or no-tax jurisdictions by providing neutral tax treatment of income attributable to intangible property, regardless of whether the property were located within or outside the United States. At the same time, the provision would

¶1006

provide a reduced U.S. tax rate on such income to the extent derived from foreign customers in recognition that it is difficult to identify precisely when the allocation of income to intangible property in foreign jurisdictions results in erosion of the U.S. tax base.

¶ 1007 SMALL BUSINESS TAX REFORM

Like large businesses, small businesses want fundamental tax reform in the shape of lower taxes and greater simplicity. Lower taxes would allow businesses to pay a lower portion of their profits to the government and allow organizations to reinvest that money in the company. Simplification of the complex U.S. tax code could decrease the cost of tax compliance, thus freeing time and capital for the business itself. Most tax reform plans suggest killing two birds with one stone. For example, the business provisions of the Tax Reform Act of 2014 attempt to address both concerns by proposing fewer marginal tax rates—meaning that many businesses would be in a lower tax bracket than they are currently—at the expense of many of the tax expenditures currently complicating the tax code. Tax reform could also introduce permanence to other provisions, such as the upfront deduction for purchases of tangible property for business use (Code Sec. 179 expensing) or the research tax credit. Such changes could simplify small business tax planning by infusing it with a certainty hitherto lacking. Following are more detailed descriptions of various reform proposals that would affect small businesses.

Tax Rates

The Tax Reform Act of 2014, following on the heels of past reform proposals, would drastically reduce the number of marginal tax brackets in the tax code. For the 2014 tax year there are seven income tax brackets for individuals and unincorporated businesses that are taxed at the individual rates (10, 15, 25, 28, 33, 35, and 39.6 percent). Camp's proposal would reduce the seven rates to only two individual rates: 10 and 25 percent. The intended effect is to lower taxes considerably for most taxpayers.

> **COMMENT:** This two-rate plan has been advocated before, notably by Camp himself and by others such as Rep. Paul Ryan (R-Wis.) in the "Path to Prosperity" FY 2015 budget resolution published by the House Budget Committee during the 2012 presidential campaign.

Code Sec. 179 Expensing

Code Sec. 179 provides an expense deduction to business taxpayers other than estates, trusts, or certain noncorporate lessors who elect to treat the cost of qualifying property as a current-year expense rather than a capital expenditure that must be depreciated and deducted slowly over the life of the property. The amount of the deduction that can be taken (the "dollar limit") and the cost of the property that qualifies (the "investment limit") are both limited by legislation, which must be reenacted from time to time. Congress often changes the limits from year to year, thus making it difficult for small businesses to plan how a particular asset purchase will affect their taxes in the future.

Table 3 recaps recent years' dollar limit for the Code Sec. 179 deduction. For the preceding three tax years, from 2010 through 2013, the limit was $500,000. However, for most of the 2012 tax year, the limit was presumed to be $125,000 until the $500,000 limit was retroactively extended by Congress in the *American Taxpayer Relief Act of 2012*. The table illustrates how the investment limit has also changed several times over the years, as has the percentage of available bonus depreciation.

Table 3. Changes in the Code Sec. 179 Deduction for 2007 Through 2014

Tax year	Dollar Limit	Investment Limit	Bonus Depreciation (%)
2007	$125,000	$ 500,000	—
2008-2009	$250,000	$800,000	50
2010	$500,000	$2,000,000	50
2011	$500,000	$2,000,000	100*
2012	$500,000	$2,000,000	50
2013	$500,000	$2,000,000	50
2014	$ 25,000	$200,000	50

* For qualifying MACRS property acquired after September 8, 2010, and before January 1, 2012, and placed in service before January 1, 2012.

> **COMMENT:** The definition of *qualified property* for Code Sec. 179 expensing purposes also is subject to change. Real property costs, for example, are not generally considered to be eligible for the deduction. However, there was a temporary exception that expired at the end of 2013 for certain costs associated with qualified leasehold, retail, or restaurant properties.

Camp's plan. The Tax Reform Act of 2014 would make permanent the dollar and investment limits under Code Sec. 179 (although with adjustments for inflation). Specifically, the draft bill would:

- Permanently increase the dollar limit for the deduction to $250,000;
- Begin to phase out the deduction for investments exceeding $800,000; and
- Permanently include certain computer software, qualified retail property, leasehold property, and restaurant property as "qualified property" for Code Sec. 179 purposes.

President's plan. In contrast, President Obama proposed in his FY 2015 budget proposal that the dollar limit and investment limit be permanently increased to $500,000 and $2 million, respectively, for tax years beginning after December 31, 2013. The president's plan did not address expensing rules for qualified retail and restaurant improvements.

Senate's plan. The Senate Finance Committee, formerly chaired by Max Baucus, released its own discussion draft in November 2013. The SFC draft also proposes increasing the investment limit to $2 million. The dollar limit would be significantly higher than in either Camp's or the president's proposals: $1 million. In addition the SFC would expand the definition of qualifying property to include off-the-shelf computer software, research and experimental expenditures, and certain advertising costs that are required to be capitalized and amortized.

> **COMMENT:** Although the SFC's proposals for Code Sec. 179 have not churned up any significant discussion of late, they were based on the Bipartisan Tax Fairness and Simplification Act of 2011 (S. 727, 112th Congress), which was cosponsored by Baucus's successor, Sen. Ron Wyden. With Wyden chairing the SFC, the committee's draft proposals may surface again in the future.

STUDY QUESTION

4. The dollar limit of $1 million for Code Sec. 179 deductions has been proposed in:

    a. President Obama's FY 2015 budget
    b. Camp's proposed Tax Reform Act of 2014
    c. The Senate Finance Committee discussion draft of November 2013
    d. The *American Taxpayer Relief Act of 2012*

Other Business Tax Reform Proposals

Creating an online platform for Form 1099 preparation. The SFC's November 2013 draft bill would require the IRS to develop an online platform for preparing and filing Form 1099. Additionally, businesses would be required to show how much of their gross receipts and expenses are reflected in separately filed Forms 1099 by breaking the amounts out on their Form 1040, Schedule C.

Like-kind exchanges. Also at stake in the tax reform debate is the Code Sec. 1031 like-kind exchange. In brief, Code Sec. 1031 provides that no gain or loss is recognized upon the exchange of property held for productive use in a trade or business or for investment if the property received is of a like kind and is held either for productive use in a business or for investment. This provision has been subject to some abuse, notably by related parties who claimed that exchanges of property fell under Code Sec. 1031 in order to avoid taxes.

Camp has proposed Code Sec. 1031's complete repeal. The president in his various budget proposals and the SFC would severely limit the reach of Code Sec. 1031. The SFC proposal, for example, would eliminate like-kind exchanges of real property.

Carried interest. President Obama has proposed taxation of carried interest paid to hedge fund managers as ordinary income, rather than as capital gain. The reasoning behind this is that much of the carried interest income is received in connection with the performance of services and is not attributable to an investment in the partnership, Treasury indicated.

    COMMENT: The president reasserted his intention to tax carried interest during a July 2014 interview. "If you're making a billion dollars a year and you're paying 15 percent on that, when your secretary is paying 23 percent, that's not fair."

REITs. A corporation, trust, or association that acts as an investment agent specializing in real estate and real estate mortgages may elect to be a real estate investment trust (REIT) under Code Sec. 856. In general, REITs, unlike ordinary corporations, are entitled to claim a deduction for dividends paid to shareholders against their ordinary income and net capital gains.

In recent years a large number of C corporations have begun to convert themselves into REITs, leading many reformers to suspect abuse of the tax code. Camp's Tax Reform Act of 2014 addresses these concerns by adding stringent restrictions on the ability of C corporations to convert to REITs. For example, the proposal would require immediate taxation of all built-in gains upon a C corporation's conversion. Previously, built-in gains were taxed over a 10-year period.

Eliminating estate taxes. Many small business owners have suggested that Congress eliminate the estate tax. Because small businesses are so often owned by families or closely held among a small number of people, the death of one owner can significantly impact business operations and/or the division of assets. Small businesses must plan for the estate tax if they want to keep the business operating after the death or retirement of their owner; repeal of the estate tax could save time and money.

¶1007

Passthrough Reform

In his 2013 small business discussion draft, Camp also proposed a more drastic reform of passthrough business taxation, which would revise the rules under Subchapter S and Subchapter K governing, respectively, S corps and partnerships. These existing rules would be replaced by one unified set of rules. These new rules would:

- Expand eligibility of most passthrough corporations to elect S corp treatment;
- Loosen current restrictions on who may be an S corp shareholder; and
- Impose a withholding requirement on a passthrough with respect to certain amounts of each passthrough owner's distributive share, and more.

Specifics of the proposals follow.

Built-in gain and S corps. For S corps, Camp proposed reduction of the recognition period for computing the Code Sec. 1374 tax on built-in gains from 10 years to 5 years.

Passive investment income rules. Camp proposed increasing the Code Sec. 1375 threshold percentage over which an S corp's net passive income is subject to the highest corporate tax rate. Camp's draft proposal would increase the current 25 percent threshold for net passive income in excess of gross receipts to 60 percent. This would enable S corps with passive net investment income between 25 and 60 percent of their gross receipts to retain their S corp status.

Passthroughs, basis, and tax avoidance. Camp suggested that one means of curbing the use of passthroughs in tax avoidance schemes would be to limit loss deductions to an investor's basis in his or her passthrough interest, while allowing excess losses to be carried forward indefinitely.

> **COMMENT:** Camp emphasized that his plan for passthrough reform is meant to accompany tax cuts for individuals and corporations. In contrast, former Sen. Max Baucus, who in 2013 was Camp's tax reform counterpart in the SFC, only supported corporate tax cuts. Some experts have stated that it is logically incongruous to attempt to stimulate U.S. business by lowering corporate tax rates but leaving passthrough tax rates (meaning the individual rates) high.

STUDY QUESTION

---

5. Camp's passthrough entity taxation rules would provide all of the following *except:*

    a. A withholding requirement for shareholders

    b. Expanded eligibility to elect treatment as an S corp

    c. Requiring built-in gains to be recognized in the current tax year

    d. Easing current restrictions on taxpayers seeking to be S corp shareholders

---

¶ 1008 INDIVIDUAL TAX REFORMS

Comprehensive reform of the tax code provisions affecting individuals could also involve drastic reduction of tax rates. In exchange for this, however, a number of tax incentives for individuals would need to be enhanced or repealed to retain revenue neutrality. Camp's proposal, for example, would cut tax rates for most individuals and increase the amount of the child tax credit. But it would repeal the deduction for personal exemptions, the medical expense deduction for itemizers, and most tax preferences for taxpayers in the 35 percent bracket. Camp's plan even proposes modification of the previously sacrosanct mortgage interest deduction and charitable contributions deduction.

Mortgage Interest Deduction

The mortgage interest deduction is one of the most costly tax benefits for individuals, and some law and policymakers have acknowledged that if revenue neutral tax reform is to take place, the mortgage interest deduction must be altered in some way. The Tax Reform Act of 2014, for example, would effectively reduce the amount of the deduction by limiting it to interest paid on the first $500,000 of acquisition indebtedness after a gradual four-year phaseout of the current limit. At present the limit is on the first $1 million of acquisition debt. The proposal would also eliminate the deduction for interest accruing on a home equity loan.

> **COMMENT:** Proponents of reform of the mortgage interest deduction have argued that the tax benefit favors higher-income households far and away above lower-and middle-income households. The Center on Budget and Policy Priorities stated that approximately 77 percent of the total tax benefits from the deduction went to homeowners with incomes above $100,000.

Charitable Deductions

The Tax Reform Act of 2014 would limit the amount that a taxpayer could deduct for contributions to charity to the excess of donations over 2 percent of the taxpayer's gross income. Camp argued that the bill as a whole would stimulate the economy and thereby increase charitable giving. Many nonprofit organizations argue on the other hand that the 2 percent floor on giving would reduce the number of taxpayers eligible to take the deduction and reduce incentive for many to make charitable contributions.

Repealing the Deduction for State and Local Taxes

Camp would also eliminate the deduction for state and local taxes to pay for his proposed the across-the-board tax rate cuts. The state and local tax deduction has been in place since the inception of the U.S. income tax code in 1913. The deduction allows individual income taxpayers who itemize to deduct from their income the cost of income taxes, property taxes, and sales taxes paid to state and local governments. The Committee for a Responsible Federal Budget (CRFB), a Washington, D.C., public policy organization, reported in 2013 that with an estimated cost of $1.1 trillion for the deductions between 2013 and 2023, the state and local tax deduction was the seventh largest tax expenditure in the tax code.

Alternative Minimum Tax

The AMT is a separate method of determining tax liability designed to ensure that taxpayers do not completely avoid income tax through the use of deductions, exemptions, losses, and credits. Many lawmakers and others have complained that the AMT represents an ineffectual means of curtailing the use of certain tax preferences and that the purpose of the AMT can be fulfilled within the regular tax system. As such, many proposals for tax reform, including the Tax Reform Act of 2014, would eliminate this parallel system for individuals as well as small businesses with taxes paid at the individuals' rate. Camp noted that repeal of the AMT would cost more than $1.3 trillion over 10 years.

STUDY QUESTION

6. Which change to the residential interest deduction is proposed in the Tax Reform Act of 2014?

    a. Eliminating the mortgage interest deduction

    b. Increasing the deduction for interest on a home equity loan

    c. Capping the amount of acquisition debt eligible for the deduction

    d. Eliminating any residential interest deduction for taxpayers with annual incomes exceeding $100,000

¶ 1009 CONCLUSION

Tax reform is not easy. Rep. Dave Camp's proposed Tax Reform Act of 2014 was years in the making. It was designed to drum up serious discussion that would lead to legislation. In reality it did little to reanimate immediate tax reform talks. Nevertheless, there is a strong consensus that comprehensive tax reform is necessary, in the international arena in particular. As more U.S. corporations move their headquarters offshore for tax reasons, Congress is sitting up to take notice. Some lawmakers are poised for action but cannot agree on key points: the proper corporate tax rate, the number of expenditures to cut, the degree of the cuts, the role of the energy sector in tax reform, and more. Consensus at the present time seems to be that tax reform is inevitable because it is necessary; that the detailed discussions and research on tax reform over the past several years have provided the framework upon which eventual tax reform will eventually rest; and that the "political will" necessary to move tax reform forward to its conclusion will be found—if not sometime after the 2014 mid-term Congressional elections, then as a centerpiece of the next administration in 2016.

¶ 10,100 Answers to Study Questions
¶ 10,101 MODULE 1—CHAPTER 1

1. a. *Incorrect.* Receipt of the tax credit is a trigger for both types of the liability.

b. *Correct.* **Section 4980H(a) liability applies when no higher than 70 percent (for 2015) of employees may enroll in minimum essential coverage; for Code Sec. 4980H(b), it is 95 percent.**

c. *Incorrect.* Salary differences do not determine the type of liability triggered.

d. *Incorrect.* Both types of liability are credited by applicable large employers.

2. a. *Correct.* **Hours of part-time employees are aggregated to determine full-time equivalent employees.**

b. *Incorrect.* Volunteer hours are not measured even if volunteers are reimbursed for expenses.

c. *Incorrect.* Leased employees are not considered employees under Code Sec. 4980H.

d. *Incorrect.* Hours of student interns as well as work-study program participants are not counted for Code Sec. 4980H.

3. a. *Correct.* **The safe harbors enable employers to calculate affordability of their health plans based on numbers they know—the employees' wages, rate of pay, and federal poverty line—rather than the unknown total household income of the employees**

b. *Incorrect.* All of the safe harbors figure plan affordability based on self-only coverage.

c. *Incorrect.* Small employers were already exempt from providing coverage under the Affordable Care Act.

d. *Incorrect.* The effective date for applicable large employers remains the 2015 tax year.

4. a. *Correct.* **Months are not a unit for measuring hours of service; plus, salaried employees may be assumed to work some hours every month.**

b. *Incorrect.* Both hourly and salaried workers' actual hours of service may be totaled in calculating the employer's assessable payment.

c. *Incorrect.* The employer may use the salaried person's weeks-worked equivalency of 40 hours of service.

d. *Incorrect.* Salaried employees may be credit with 40 hours of service per week using the days-worked equivalency.

5. a. *Incorrect.* A spouse, even when unemployed, is not a dependent under Code Sec. 4980H.

b. *Incorrect.* A foster child is not considered a dependent for employer plan coverage under Code Sec. 4980H rules.

c. *Correct.* **Biological children younger than age 26 are dependents under Code Sec. 4980H.**

d. *Incorrect.* A stepchild is not a dependent for employer plan coverage under Code Sec. 4980H.

6. a. *Incorrect.* Transition relief commences later than January 1, 2014.

b. *Correct.* **Maintenance of workforce and health plan coverage for this period is required for transition relief.**

c. *Incorrect.* A shorter period is being used to qualify employers for transition relief.

d. *Incorrect.* Requirements became effective for transition relief earlier than 2015.

¶ 10,102 MODULE 1—CHAPTER 2

1. a. *Correct.* **The optional method does not apply to standby emergency spare parts; they are not intended to be installed as are the parts that are deductible upon installation and included in income when removed.**

b. *Incorrect.* The optional method is applicable to rotable spare parts whose costs are deductible when installed and included in gross income when removed.

c. *Incorrect.* Temporary spare parts installed until new or repaired parts can be installed may be deducted using the optional method if their fair market value is included in income when removed.

d. *Incorrect.* One category of spare parts may not use the optional method.

2. a. *Correct.* **Other routine maintenance activities include inspection and cleaning of the equipment.**

b. *Incorrect.* The taxpayer must expect to perform the activities more than once during the class life of the unit of property, and for buildings, more than once during the 10 years after placement in service.

c. *Incorrect.* Betterment expenses are a type of capitalized improvement rather than currently deductible as routine maintenance expenses.

d. *Incorrect.* Taxpayers are cautioned against using the safe harbor for scheduled maintenance performed shortly after purchase of the used machine or existing building. Routine maintenance only includes maintenance that is required on account of wear and tear occurring while the taxpayer owned the property.

3. a. *Incorrect.* The costs of replacing major components when the taxpayer rebuilds a unit of property are capitalized. The reuse or replacement of major components when the taxpayer rebuilds an asset to a like-new condition is not determinative of whether other costs are deductible.

b. *Correct.* **After the end of the unit of property's class life, all costs are capitalized, but rebuilding prior to the end of the class life enables some portions to be deductible as repairs.**

c. *Incorrect.* For rebuilding projects, the purchase date is not the determinant of whether costs must be capitalized or deducted.

d. *Incorrect.* The owner's intent in selling the rebuilt the property does not dictate whether costs are deducted or capitalized.

4. a. *Incorrect.* Because the Code Sec. 481(a) adjustment is equal to the difference between the amount deducted as a repair expense and the amount of the repair expense that would have been depreciated prior to the year of change if it were capitalized, there is no adjustment if the capitalized amount would be fully depreciated prior to the year of change.

b. *Incorrect.* There is no accounting method change and, therefore, no Code Sec. 481(a) adjustment, if an item has only been erroneously treated on one filed tax return. An amended return is filed in such a case.

c. *Correct.* **The cost of replacing a major component must be capitalized unless the routine maintenance safe harbor applies and a taxpayer who claimed a repair expense for such a replacement is not excepted from filing Form 3115 and computing a Code Sec. 481(a) adjustment solely on the basis of the fact that a major component was involved.**

d. *Incorrect.* No Code Sec. 481(a) adjustment is required to change to a method that applies to amounts paid or incurred in tax years beginning on or after January 1, 2014, if the amount was paid or incurred in a tax year beginning before that date.

5. a. *Incorrect.* There is no IRS filing fee for automatic consent changes, but a $7,000 filing fee applies for nonautomatic advance consent changes.

b. *Incorrect.* Rev. Proc. 2012-19 provided the procedures for compliance with the temporary regulations for Form 3115 filings on or before January 24, 2014.

c. *Correct.* **Rev. Proc. 2014-16 supersedes Rev. Proc. 2012-19 and lists procedures for securing IRS consent to change to an accounting method under the final or temporary repair regulations effective for Forms 3115 filed after January 24, 2014.**

d. *Incorrect.* Rev. Proc. 2014-16 only waves the scope limitations for tax years beginning before January 1, 2015.

6. a. *Incorrect.* Schedule E is not used to indicate use of one of the safe harbors.

b. *Incorrect.* Schedule E is not completed to indicate a change to comply with UNICAP rules; rather, the change is reported on the same Form 3115 used for the repair regulations.

c. *Incorrect.* The Code Sec. 481(a) adjustment is reported directly on Form 3115, Part IV, line 25.

d. *Correct.* **The taxpayer uses Schedule E to report the depreciation period, method, and convention used for a prior repair expense that is now capitalized as well as reasons the repair expense is now treated as depreciable.**

¶ 10,103 MODULE 1—CHAPTER 3

1. a. *Incorrect.* The material participation rules require substantial participation in the trade or business—for most individuals, at least 500 hours per year.

b. *Correct.* **The individual need not serve in a managerial capacity if other requirements for material participation are satisfied.**

c. *Incorrect.* To qualify as material participation, the individual must participate in the activity continuously, as substantiated by daily time reports or logs.

d. *Incorrect.* Material participation must be regular, as substantiated by daily reports or logs, or alternatively for most individuals, for more than 500 hours during the year.

2. a. *Incorrect.* Merely aggregating the income and expenses on tax returns does not constitute the election.

b. *Incorrect.* The election is not made on Schedule K-1, which is completed by the entity, not the individual.

c. *Correct.* **The statement of election should accompany the individual's tax return.**

d. *Incorrect.* Multiply real estate activities may not be grouped and do not signify an election to aggregate real estate activities.

3. a. *Incorrect.* Currently one determination of eligibility to be a limited partner is limited liability under applicable state law, but the proposed regulations change the criterion.

b. *Incorrect.* Currently one determination of eligibility to be a limited partner is designation as a limited partner in the partnership agreement, but the proposed regulations change the criterion.

c. *Correct.* **The proposed regulations eliminate the reliance of the limited partner designation in the partnership agreement or state law, so the sole requirement is the individual's right to participate in management of the entity.**

d. *Incorrect.* The criterion provided in the proposed regulations does not require any certain percentage of allocable income and expenses for the limited partner.

4. a. *Correct.* **The self-charged interest rules apply to both owners' loans to a passthrough entity and the entity's loans to its owners, as well as loans between passthrough entities.**

b. *Incorrect.* The self-charged interest rules are applied to additional circumstances than owners' loans to the passthrough entity.

c. *Incorrect.* Additional transactions trigger the use of the self-charged interest rules for passthrough entities.

d. *Incorrect.* Other transactions are also subject to the self-charged interest rules.

5. a. *Incorrect.* Exploring for or exploiting geothermal deposits must not be grouped with activities for oil and gas.

b. *Correct.* **Such holding, production, and distribution activities may be grouped for films along with video tapes.**

c. *Incorrect.* Real property rental activities must not be grouped with activities involving personal property rentals.

d. *Incorrect.* Interests in publicly traded partnerships must be treated separately from activities of other entities.

6. a. *Incorrect.* Recognition of suspended losses is triggered by death of the taxpayer.

b. *Incorrect.* The owner's complete abandonment of an interest in a passive activity triggers recognition of the suspended losses.

c. *Correct.* **An exchange under Code Sec. 351 or transfer under Code Sec. 721 does not trigger suspended loss recognition.**

d. *Incorrect.* Treatment of a security as a sale or exchange triggers the suspended loss recognition if the security is worthless.

¶ 10,104 MODULE 2—CHAPTER 4

1. a. *Incorrect.* The public key identifies the digital wallet and is visible on the block chain.

¶10,104

b. *Incorrect.* Sites such as Blockchain.info enable users to create free wallets, and few merchants charge transaction fees to purchasers.

c. *Correct.* **The wallet's owner holds the private key to access the wallet and make payments in Bitcoin.**

d. *Incorrect.* Virtual currency transactions may not be reversed.

2. a. *Incorrect.* Virtual currency has been used to avoid tax assessments for foreign accounts under FATCA rules.

b. *Incorrect.* Bitcoin transactions have been associated with illicit transactions involving narcotics and money laundering.

c. *Incorrect.* Hackers have infected users' computers with viruses that lock files until users render Bitcoins to the hackers' addresses.

d. *Correct.* **"Conversions" do not occur with virtual currency, and transactions are fee-free or inexpensive with currency like Bitcoin.**

3. a. *Incorrect.* Virtual currency miners are not traders in currency conversions because virtual currencies are not currencies for federal tax purposes.

b. *Incorrect.* Virtual currencies are not considered investments, so miners are not treated as counselors or brokers.

c. *Correct.* **As financial services providers, miners realize gross income on receipt, not sale, or virtual currency.**

d. *Incorrect.* A taxpayer creating virtual currency is not treated as a prospector and its income is taxed as ordinary income.

4. a. *Correct.* **California treats virtual currencies as cash alternatives, not transactions of currency.**

b. *Incorrect.* California law facilitates use of virtual currencies and other exchange media as cash alternatives.

c. *Incorrect.* States considering virtual currencies as high-risk investments include Massachusetts, Wisconsin, and Florida.

d. *Incorrect.* Massachusetts, Wisconsin, and Florida regulations treat crypto-currencies as investments.

5. a. *Incorrect.* Because they accept deposits regularly, the exchanges are considered FFIs subject to FATCA rules.

b. *Correct.* **Online wallets do not need to be reported.**

c. *Incorrect.* Under FATCA, foreign Bitcoin entities are considered FFIs if controlled by U.S. taxpayers.

d. *Incorrect.* Summary information about Bitcoin deposit accounts should be reported in Part V of Form 8938.

6. a. *Correct.* **Sales or exchanges of virtual currencies do not create income and should be included as subpart F income of CFOs.**

b. *Incorrect.* Virtual currencies are not expressly included or covered under like-kind exchange rules for deferral of recognition of gain or loss.

c. *Incorrect.* Rules remain unclear regarding whether contributions of virtual currency are intangible or tangible property.

d. *Incorrect.* It remains unclear whether virtual currency exchange rates should be considered a specified index for virtual currency payments.

¶ 10,105 MODULE 2—CHAPTER 5

1. a. *Correct.* **A foreign estate is not a U.S. person under FATCA, although other estates are.**

b. *Incorrect.* A domestic corporation or partnership is considered a U.S. person under FATCA.

c. *Incorrect.* A specified person holding an interest in a specified foreign financial asset must file Form 8938 even if the reported assets do not affect his or her tax liability.

d. *Incorrect.* Any domestic entity serving to hold specified foreign financial assets is a specified person.

2. a. *Incorrect.* Under FATCA requirements, unless the account is owned by a bona fide resident of the U.S. territory, it is subject to reporting on Form 8938.

b. *Incorrect.* A currency swap and similar agreements with a foreign counterparty are other specified foreign financial assets.

c. *Correct.* **The stock is not reportable on Form 8938 if a bona fide resident of Guam (a U.S. possession) is the owner.**

d. *Incorrect.* An interest in a foreign entity is reportable on Form 8938 even if the account is not maintained by an FFI.

3. a. *Correct.* **Each spouse includes just half of the value of the jointly owned assets in his or her foreign financial assets for reporting.**

b. *Incorrect.* Each of the owners not married to each other must list the entire value of the jointly owned asset in determining his or her total assets.

c. *Incorrect.* A parent electing to include a child's unearned income by filing Form 8814 lists the jointly owned asset's value on the parent's Form 8938.

d. *Incorrect.* When one spouse is not a specified person, each spouse includes the entire value of the jointly owned asset in determining the total specified foreign financial assets.

4. a. *Incorrect.* The limitations period is extended to six years even for classes of assets that the IRS excepts from the reporting requirements if the assets increase gross income by $5,000 or more.

b. *Incorrect.* The statutory period is extended to six years even when omissions of gross income of more than $5,000 are properly reported.

c. *Correct.* **If the omitted income is less than $5,000, the normal three-year limitations period applies.**

d. *Incorrect.* The duration of the limitations period is extended to six years even when the assets' value is less than the reporting threshold if gross income from the assets increases by at least $5,000.

5. a. *Incorrect.* The maximum fine for tax evasion is $250,000.

b. *Incorrect.* Filing a false return incurs up to a $250,000 fine, which is half as much as the fine for another individual tax violation.

c. *Correct.* **Failure to file an FBAR carries a fine of up to $500,000, double the fine applied to other individual tax law violations.**

d. *Incorrect.* Defrauding the government carries a fine of up to $250,000; the violation's maximum prison term is five years.

6. a. *Incorrect.* All penalties for U.S. citizens dwelling in the United States have not been eliminated, but the procedure applies to more noncompliant taxpayers.

b. *Correct.* **Starting in 2014, the procedures apply to taxpayers whose failure to disclose offshore assets was nonwillful, and the low-risk threshold is not required.**

c. *Incorrect.* The Streamlined Procedure has been expanded to include more taxpayers, not narrowed in scope.

d. *Incorrect.* The liability threshold for eligibility to use the procedure was not raised.

¶ 10,106 MODULE 3—CHAPTER 6

1. a. *Incorrect.* Single taxpayers with incomes of less than $601,000 are eligible to make nondeductible contributions for 2014.

b. *Incorrect.* Total earned income of less than $96,000 for 2014 qualifies joint filers to make a full nondeductible IRA contribution.

c. *Incorrect.* Taxpayers age 50 and older may contribute $6,500 of earned income for 2014.

d. *Correct.* **Taxpayers must have earned compensation to make a nondeductible contribution for 2014.**

2. a. *Incorrect.* Hardship distributions from qualified plans may not be used as rollover amounts.

b. *Incorrect.* Required minimum distributions are not eligible for rollover treatment.

c. *Correct.* **Nongovernmental 457(b) plans of tax-exempt organizations are not eligible for rollovers.**

d. *Incorrect.* Corrective distributions may not be rolled over.

3. a. *Correct.* **The receiving employer plan may refuse or limit the transfer.**

b. *Incorrect.* Withholding does not apply unless the trustee-to-trustee transfer is partial, in which case withholding would apply to the amount distributed to the taxpayer if the amount is more than $200.

c. *Incorrect.* Inherited IRAs may not be transferred to an employer plan.

d. *Incorrect.* Trustee-to-trustee transfers often entail the individual delivering a check payable to the new plan or trustee.

4. a. *Correct.* **The taxpayer must wait until the beginning of the next tax year after the conversion to reconvert.**

b. *Incorrect.* Although typically implemented when the traditional IRA's value has *decreased,* a reconversion is allowed even for account whose value has increased.

c. *Incorrect.* If the recharacterization is done within 30 days of the end of the year of the conversion, the delay is extended 30 days, beginning on the date the owner recharacterized the account as a Roth.

d. *Incorrect.* The rules do not disallow reconversions to the same Roth account from which the taxpayer recharacterized the assets.

5. a. *Incorrect.* Lacking a rollover, the tax is due when the distribution is made, with some plans spreading the distribution over five years if the beneficiary so chooses.

b. *Correct.* **The nonspouse beneficiary may establish an inherited IRA for the assets, with RMDs required thereafter annually.**

c. *Incorrect.* The nonspouse beneficiary may take distributions before he or she reaches age 591/2 without incurring an early withdrawal penalty, though he or she may be subject to a 10 percent early withdrawal penalty, depending on the decedent's age.

d. *Incorrect.* A domestic partner does not have the same rights as a same-sex spouse for distributions from the decedent's account.

6. a. *Incorrect.* The 10 percent tax applies to early withdrawals (for employees younger than age 591/2) from IRAs, 401(k)s, and 403(b) accounts.

b. *Correct.* **Early withdrawals during the two-year period starting on the date of first participation are subject to a 25 percent tax unless one of the exceptions applies.**

c. *Incorrect.* No tax of 50 percent is applied to SIMPLE plan early withdrawals.

d. *Incorrect.* Early withdrawals are permitted but subject to a tax within two years of the employee's first participation.

¶ 10,107 MODULE 3—CHAPTER 7

1. a. *Incorrect.* Simply having a second office at home does not allow an employee to deduct its expenses.

b. *Incorrect.* The exclusive use test applies to employees, and any use for personal activities is not allowed if a deduction is claimed.

c. *Incorrect.* An employee's home office use must be regular to be deductible.

d. *Correct.* **All of the exclusive and regular use requirements must be met and the office must be for the employer's convenience.**

2. a. *Incorrect.* More space for a home office may be deductible using the actual expense method.

b. *Incorrect.* Losses may be carried forward under the actual expense method but not the safe harbor method.

c. *Correct.* **Gain is potentially taxable on the portion of the residence claimed as a home office using either method.**

d. *Incorrect.* Only the actual expense method allows deductions for home offices in multiple homes.

3. a. *Incorrect.* An urban office worker with a regular place of business may deduct bus fare for a two-week suburban assignment because the temporary assignment is located in a densely populated and socially integrated area around the city.

b. *Correct.* **Expenses of any type of vehicle used for a two-year period at the same location are not considered deductible commuting costs to a temporary location.**

c. *Incorrect.* A one-week commute by a self-employed person to attend a professional gathering is considered temporary.

d. *Incorrect.* Costs of a temporary commute for professional duties within the same metropolitan area are deductible.

4. a. *Correct.* **Separately deductible expenses for the business standard mileage rate include interest on the vehicle's loan as well as parking fees, tools, and property taxes attributed to the business use of the vehicle.**

b. *Incorrect.* Fuel costs are included in the standard mileage rate deduction; such costs must be recorded if the taxpayer opts to use the actual cost method.

c. *Incorrect.* Repairs of any cost are included as part of the standard business mileage rate deduction but may be recorded if the taxpayer uses the actual cost method.

d. *Incorrect.* Depreciation of the vehicle is included in the deduction when the business standard mileage rate is used.

5. a. *Incorrect.* Listed property is not totally nondeductible.

b. *Correct.* **Listed property used less than half the time for business must be depreciated using the straight-line method of the alternative depreciation system.**

c. *Incorrect.* Under Code Sec. 280F, listed property is not 50 percent deductible when purchased.

d. *Incorrect.* Listed property used less than half the time for business purposes is not fully deductible even if the taxpayer must purchase it as a condition of employment.

6. a. *Correct.* **A U.S. citizen is subject to federal taxation on all of his or her worldwide income, regardless of where it is earned.**

b. *Incorrect.* The foreign tax credit gives a U.S. international telecommuters credit for taxes they pay to the resident country.

c. *Incorrect.* The foreign earned income exclusion, which is $99,200 for the 2014 tax year, helps to mitigate taxes of U.S. citizens for foreign income earned in the telecommuter's residence abroad; it does not, however, lower the tax burden on U.S. income.

d. *Incorrect.* Tax treaties enable U.S. citizens residing in countries with which the United States holds treaties to exempt or receive credit for some of their foreign income when the taxpayers file U.S. returns.

¶ 10,108 MODULE 3—CHAPTER 8

1. a. *Correct.* **Generally, beneficiaries are in a lower income tax bracket than trusts; the threshold triggering the 39.6 percent rate is just $12,150 for trusts in 2014.**

b. *Incorrect.* In computing DNI, no deduction is allowed for distributions to beneficiaries.

c. *Incorrect.* The trustee, not the beneficiary, has the authority for allocating receipts of the trust (such as capital gains) between principal (corpus) and income.

d. *Incorrect.* No deduction for the personal exemption is allowed in calculating DNI.

2. a. *Correct.* **Dividends are subject to the NII tax.**

b. *Incorrect.* Distributions from IRAs are not subject to the NII tax.

c. *Incorrect.* Income derived from in the ordinary course of a trade or business is not subject to the NII tax.

d. *Incorrect.* Although individuals are allowed a higher threshold for triggering the NII tax than trusts, individuals with $200,000 or higher incomes (for single filers) or $250,000 (for joint filers) may be subject to NII tax.

3. a. *Incorrect.* The trust does not recognize gain on an in-kind distribution of appreciated property.

b. *Incorrect.* The NII tax is imposed on the net gain attributable to the disposition of the property, not its fair market value.

c. *Correct.* **The beneficiary, who will typically be in a lower tax bracket than the trust, will be subject to any NII tax resulting from the disposition of the property, rather than the trust.**

d. *Incorrect.* In an in-kind distribution, the trust's basis in the property "carries over" to the beneficiary.

¶ 10,109 MODULE 3—CHAPTER 9

1. a. *Incorrect.* Preserving land areas for outdoor recreation or education is one of the four purposes.

b. *Incorrect.* Preserving open space for scenic enjoyment by the general public is one of the four purposes.

c. *Correct.* **Population density of specific neighborhoods is not a direct purpose of the qualifications, although preserving land for other reasons is.**

d. *Incorrect.* Retaining the character of a historically significant land area or structure is one of the purposes.

2. a. *Incorrect.* A remainder interest is considered part of a qualified real property interest.

b. *Correct.* **This type of donation is treated like that of a used vehicle or household goods.**

c. *Incorrect.* A donation of property for a tax deduction is not a like-kind exchange.

d. *Incorrect.* A donation of property to claim a tax deduction does not constitute a donation of cash.

3. a. *Incorrect.* The donor used the comparable-sales, not FMV, method.

b. *Correct.* **The Tax Court's valuation was found not clearly in error and the easement was less restrictive than comparable ones.**

c. *Incorrect.* The Tax Court valued the easement's value at $500,000; the taxpayer's valuation was $2.2 million for the deduction.

d. *Incorrect.* The Tax Court's valuation was $500,000; the IRS valued the easement at $485,000, then at zero.

4. a. *Correct.* **The IRS and Tax Court maintain that taxpayers often overstate the value of land.**

b. *Incorrect.* Although the methodology is correct for valuing easements in cases such as *Esgar Corporation,* other issues arise in disputes of qualified conservation contributions of land.

c. *Incorrect.* In cases such as *Esgar Corporation,* the IRS and Tax Court lower valuations, maintaining that agriculture is the land's highest and best use.

d. *Incorrect.* Before-and-after values are the more common method preferred by the IRS and Tax Court for valuing contributions of land, as in the *Trout Ranch* case.

5. a. *Incorrect.* The appraiser's membership in the board of accountancy was not argued in *Friedberg.*

b. *Correct.* **Even though the appraiser had never appraised other development rights, he had made the proper declarations and was qualified to appraise that type of property.**

c. *Incorrect.* The appraiser had never appraised other development rights.

d. *Incorrect.* The Tax Court upheld the taxpayer's argument that the appraisal's reliability was not a factor in whether the appraisal was qualified.

6. a. *Incorrect.* The exclusion amount must be reduced by claimed charitable deductions under Code Sec. 2055(f).

b. *Correct.* **The date of contribution, not the donor's death, is used in the valuation.**

c. *Incorrect.* The exclusion applies to up to 40 percent of the land's value, up to $500,000.

d. *Incorrect.* The election, made on Schedule U of Form 706, is irrevocable.

¶ 10,110 MODULE 4—CHAPTER 10

1. a. *Correct.* **Rep. Camp released the bill through the House Ways and Means Committee, which he chairs.**

b. *Incorrect.* That bill, S. 1616, introduced October 30, 2013, by Sen. Mike Lee (R-UT) aims to consolidate the tax brackets, add personal and dependent credits, and eliminate most deductions.

c. *Incorrect.* This bill would replace the entire existing federal income tax system with one that taxes consumption.

d. *Incorrect.* The Flat Tax Act (H.R. 1040) would substitute a flat tax for the current complex system of incentives, penalties, and deductions.

2. a. *Incorrect.* A higher percentage of the inverted corporation's shares must be held by the foreign company's shareholders after the merger.

b. *Correct.* **The current law for inversions allows U.S. corporations to pay the foreign jurisdiction's (lower) tax rates if 20 percent or more of shares are held by the foreign company's shareholders after the merger.**

c. *Incorrect.* Current law allows U.S. corporations to pay the foreign jurisdiction's tax rate if a different percentage of shares of the foreign company is held its shareholders after the merger.

d. *Incorrect.* The current system does not require a majority of shares to be held by the foreign company's shareholders after the merger.

3. a. *Incorrect.* The international financial reporting standards do not allow use of the LIFO accounting method, so repealing LIFO would better align U.S. standards with IFRS.

b. *Incorrect.* Repeal is estimated to generate more than $78 billion additional revenue between 2013 and 2023.

c. *Correct.* **LIFO users have used that accounting system for 70 years and maintain that their tax burden would increase if another system were adopted.**

d. *Incorrect.* LIFO can be misused to manipulate the cost of goods sold and improperly reflect profit margins and tax liability.

4. a. *Incorrect.* President Obama's budget proposed a permanent dollar limit of $500,000.

b. *Incorrect.* The Tax Reform Act of 2014 would permanently increase the Code Sec. 179 deduction's dollar limit to $250,000 from its 2014 limit of $25,000.

c. *Correct.* **The SFC plan should set the dollar limit at $1 million and the investment limit at $2 million.**

d. *Incorrect.* The act extended the $500,000 retroactively for the 2012 tax year.

5. a. *Incorrect.* The new rules would impose withholding requirements on certain amounts of the passthrough owner's distributive share of revenue.

b. *Incorrect.* Under Camp's plan, most passthrough corporations would have expanded opportunities to elect treatment as S corps.

c. *Correct.* **Camp's proposal would reduce the recognition period from 10 to 5 years, not 1.**

d. *Incorrect.* Camp's passthrough reform proposal would loosen existing restrictions on who is eligible to be an S corp shareholder.

6. a. *Incorrect.* Camp's proposal would not eliminate but reduce the amount of the home mortgage interest deduction.

b. *Incorrect.* Camp's proposal would eliminate the deduction for interest on a home equity loan.

c. *Correct.* **The bill limits the amount of acquisition indebtedness eligible for the deduction to the first $500,000 from the current $1 million.**

d. *Incorrect.* The bill does not propose eliminating the deduction based on taxpayers' income levels.

Index

References are to paragraph (¶) numbers.

FOR

¶ 10,200 CPE Quizzer Instructions

This CPE Quizzer is divided into four Modules. To obtain CPE Credit, go to **CCH-Group.com/PrintCPE** to complete your Quizzers online for immediate results and no Express Grading Fee. There is a grading fee for each Quizzer submission.

Processing Fee:	Recommended CPE:	Recommended CFP:
$84.00 for Module 1	6 hours for Module 1	3 hours for Module 1
$56.00 for Module 2	4 hours for Module 2	2 hours for Module 2
$98.00 for Module 3	7 hours for Module 3	3 hours for Module 3
$28.00 for Module 4	2 hours for Module 4	1 hours for Module 4
$266.00 for all Modules	19 hours for all Modules	9 hours for all Modules
IRS Program Number:	**Federal Tax Law Hours:**	
4VRWB-T-00981-14-S for Module 1	6 hours for Module 1	
4VRWB-T-00990-14-S for Module 2	4 hours for Module 2	
4VRWB-T-00982-14-S for Module 3	7 hours for Module 3	
4VRWB-T-00983-14-S for Module 4	2 hours for Module 4	
	19 hours for all Modules	

Instructions for purchasing your CPE Tests and accessing them after purchase are provided on the **CCHGroup.com/PrintCPE** website.

To mail or fax your Quizzer, send your completed Answer Sheet for each Quizzer Module to **CCH Continuing Education Department, 4025 W. Peterson Ave., Chicago, IL 60646**, or fax it to (773) 866-3084. Each Quizzer Answer Sheet will be graded and a CPE Certificate of Completion awarded for achieving a grade of 70 percent or greater. The Quizzer Answer Sheets are located at the back of this book.

Express Grading: Processing time for your mailed or faxed Answer Sheet is generally 8-12 business days. To use our Express Grading Service, at an additional $19 per Module, please check the "Express Grading" box on your Answer Sheet and provide your CCH account or credit card number **and your fax number**. CCH will fax your results and a Certificate of Completion (upon achieving a passing grade) to you by 5:00 p.m. the business day following our receipt of your Answer Sheet. **If you mail your Answer Sheet for Express Grading, please write "ATTN: CPE OVERNIGHT" on the envelope.** NOTE: CCH will not Federal Express Quizzer results under any circumstances.

Recommended CPE credit is based on a 50-minute hour. Participants earning credits for states that require self-study to be based on a 100-minute hour will receive 1/2 the CPE credits for successful completion of this course. Because CPE requirements vary from state to state and among different licensing agencies, please contact your CPE governing body for information on your CPE requirements and the applicability of a particular course for your requirements

---

Date of Completion: If you mail or fax your Quizzer to CCH, the date of completion on your Certificate will be the date that you put on your Answer Sheet. However, you must submit your Answer Sheet to CCH for grading within two weeks of completing it.

Expiration Date: December 31, 2015

Evaluation: To help us provide you with the best possible products, please take a moment to fill out the course Evaluation located after your Quizzer. A copy is also provided at the back of this course if you choose to mail or fax your Quizzer Answer Sheets.

Wolters Kluwer, CCH is registered with the National Association of State Boards of Accountancy (NASBA) as a sponsor of continuing professional education on the National Registry of CPE Sponsors. State boards of accountancy have final authority on the acceptance of individual courses for CPE credit. Complaints regarding registered sponsors may be submitted to the National Registry of CPE Sponsors through its website: www.learningmarket.org.

One **complimentary copy** of this course is provided with certain copies of CCH publications. Additional copies of this course may be downloaded from **CCHGroup.com/PrintCPE** or ordered by calling 1-800-248-3248 (ask for product 10024491-0002).

¶ 10,301 Quizzer Questions: Module 1

1. The effective date of the employer mandate for _____ is 2016.

   a. Small

   b. Midsize

   c. Large

   d. 2016 is not an effective date for any size of employer

2. If at least one employee receives the premium assistance tax credit, an applicable large employer must offer minimum essential coverage to at least _____ in 2015 to avoid making a shared responsibility payment under Code Sec. 4980H(a).

   a. 51 percent

   b. 60 percent

   c. 70 percent

   d. 95 percent

3. Both the monthly measurement and lookback measurement methods use _____ per _____ of service to determine am employer's number of full-time employees.

   a. 20; week

   b. 30; pay period

   c. 130; month

   d. 390; quarter

4. The seasonal worker exception applies to measuring an employer's workforce is the company's workforce exceeds 50 full-time employees (including full-time equivalent employees) for _____ or fewer during the calendar year.

   a. 50 days

   b. 90 days

   c. 100 days

   d. 120 days

5. An employer-sponsored health plan offers minimum essential coverage if:

   a. The plan's share of the cost of benefits is 51 percent

   b. The cost for self-only coverage is less than 15 percent of the employee's annual household income

   c. The employer's plan qualifies for the rate of pay safe harbor

   d. The plan provides coverage for on-site medical clinics

6. The three safe harbors an employer may use to determine that a plan is affordable apply when coverage does not exceed _____ of the employee's annual household income.

   a. 5 percent

   b. 7 percent

   c. 9.5 percent

   d. 15 percent

7. The shared responsibility payment for Section 4980H(a) or 4980H(b) liability is the:

    a. Assessable payment

    b. Applicable large employer penalty tax

    c. Premium assistance assessment

    d. Marketplace accessibility payment

8. The maximum waiting period before an employee becomes eligible for an employer's group health coverage is:

    a. 20 days

    b. 30 days

    c. 60 days

    d. 90 days

9. To qualify for transition relief from the employer mandate in 2015, employers must:

    a. Maintain a workforce of at least 50 but fewer than 100 full-time employees, including full-time equivalent employees

    b. Implement a new health plan for spouses and dependents

    c. Amend their health plans to increase eligibility requirements

    d. Offer coverage to 95 percent of full-time employees

10. The deadline for electronic filing of Code Sec. 6056 health care coverage information for 2015 is:

    a. December 31, 2015

    b. March 31, 2016

    c. April 15, 2016

    d. June 30, 2016

11. Materials and supplies are _____ if no record of their consumption is kept.

    a. Reduced

    b. Nondeductible

    c. Incidental

    d. Ignored

12. A _____ is a component of a particular item of machinery or equipment set aside for use as a replacement to avoid substantial operational time loss.

    a. Temporary spare part

    b. Standby emergency part

    c. Rotable spare part

    d. Installable part

13. Which of the following is true for the *de minimis* safe harbor election?

    a. It is elected annually before December 31

    b. It is irrevocable

    c. It requires an applicable financial statement

    d. The electing taxpayer may not lower the dollar limit for the deduction

14. A taxpayer may elect the small building-small taxpayer safe harbor if:

    a. Average annual gross receipts during the previous three tax years do not exceed $20 million

    b. The building's unadjusted basis is $5 million or less

    c. The total amount for repairs, maintenance, and improvements during the tax year does not exceed the lesser of $10,000 or 2 percent of the building's unadjusted basis

    d. Expenditures for property located outside of the building are included in calculating the deduction

15. An expenditure that ameliorates a material defect that existed before the taxpayer's acquisition of a unit of property is a:

    a. Capitalized restoration

    b. Capitalized adaptation

    c. Structural replacement

    d. Capitalized betterment

16. Regrading farmland to enable its development for residences is an example of a:

    a. Capitalized restoration

    b. Capitalized adaptation

    c. Structural replacement

    d. Capitalized betterment

17. A repair expense that was previously capitalized may be claimed as a deduction under the repair regulations if:

    a. The taxpayer files Form 3115 showing a negative Code Sec. 481(a) adjustment

    b. The taxpayer files Form 3115 and the capitalized amount is fully depreciated

    c. The Code Sec. 481(a) adjustment totals less than $5,000

    d. The amount was incurred during calendar year 2014

18. The deadline for filing Form 3115 for a calendar year individual having an extension to file Form 1040 for 2014 is:

    a. January 1, 2015

    b. April 15, 2015

    c. October 15, 2015

    d. December 31, 2015

19. Unit of property method changes:

    a. Do not require computing a Section 481(a) adjustment

    b. May be made without filing Form 3115

    c. Are not required if the taxpayer previously filed a method change on Form 3115 that treated the entire building as a unit of property for purposes of determining whether an expenditure was a repair

    d. Are not allowed under the repair regulations

20. Removal costs are not deductible if:

   a. The taxpayer makes a partial disposition election

   b. An entire asset is removed

   c. A component is replaced, a partial disposition election is not made, and the removal costs are incurred by reason of an improvement to the property

   d. A component is replaced, a partial disposition election is not made, and the removal costs are incurred by reason of a repair to the property

21. Under the passive activity rules, losses and expenses arising from passive activities:

   a. May not be carried forward to later tax years

   b. May only be netted with income attributed to passive activities

   c. Are lost when the taxpayer disposes of the entire interest in the passive activities

   d. Apply to the entity's taxable income

22. Excess passive activity losses in one tax year are:

   a. Lost

   b. Applied against the entity's taxable income

   c. Suspended

   d. Applied to the partners' or shareholders' taxable income

23. Under Code Sec. 707(c), a partner's guaranteed payments for use of property:

   a. Are not treated as income from a rental activity

   b. Are netted against the partner's passive activity losses

   c. Are passive activity income

   d. Are considered to be third-party charges

24. One test used to qualify a taxpayer as a real estate professional requires him or her to perform more than _____ hours per tax year in real property trades or businesses.

   a. 500

   b. 750

   c. 1,000

   d. 1,200

25. A limited partner satisfies a material participation test if he or she satisfies all of the following *except:*

   a. Participation in partnership activities for more than 500 hours in the tax year

   b. Materially participation for 5 of the 10 preceding tax years

   c. Becoming a general partner within the first month of the partnership's tax year

   d. Material participation in the partnership's personal services activity for any tax year

26. The self-charged interest rules treat interest expenses allocable to the lender as:

   a. Passive activity deductions

   b. Passive activity income

   c. Ordinary losses

   d. Ordinary gross income

27. Net rental income from property rented for use in a trade or business of a material participant is nonpassive income under the:

    a. Rental contractual rule

    b. General partnership regulations

    c. Self-rental rule

    d. Net income rule

28. Grouping activities are *not* limited under passive activity rules for:

    a. Limited partners and limited entrepreneurs

    b. Rental activities and nonrental activities

    c. Real property rentals and personal property rentals

    d. Immediate income items versus long-range income items

29. Income received by a partner who lends funds to a partnership is treated as:

    a. A sale of the partner's interest

    b. A nontaxable return on investment

    c. Suspended passive income

    d. Interest

30. Excess suspended loss remaining after the disposition of an entire interest in a passive activity:

    a. May be applied to prior years' passive income on amended returns

    b. May offset nonpassive income in that tax year

    c. Is forfeited by the taxpayer

    d. Is carried over to subsequent tax years for other activities

¶ 10,302 Quizzer Questions: Module 2

31. A virtual currency payment transaction includes all of the following information *except:*

    a. Address from which the currency was sent

    b. Fees paid by the buyer

    c. Amount being sent

    d. Seller's address

32. Bitcoin transactions are verified and put into a transaction block by the:

    a. Seller

    b. Buyer

    c. Miner

    d. Public key holder

33. A _____ is software that an individual or business uses to manage virtual currency.

    a. Block chain

    b. Digital wallet

    c. Mining algorithm

    d. Third-party settlement application

34. A limit of _____ exists.

    a. 10 million

    b. 12 million

    c. 15 million

    d. 21 million

35. Which of the following is a benefit of using virtual currency?

    a. Low volatility

    b. Ability to be traded as investments exempt from security laws

    c. Low fees for merchants

    d. Ability to trace amounts to their owners

36. Notice 2014-21 treats virtual currency as _____ for federal tax purposes.

    a. Property

    b. Legal tender

    c. Convertible currency

    d. Capital assets

37. Payors are *not* required to file _____ if payments are made in virtual currency.

    a. Form W-2 for annual employee wages of more than $600

    b. Form 1099-MISC for independent contractor payments

    c. FinCEN Form 114 for virtual currency exchanges holding the equivalent of $600 in Bitcoins

    d. Form 1099-K for merchant payments exceeding the equivalent of $20,000

38. FinCEN regulations address whether virtual currency dealers should be considered:

   a. Currency producers

   b. Fiscal intermediaries

   c. Money services businesses

   d. Banking institutions

39. The AICPA recommends that foreign virtual currency deposit accounts:

   a. Follow FATCA foreign financial asset rules

   b. Comply with FinCEN requirements except for FBAR filings

   c. Be reported as ordinary income sources

   d. Be treated as currency exchanges for reporting purposes

40. Bitcoin transactions are permitted and considered safer than official currency in:

   a. China

   b. Argentina

   c. India

   d. Japan

41. FATCA currently requires all of the following specified persons with foreign assets exceeding the threshold to file Form 8938 *except:*

   a. Specified domestic closely held corporations and partnerships

   b. Domestic entities indirectly holding specified foreign assets

   c. Nonresident aliens electing to be resident aliens to file joint returns

   d. Any individual who is a resident alien for any part of the year

42. If a foreign financial institution (FFI) fails to meet FATCA requirements, a U.S. withholding agent must withhold _____ on any withholdable payment to the FFI.

   a. 10 percent

   b. 20 percent

   c. 30 percent

   d. 40 percent

43. Under FATCA requirements, _____ is a reportable specified foreign financial asset.

   a. A financial accounts in a domestic branch of a foreign bank

   b. A security issued by a person other than a U.S. person

   c. All assets in a financial account subject to the mark-to-market rules

   d. An account at a foreign branch of a U.S. financial institution

44. Specified persons who are joint filers living abroad are subject to FATCA requirements when their specified foreign assets exceed _____ on the last day of the year or _____ anytime during the year.

   a. $50,000; $100,000

   b. $100,000; $150,000

   c. $200,000; $300,000

   d. $400,000; $600,000

45. To report the value of a specified foreign financial asset for Form 8938, the taxpayer:

    a. Lists its total worth in the currency type used for the account

    b. Averages the monthly or quarterly exchange rates used for paying estimated tax

    c. Uses the Treasury Department's year-end spot rate

    d. Converts the beginning value of the asset for that tax year

46. An accuracy-related penalty of _____ applies under FATCA to tax underpayments involving undisclosed foreign financial assets.

    a. 10 percent

    b. 20 percent

    c. 30 percent

    d. 40 percent

47. For the FBAR rules, a U.S. person can have a financial interest in a foreign account unless he or she:

    a. Is a deemed owner of the financial interest's account

    b. Is a constructive owner acting on behalf of the U.S. person who owns the foreign account

    c. Is a discretionary beneficiary in a discretionary trust

    d. Is the owner of record or holder of legal title of the foreign financial account

48. Which officers or employees are subject to FBAR requirements?

    a. Ones with signature or other authority of a bank-owned account

    b. Ones having a financial interest in an account of the institution

    c. Ones registered with and examined by the Commodity Futures Trading Commission

    d. Ones of an entity with a class of security listed on any U.S. national securities exchange

49. An exception to FBAR reporting applies to:

    a. Employee welfare plan accounts of government entities

    b. Annuity policies with cash value

    c. Mutual fund accounts issuing shares to the general public

    d. Accounts with brokers or deals for futures or options

50. The 2014 Offshore Voluntary Disclosure Program imposes an accuracy-related penalty for offshore taxpayers' noncompliance of:

    a. 10 percent

    b. 20 percent

    c. 30 percent

    d. 40 percent

¶ 10,303 Quizzer Questions: Module 3

51. The regular maximum salary deferral limit for individuals younger than age 50 for 401(k), 403(b), and 457(b) plans for 2014 is:

    a. $5,500

    b. $6,500

    c. $10,000

    d. $17,500

52. Which of the following designated Roth accounts does **not** allow tax-free distribution?

    a. Designated 401(k) accounts

    b. Designated 403(b) accounts

    c. Designated 457(b) accounts

    d. 401(k), 403(b), and 457(b) designated Roth accounts all allow tax-free distributions of contributions and earnings

53. Which type of qualified plan distribution is eligible for rollovers?

    a. Hardship distributions

    b. Loans treated as distributions

    c. Lump-sum payment made when an employee terminates employment

    d. Required minimum distributions

54. Rollovers are taxable when made from:

    a. Nondeductible IRA contributions rolled over to Roth IRAs

    b. Pretax contributions and earnings in a traditional 401(k) rolled over to a designated Roth account

    c. After-tax contributions from employer plans to Roth IRAs

    d. Roth IRA accounts to other Roth accounts

55. Taxpayers receiving distributions of rollover amounts to switch accounts must deposit the funds within:

    a. 30 days

    b. 60 days

    c. 90 days

    d. The same tax year as funds were received

56. Which of the following is true for the one-in-12-months rule for 2015?

    a. A taxpayer is limited to one rollover from all of the taxpayer's IRA accounts per 12-month period

    b. The rule will be applied on a IRA-by-IRA basis

    c. Taxpayers will be allowed free access to all of their multiple IRA funds throughout the year

    d. The rule will apply only to trustee-to-trustee transfers

57. Rollovers from traditional IRAs to Roth IRAs:

   a. Are tax-free

   b. Have no AGI limits for taxpayers

   c. Have the same income limits as annual IRA contributions

   d. Impose traditional IRA RMD requirements on the amounts converted

58. Recharacterization of a Roth conversion:

   a. Is commonly done to undo a conversion done just prior to a market crash to avoid paying tax on a balance that was much higher than the current postcrash balance

   b. Is not reported on the tax return for the year of the contribution was made

   c. Does not trigger tax on the entire converted amount if its value declines in the same tax year

   d. Cannot be made for a conversion from an employer's designated Roth account

59. An advantage of leaving assets in a former employer's 401(k) plan upon leaving a job is:

   a. Avoiding mandatory RMDs if the employee works past age 701/2

   b. Charitable giving is easier to plan from a 401(k) account

   c. The ability to take distributions for education and first-time home purchases

   d. Maximum flexibility for choosing investments with low fees

60. Hardship distributions from 401(k), 403(b), or 457(b) accounts:

   a. Do not apply to burial or funeral expenses paid from the employee's account for a deceased parent, spouse, or child

   b. May be used to pay ongoing mortgage payments

   c. May not be taken from earnings on deferrals

   d. May be rolled over without incurring the additional 10 percent tax

61. The following entity types may claim a home office deduction *except:*

   a. Estates

   b. Partnerships

   c. C corporations

   d. S corporations

62. An exception to the exclusive use test for home office deductions applies to a taxpayer who:

   a. Is a sole proprietor

   b. Regularly uses the space to store inventory or product samples

   c. Occasionally meets with customers or patients there

   d. Uses the simplified safe harbor method to claim the deduction

63. Indirect expenses of a home office, such as mortgage interest and homeowner's insurance:

   a. Are not deductible

   b. Are depreciable for 39 years

   c. Are deductible based on the percentage of the home used for the office

   d. Are deductible as itemized deductions on Schedule A of Form 1040

¶10,303

64. In 2014, the maximum annual deduction for a home office under the simplified safe harbor rule is:

   a. $1,500 (300 square feet × $5 prescribed rate)

   b. $2,000 (400 square feet × $5 prescribed rate)

   c. $2,500 (500 square feet × $5 prescribed rate)

   d. $3,000 (600 square feet × $5 prescribed rate)

65. Under the simplified safe harbor method, a home office is only deductible for months when it was used at least _____.

   a. 5 days

   b. 10 days

   c. 15 days

   d. 20 days

66. An entirely deductible travel expense is:

   a. A one-night hotel stay during a trade show 300 miles from home

   b. Costs for treating a client to dinner

   c. Traveling to a destination where one day out of a week-long trip is spent in a business meeting; the remaining days are spent sight-seeing

   d. Hotel costs for an employee and his nonemployee daughter during his business conference

67. Prorating business versus personal expenses for an international trip is based on:

   a. Whether a spouse or dependent accompanies the individual

   b. The distance of the side trip(s)

   c. The deductibility of the business trip by the employer

   d. The time spent on personal versus business activities

68. Self-employed individuals can use the federal government's per diem travel allowance to figure deductions of:

   a. Lodging

   b. Meals and incidental expenses

   c. Airfare or train expenses

   d. Shipping business equipment

69. Unreimbursed actual costs of meals consumed away from home have a _____ prorated deduction for most employees but a(n) _____ limit for interstate truck drivers.

   a. 25 percent; 50 percent

   b. 50 percent; 80 percent

   c. 60 percent; 90 percent

   d. 75 percent; 100 percent

70. An employee must include reimbursed expenses in income if:

   a. The employee and employer use an accountable plan

   b. The reimbursement constitutes less than 10 percent of the employee's annual gross income

   c. A business connection exists between advances and incurred expenses

   d. The employer uses a per diem rate exceeding the federal government's rate

71. Under the *Uniform Principal and Income Act* and IRS regulations, _____ is (are) generally allocated to trust principal.

    a. Interest on promissory notes

    b. Rent received from real property

    c. Capital gains

    d. Ordinary dividends

72. For 2014 returns, the top tax rate of 39.6 percent applies to a trust's taxable income exceeding:

    a. $11,950

    b. $12,150

    c. $406,750

    d. $457,600

73. All of the following are benefits of making in-kind distributions of trust property *except:*

    a. The trust is not liable for capital gains tax on the property

    b. Income tax liability is completely avoided when the beneficiary subsequently sells the property

    c. Income attributable to any disposition of the property can be shifted from the trust to a beneficiary in a lower tax bracket

    d. The beneficiary will not be liable for capital gains tax until he or she sells the property, which potentially gives the beneficiary flexibility as to the timing of gain recognition

74. The _____ is applied to administrative costs of the trust:

    a. Business and trade costs test

    b. More-likely-than-not test

    c. Commonly or customarily test

    d. Nonitemizable test

75. All of the following are benefits for trusts of making the 65-day election *except:*

    a. It is revocable for a tax year if the trust files an amended return

    b. It enables the trustee to assess whether additional distributions for the year would be advantageous

    c. The trustee simply makes the election with the trust's Form 1041 for the year

    d. The trustee may adjust distributions once he or she is aware of the beneficiary's level of income at the close of the trust's tax year

76. The charitable conservation easement deduction was established to:

    a. Override local zoning ordinances for historic façade easements

    b. Enable recipient charities to develop land

    c. Offset costs and losses associated with preserving property

    d. Take decisions regarding conservation easements out of the IRS and Tax Court's jurisdiction

77. A donor benefits from making a qualified conservation easement contribution because:

    a. There is no requirement to actually transfer the easement property to the charity

    b. The deduction is not tied to the donor's adjusted gross income

    c. The donor may determine the use to which the property may be put

    d. The income tax deduction may be deferred to future tax years

78. President Obama's 2013 and 2014 budget proposed limiting easements on golf course land because:

    a. The easements do not provide for affordable housing development

    b. Deduction amounts may be excessive and promote the owners' private interests

    c. The land donated is not preserved using native vegetation

    d. The type of property donated for golf course development is not put to its highest and best use

79. A qualified conservation contribution is *not* required to prove it is:

    a. For property that has never been developed

    b. Exclusively for conservation purposes

    c. To a qualified organization

    d. For a qualified real property interest

80. A deduction for donors in the *Graev* case was disallowed because:

    a. The conservation was not protected in perpetuity

    b. The conservation agreement permitted property substitutions

    c. The transaction used the comparable-sales method of valuation

    d. The cash and façade conservation easement were conditional

81. In *Belk,* the Tax Court disallowed the taxpayer's charitable deduction because:

    a. The contribution was a floating easement allowing substitutions of real property

    b. The easement allowed some commercial development in the golf course

    c. The easement lacked provisions for qualified mineral interests

    d. Belk's LLC did not pass the charitable contribution deduction through to the taxpayer

82. In *Mitchell,* the FLP's deduction was disallowed because:

    a. The recipient organization was not qualified

    b. The probability of default on the note was negligible

    c. No subordination agreement was in place at the time of gifting the easement

    d. The mortgage subordinated its property rights

83. The IRS imposes an overvaluation penalty of _____ under Code Sec. 6662(a).

    a. 10 percent

    b. 25 percent

    c. 40 percent

    d. 50 percent

84. The focus of the Tax Court's position on the deduction for a conservation easement in *Rothman* was:

    a. The appraisal of the easement was not qualified

    b. The appraiser overvalued the easement

    c. The basis for the valuation was misstated

    d. The cause for failing to obtain a qualified appraisal was unreasonable

85. A restriction of a qualified conservation contribution of qualified real property:

    a. May not be claimed for a single easement by multiple donors

    b. Must be stated in state law

    c. Must be due to an inevitable event

    d. Must be granted in perpetuity

¶ 10,304 Quizzer Questions: Module 4

86. The concept of reforming the tax structure so the government receives the same tax revenue as before the reform is:

   a. Base-broadening

   b. Alternative revenue building

   c. Revenue neutrality

   d. Revenue restructuring

87. Which new tax being considered is levied only at the retail stage?

   a. Value-added tax

   b. Environmental tax

   c. Retail alternative minimum tax

   d. Federal sales tax

88. The current statutory tax rate for U.S.-owned corporations with taxable incomes of more than $10 million is:

   a. 25 percent

   b. 34 percent

   c. 35 percent

   d. 42 percent

89. The proposed Tax Reform Act of 2014 would _____ the domestic production activities income deduction after 2016.

   a. Phase out

   b. Increase

   c. Phase in

   d. Leave unchanged

90. Under the proposed Tax Reform Act of 2014, businesses with annual gross receipts of _____ or less could use cash accounting for tax purposes.

   a. $10 million

   b. $15 million

   c. $20 million

   d. $50 million

91. Changing the U.S. international tax system to be territorial could have the negative effect of:

   a. Incentivizing firms to avoid repatriating foreign earnings

   b. Encouraging firms to location operations overseas

   c. Increasing intangible income from foreign subsidiaries that were untaxed

   d. Exempting all foreign intangible income from taxation

92. The dividend-exemption system of the proposed Tax Reform Act of 2014:

    a. Would not apply to capital gains for 1 percent U.S. corporate shareholders

    b. Would eliminate the foreign tax credit or deduction for foreign taxes paid on any part of an exempt dividend

    c. Would further discourage repatriation of foreign earnings

    d. Would continue the deduction for withholding taxes paid on exempt dividends

93. The proposed Tax Reform Act of 2014 would compress individual income tax brackets to:

    a. Three: 15, 25, and 28 percent

    b. Two: 10 and 25 percent

    c. Four: 10, 25, 28, and 33 percent

    d. One: a flat tax of 25 percent

94. Which tax reform proposal(s) would completely repeal Code Sec. 1031 tax breaks from like-kind exchanges?

    a. Camp's Tax Reform Act of 2014

    b. President Obama's budget proposals

    c. The Senate Finance Committee's proposal

    d. Rep. Camp, President Obama, and the SFC all do not propose repeal

95. Camp's proposed Tax Reform Act of 2014 would eliminate:

    a. The home mortgage interest deduction

    b. The charitable contributions deduction

    c. The deduction for state and local taxes paid

    d. The child tax credit

¶ 10,400 Answer Sheets

¶ 10,401 Top Federal Tax Issues for 2015 CPE Course: MODULE 1

(10014583-0003)

Go to **CCHGroup.com/PrintCPE** to complete your Quizzer online for instant results and no Express Grading Fee.

A $84.00 processing fee will be charged for each user submitting Module 1 for grading. If you prefer to mail or fax your Quizzer, remove both pages of the Answer Sheet from this book and return them with your completed Evaluation Form to: CCH Continuing Education Department, 4025 W. Peterson Ave., Chicago, IL 60646-6085 or fax your Answer Sheet to CCH at 773-866-3084. You must also select a method of payment below.

NAME _____

COMPANY NAME _____

STREET _____

CITY, STATE, & ZIP CODE _____

BUSINESS PHONE NUMBER _____

E-MAIL ADDRESS _____

DATE OF COMPLETION _____

CFP REGISTRANT ID (for Certified Financial Planners) _____

PTIN ID (for Enrolled Agents or RTRPs only) _____

METHOD OF PAYMENT:

☐ Check Enclosed ☐ Visa ☐ Master Card ☐ AmEx

☐ Discover ☐ CCH Account* _____

Card No. _____ Exp. Date _____

Signature _____

EXPRESS GRADING: Please fax my Course results to me by 5:00 p.m. the business day following your receipt of this Answer Sheet. By checking this box I authorize CCH to charge $19.00 for this service.

☐ Express Grading $19.00 Fax No. _____

* Must provide CCH account number for this payment option

 Wolters Kluwer

Module 1: Answer Sheet

(10014583-0003)

Please answer the questions by indicating the appropriate letter next to the corresponding number.

1. _____	6. _____	11. _____	16. _____	21. _____	26. _____
2. _____	7. _____	12. _____	17. _____	22. _____	27. _____
3. _____	8. _____	13. _____	18. _____	23. _____	28. _____
4. _____	9. _____	14. _____	19. _____	24. _____	29. _____
5. _____	10. _____	15. _____	20. _____	25. _____	30. _____

Please complete the Evaluation Form (located after the Module 4 Answer Sheet) and return it with this Quizzer Answer Sheet to CCH at the address on the previous page. Thank you.

¶ 10,402 Top Federal Tax Issues for 2015 CPE Course: MODULE 2

(10014584-0003)

Go to **CCHGroup.com/PrintCPE** to complete your Quizzer online for instant results and no Express Grading Fee.

A $56.00 processing fee will be charged for each user submitting Module 2 for grading. If you prefer to mail or fax your Quizzer, remove both pages of the Answer Sheet from this book and return them with your completed Evaluation Form to: CCH Continuing Education Department, 4025 W. Peterson Ave., Chicago, IL 60646-6085 or fax your Answer Sheet to CCH at 773-866-3084. You must also select a method of payment below.

NAME _____

COMPANY NAME _____

STREET _____

CITY, STATE, & ZIP CODE _____

BUSINESS PHONE NUMBER _____

E-MAIL ADDRESS _____

DATE OF COMPLETION _____

CFP REGISTRANT ID (for Certified Financial Planners) _____

PTIN ID (for Enrolled Agents or RTRPs only) _____

METHOD OF PAYMENT:

☐ Check Enclosed	☐ Visa	☐ Master Card	☐ AmEx
☐ Discover	☐ CCH Account* _____		

Card No. _____ Exp. Date _____

Signature _____

EXPRESS GRADING: Please fax my Course results to me by 5:00 p.m. the business day following your receipt of this Answer Sheet. By checking this box I authorize CCH to charge $19.00 for this service.

☐ Express Grading $19.00   Fax No. _____

* Must provide CCH account number for this payment option

 Wolters Kluwer

Module 2: Answer Sheet

(10014584-0003)

Please answer the questions by indicating the appropriate letter next to the corresponding number.

31. _____	35. _____	39. _____	43. _____	47. _____
32. _____	36. _____	40. _____	44. _____	48. _____
33. _____	37. _____	41. _____	45. _____	49. _____
34. _____	38. _____	42. _____	46. _____	50. _____

Please complete the Evaluation Form (located after the Module 4 Answer Sheet) and return it with this Quizzer Answer Sheet to CCH at the address on the previous page. Thank you.

¶ 10,403 Top Federal Tax Issues for 2015 CPE Course: MODULE 3

(10014585-0003)

Go to **CCHGroup.com/PrintCPE** to complete your Quizzer online for instant results and no Express Grading Fee.

A $98.00 processing fee will be charged for each user submitting Module 3 for grading. If you prefer to mail or fax your Quizzer, remove both pages of the Answer Sheet from this book and return them with your completed Evaluation Form to: CCH Continuing Education Department, 4025 W. Peterson Ave., Chicago, IL 60646-6085 or fax your Answer Sheet to CCH at 773-866-3084. You must also select a method of payment below.

NAME _____

COMPANY NAME _____

STREET _____

CITY, STATE, & ZIP CODE _____

BUSINESS PHONE NUMBER _____

E-MAIL ADDRESS _____

DATE OF COMPLETION _____

CFP REGISTRANT ID (for Certified Financial Planners) _____

PTIN ID (for Enrolled Agents or RTRPs only) _____

METHOD OF PAYMENT:

☐ Check Enclosed ☐ Visa ☐ Master Card ☐ AmEx

☐ Discover ☐ CCH Account* _____

Card No. _____ Exp. Date _____

Signature _____

EXPRESS GRADING: Please fax my Course results to me by 5:00 p.m. the business day following your receipt of this Answer Sheet. By checking this box I authorize CCH to charge $19.00 for this service.

☐ Express Grading $19.00 Fax No. _____

* Must provide CCH account number for this payment option

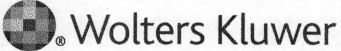
®. Wolters Kluwer

Module 3: Answer Sheet

(10014585-0003)

Please answer the questions by indicating the appropriate letter next to the corresponding number.

51. _____	58. _____	65. _____	72. _____	79. _____
52. _____	59. _____	66. _____	73. _____	80. _____
53. _____	60. _____	67. _____	74. _____	81. _____
54. _____	61. _____	68. _____	75. _____	82. _____
55. _____	62. _____	69. _____	76. _____	83. _____
56. _____	63. _____	70. _____	77. _____	84. _____
57. _____	64. _____	71. _____	78. _____	85. _____

Please complete the Evaluation Form (located after the Module 4 Answer Sheet) and return it with this Quizzer Answer Sheet to CCH at the address on the previous page. Thank you.

¶ 10,404 Top Federal Tax Issues for 2015 CPE Course: MODULE 4

(10014586-0003)

Go to **CCHGroup.com/PrintCPE** to complete your Quizzer online for instant results and no Express Grading Fee.

A $28.00 processing fee will be charged for each user submitting Module 4 for grading. If you prefer to mail or fax your Quizzer, remove both pages of the Answer Sheet from this book and return them with your completed Evaluation Form to: CCH Continuing Education Department, 4025 W. Peterson Ave., Chicago, IL 60646-6085 or fax your Answer Sheet to CCH at 773-866-3084. You must also select a method of payment below.

NAME _____

COMPANY NAME _____

STREET _____

CITY, STATE, & ZIP CODE _____

BUSINESS PHONE NUMBER _____

E-MAIL ADDRESS _____

DATE OF COMPLETION _____

CFP REGISTRANT ID (for Certified Financial Planners) _____

PTIN ID (for Enrolled Agents or RTRPs only) _____

METHOD OF PAYMENT:

☐ Check Enclosed   ☐ Visa   ☐ Master Card   ☐ AmEx

☐ Discover   ☐ CCH Account* _____

Card No. _____   Exp. Date _____

Signature _____

EXPRESS GRADING: Please fax my Course results to me by 5:00 p.m. the business day following your receipt of this Answer Sheet. By checking this box I authorize CCH to charge $19.00 for this service.

☐ Express Grading $19.00   Fax No. _____

* Must provide CCH account number for this payment option

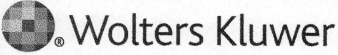 Wolters Kluwer

Module 4: Answer Sheet

(10014586-0003)

Please answer the questions by indicating the appropriate letter next to the corresponding number.

86. _____   89. _____   92. _____   95. _____

87. _____   90. _____   93. _____

88. _____   91. _____   94. _____

Please complete the Evaluation Form (located after the Module 4 Answer Sheet) and return it with this Quizzer Answer Sheet to CCH at the address on the previous page. Thank you.

¶ 10,500 Top Federal Tax Issues for 2015 CPE Course: Evaluation Form

(10024491-0002)

Please take a few moments to fill out and mail or fax this evaluation to CCH so that we can better provide you with the type of self-study programs you want and need. Thank you.

About This Program

1. Please circle the number that best reflects the extent of your agreement with the following statements:

		Strongly Agree				Strongly Disagree
a.	The Course objectives were met.	5	4	3	2	1
b.	This Course was comprehensive and organized.	5	4	3	2	1
c.	The content was current and technically accurate.	5	4	3	2	1
d.	This Course was timely and relevant.	5	4	3	2	1
e.	The prerequisite requirements were appropriate.	5	4	3	2	1
f.	This Course was a valuable learning experience.	5	4	3	2	1
g.	The Course completion time was appropriate.	5	4	3	2	1

2. This Course was most valuable to me because of:

_____ Continuing Education credit   _____ Convenience of format

_____ Relevance to my practice/employment   _____ Timeliness of subject matter

_____ Price   _____ Reputation of author

_____ Other (please specify) _____

3. How long did it take to complete this Course? (Please include the total time spent reading or studying reference materials and completing CPE Quizzer).

Module 1_____   Module 2_____   Module 3_____   Module 4 _____

4. What do you consider to be the strong points of this Course?

5. What improvements can we make to this Course?

General Interests

(10024491-0002)

1. Preferred method of self-study instruction:

_____ Text   _____ Audio   _____ Computer-based/Multimedia   _____ Video

2. What specific topics would you like CCH to develop as self-study CPE programs?

_____

_____

_____

3. Please list other topics of interest to you _____

_____

_____

About You

1. Your profession:

_____ CPA   _____ Enrolled Agent

_____ Attorney   _____ Tax Preparer

_____ Financial Planner   _____ Other (please specify)

_____

2. Your employment:

_____ Self-employed   _____ Public Accounting Firm

_____ Service Industry   _____ Non-Service Industry

_____ Banking/Finance   _____ Government

_____ Education   _____ Other _____

3. Size of firm/corporation:

_____ 1   _____ 2-5   _____ 6-10   _____ 11-20   _____ 21-50   _____ 51+

4. Your Name _____

Firm/Company Name _____

Address _____

City, State, Zip Code _____

E-mail Address _____

THANK YOU FOR TAKING THE TIME TO COMPLETE THIS SURVEY!